Y0-ASD-754

MONADNOCK REGION ODYSSEYS

MONADNOCK REGION ODYSSEYS

HIKING
PADDLING
CYCLING
OBSERVING

DICK JENKINS

MONADNOCK REGION ODYSSEYS
by Dick Jenkins

ISBN 978-0-9795067-4-1

First Edition

Cover Photo by Jeff Topping

Surry Cottage Books
25 Roxbury Street
Keene NH 03431
(603) 499-6500
surrycottagebooks.com

Table of Contents

Part Two: Paddling

Part Three: Cycling

Part Four: Observing

Introduction: Outdoor Zen

I first saw Mt. Monadnock from the front seat of an army two and a half ton truck, part of a convoy transporting elements of the Fifth Field Hospital from Fort Devens, Massachusetts, to Vergennes, Vermont. It was the summer of 1962, and we had an interesting mission - to be the medical facility for the International Girl Scout Jamboree at Button Bay, on Lake Champlain. Our route took us through the Green Mountains, but no single peak there dominated its surroundings as did Monadnock. I didn't know it then, but the mountain and the region named for it would have a dominant role in my life. Just before I was discharged, I married a girl from Greenville, New Hampshire, and we have lived in either Greenville or Peterborough ever since.

A few years later, I was just finishing Keene State College when I was hired to work summers at Greenfield State Park by the late Charles Burrage. I began teaching the following fall, but I continued to work at the park for another four years. At that time, most teachers sought summer work, and many worked for the parks.

In 1973, I was given the opportunity to be the manager of Miller State Park on Pack Monadnock. I worked there for over twenty years. That gave me plenty of outdoor time, including hiking between South and North Pack. For most of those years, the park was located only on the summit of the mountain, so I had lots of time to contemplate the view, which included a large portion of the region. For most of those years, I also had the companionship and guidance of the late Roy Finan, who had been the fire lookout there since the 1940's. Roy was a remarkable man and a storehouse of outdoor knowledge. On days off, I tried to visit as many other mountain parks as possible, and I managed to climb Monadnock from time to time.

Since retiring from the park in the mid nineties, I have had more opportunities to hike, bicycle and paddle in the region. Having the last few summers of my teaching career free from working allowed me to pursue those hobbies. Then, in 2002, I began writing a weekly column, Outdoor Odysseys, for the *Monadnock Shopper News*, in Keene. In finding topics for the column, I have walked many paths, peddled many roads, and paddled many ponds in the region. I am grateful to the paper and its managing editor, Michelle Greene, for the experience.

This book is a compilation of the best of those columns. They were not written as guides, and they do not include all of the information such as maps and distances normally found in guides. However, these little narratives can be used that way, and I have been told by many readers that they often have been. I believe that getting outside is the best way to know any region, and I hope this book encourages and helps readers to get out and explore this part of the world.

The Monadnock Region does not have the highest mountains in New Hampshire nor the largest lakes. It does have, obviously, Mt. Monadnock, and there are a number of other, smaller mountains, all with hiking trails. The epicenter for hiking in the region is Monadnock State Park, but there are trails in Miller State Park on Pack Monadnock Mountain, on Crotched Mountain, Little Monadnock and Gap Monadnock. There are trails on just about every mountain in the area. There are also three long distance trails within the region: the Wapack Trail, the Monadnock-Sunapee Greenway, and the northern end of the Metacomet-Monadnock Trail, which begins in Connecticut. There are trails in all the state parks in the area, including many miles in Pisgah State Park. There are trails in several Audubon Nature Preserves and in a number of Nature Conservancy holdings. Most of the towns in the region have conservation lands, and many of those have well-marked paths.

There are only a few major highways in the region but many miles of country roads, and cyclists can go just about anywhere. The whole Monadnock Region can be seen as one big bicycle tour. Those who prefer mountain biking may use many of the hiking trails, several rail trails and hundreds of miles of dirt roads and old logging roads.

For those who paddle, the region includes many ponds, lakes and reservoirs, some of them free or nearly free of shore line development. There are navigable streams, as well, including the Ashuelot, Contoocook and Connecticut rivers.

If you extend the Monadnock Region a few miles to the east and north in New Hampshire, across the Connecticut into eastern Vermont, and south into the Quabbin Region of Massachusetts, the opportunities for hiking, cycling and paddling are all increased, and they are still within easy driving distance.

This book comprises narratives of over a hundred hikes, bicycle rides and canoe or kayak trips I have taken in the greater Monandock Region during the first few years of the new millennium. Some of them were more difficult than others, but all were done by me, a retired school teacher and certified codger. Most people of reasonable fitness could do any of them. Many of the trips could also be done in the comfort of a car, and most are in or near areas that offer camping, picnicking and viewing opportunities for those who prefer or are limited to less physical activity.

One thing that has surprised me on many of my outings is that I find myself alone. Not that I want to be in a crowd, but I do wonder why I so seldom encounter other hikers on the trail. To be sure, the main trails on Monadnock are often busy, even crowded, especially on weekends, but that is not true of most of the trails described in this book. I have read, lately, that visits to national parks are down, that fewer people are getting outdoors. I think one of the causes may be that people have decided that if they cannot through hike the Appalachian Trail, enter the Tour de France, or kayak the rapids of the Colorado, they would rather watch or read about others doing those spectacular things. I suppose it's the same reasoning that causes some athletes to stop playing when they realize they can't make it to the big leagues. It seems to me that it's better to get out and do what you can, even if it is just sitting by a lake or looking up at a mountain from a picnic table.

There is no reason to feel being outdoors requires constant, high-energy exercise. Outdoor experiences do not have to be endurance trials. One of the first few columns I wrote for the *Monadnock Shopper* was called "Outdoor Zen", and I think it captures my thinking about being outdoors.

Although nearly all the columns are about active pursuits such as hiking and canoeing, there is a great deal to recommend being outside and being still, at least sometimes. An odyssey has come to mean a long journey, either physical or spiritual, but every journey includes rest stops. Even the great hero of the original *Odyssey* spent more time hanging around a couple of Mediterranean islands than he did actually sailing to Ithaca.

Some of the best parts of the little journeys I have taken in the woods or on rivers and lakes have been those moments when I just sat, to rest, but also to enjoy my surroundings. There are always things to see and think about outdoors, buy you have to take some time to do it. It's very easy to become so concerned with the end of the trip that you forget that it's being outdoors that's most important. The end of the hike, after all, is also the end of the physical experience.

Probably campers understand, or at least practice this point of view better than hikers. Campers really look forward to the campfire at night, and sitting around it is often the high point of the day. Of course hikers can do that, too, but often they are so tired at the end of the day that they are sound asleep soon after dinner. There is no real reason why hikers, cyclists or paddlers can't stop and sit more often, and some do. They are the ones who are not always in a hurry to get to the next shelter or complete the day's allotted miles.

One very good reason to spend more time just sitting is that you will see more. When you are always in motion, even walking, you often pass by things well worth examining. Oh, no one passes by the large and spectacular without a pause. Who would hurry by a moose standing in a stream or an eagle perched on a limb above a lake? It's the many smaller things – flowers, insects, individual trees, birds, inviting rocks or logs to sit on, pleasant views, and on and on – that many people really just pass by without notice.

Moreover, you don't have to be on a hike or ride to do your sitting. It doesn't have to be a break from something else. Sitting in your garden or on your patio is fine. Think of all the lovely parks in our towns, all with inviting benches. Many people drive to good view points such as Miller State Park on Pack Monadnock Mountain just to watch the sunset. Sunsets, sunrises, moonrises, wind-driven clouds, ducks swimming on a pond – they are all there waiting for you to sit and watch.

Although one good reason for stopping and looking around is that you will see and learn more, it's not essential that there

SUNRISE IN PILLSBURY STATE PARK

always be something particular to see at all. It's really the sitting, the reflection, that is most important. That's where the zen enters. The literal meaning of zen is sitting meditation. I think sitting somewhere outside and just letting your mind wander a bit while your feet are resting is a really fine form of meditation, and one way to enjoy the outdoors without breaking a sweat.

February 2008

Part One

Hiking

1
MacDowell Dam Trails
Peterborough, NH

The Monadnock Region is blessed with many fine hiking and walking paths including, of course, Monadnock itself. One of the less used is the recreation area around the MacDowell Dam in Peterborough. There is a real variety of paths about the lake, paved sections, wide and level dirt roads, and a real woods path along the northern shore.

I recently walked the large loop around the area which includes a mile or so on paved roads outside the reservation.

I parked in the picnic area on the far side of the dam itself from which great views of the lake and surrounding wooded hills may be had. The picnic area is quite extensive and includes playing fields and shelters, toilet buildings, a boat launch, and a small beach. Although large groups are welcome and sometimes present, the area is most often far from crowded. I walked back across the dam, through the picnic area on the southern shore of the lake and started on the "Wetland Wander Trail" which is a broad, gravel road which closely follows the shore of the lake Widely spaced benches on the water's edge provide great spots to sit and admire the water as well as the many birds that populate the brush along the lake. I'm no expert birder, but I recognized kingbirds and one bright oriole as well as several ducks. I believe ospreys have been seen at times.

After passing another boat launch which is accessed from outside the main area, the road rises a little, leaves the reservation proper and passes a house on the road which leads to the boat launch. Just past the house is the paved Spring Road. If you turn right here, you soon reach another gravel road/trail which returns to the lake shore through a sand pit. Turn left, as I did, and after a mile or so of walking along Spring Road to just where it joins Rte. 137, another trail leads back to the dam.

This trail is a real woods path, narrow and winding. It's certainly more difficult than the gravel road along the lake, and sturdy shoes or hiking boots are probably a wise choice. The trail at first follows a swift little stream with some white water and small pools that may contain fish although I saw no evidence of fishermen. The trail is located on a fairly steep slope that leads right to the water and sometimes it climbs a bit, but never very much. There are also many large rocks and even boulders along and near the trail. Soon the little stream leads to the beginning of the lake itself and the road along the opposite shore can be seen. It's a very pleasing, thickly wooded trail, well over a mile long. There are many spots for watching for wildlife in and about the lake and its many marshy areas.

Then it's back to the dam itself, the little circle where I left my car. The whole loop, gravel trail, paved roads and woods trail is about five miles. You can do it in an hour and half, or you could take most of the day, even do a little fishing. By the way, there is no charge.

June 2002

2
Luca's Lookout
Pillsbury State Park
Washington NH

Just a bit north of the Monadnock Region, Pillsbury State Park provides opportunities for primitive camping, boating, mountain biking, snowmobiling, wildlife-viewing, and hiking. The park's more than 5000 acres include miles of snowmobile and foot trails, many on old logging roads very suitable for mountain biking and walking. The park also includes a section of the Monadnock Sunapee Greenway.

I hiked a loop from the park to Lucia's Lookout on a southern shoulder of Mt. Sunapee and back. It's an eight and a half mile hike with gradual climbs and descents and one short but steep climb to the look-out. This is a fairly strenuous day hike, but an early start gives you plenty of time to take it easy with breaks and a long lunch at the lookout.

The park entrance is on Route 31, a few miles north of Washington, a few miles south of the junction with Route 10. The park's main road leads first to the headquarters where a day use charge is collected when the park is operating, from May until October. The trails begin at the small, grassy play area on Mill Pond, about a mile from there. Mill Pond is only one of 10 ponds within the park.

The hiking begins just past the play area where a gate closes the gravel road to cars. For the first half mile, the trail passes Milll Pond and then North Pond. It is really two trails at first, the Five Summers Trail and Bear Pond Trail, and it is really more of a road than a foot trail. Snowmobile trail signs and sturdy bridges over the streams show the popularity of the park with the winter riders.

After a half mile, the Bear Pond Trail splits off to the right. I followed its blue blazes upward past Bear Pond to the junction with the Greenway, just under two miles from the parking area. The trail is more of a hiking trail and less of a forest road as you climb gradually up to the ridge. It is also very muddy in spots, especially in spring and early summer, and you should expect to get a little muddy, too. I began noticing moose tracks in that mud. Before the day was over, I saw hundreds of tracks, but never a moose. They are there, though, and are often seen in and around the many ponds, as well as crossing Route 31.

There's a sign post and a mailbox with trail info and a log for hikers at the junction with the Greenwav. I always sign in at these points. It's a safety precaution, of course, but it's also interesting to read the comments of other hikers.

Bear Pond Trail runs easterly from the park, and at the Greenway junction I turned left, to the north. This is a real footpath following the long ridge which leads to the summit of Mt. Sunapee. The trail is dry and passes under spruces and then beech trees. Nearly two miles from the junction, the Greenway's Moose Lookout Campsite is located. It's a tent platform in a small clearing with a primitive toilet nearby. Water is available from a small stream, but it should be filtered before drinking. The campsite makes a fine rest stop.

A mile beyond the campsite, the Five Summers Trail from the park joins the Greenway. This is the point where the steepest climb of the day is found. It's short, however and leads to the day's goal - Lucia's Lookout. There's another mailbox at this point, and the Greenway continues on to Mt. Sunapee, but my destination was the lookout and its great views. The first view is from the top of the climb before taking the side trail to Lucia's Lookout itself. This view is back - toward the south and east - and includes Mt. Monadnock. The lookout itself has views to the west and north and includes Mt. Sunapee, so both ends of the Greenway can be seen almost at once. Lunch at Lucia's Lookout is a good idea, and you could spend an hour or two enjoying the views and nesting up for the return hike to the park.

I took the Five Summers Trail back to the play area by Mill Pond. The trail was built by campers from Camp Union in Greenfield, and is named for the five summers it took. It leads from Pillsbury to Lake Solitude, about three miles beyond Lucia's Lookout. Most of the trail is easy walking if you don't mind getting muddy again.

It's almost four miles to the play area by Mill Pond, and the closer you get to the park, the more the trail becomes a road. The feature of this section that I remember most is water. Ponds, streams, and puddles are everywhere, and the sound of running water is prevalent. In late June, there were lots of wildflowers, too, and it was a pleasant trip.

The four miles passed quickly, and soon I was crossing streams on snowmobile bridges again. Bear Pond Trail came in from the left, the access roads to the remote campsite on North Pond showed up, and then Mill Pond, the gate across the road, and I was back at the grassy play area. Before I left the park, I took a walk on some of the park roads and checked out some of the tent sites. I plan to return to the park soon and spend a few nights camping.

July 2002

ELIZA ADAMS GORGE, DUBLIN NH

3
Eliza Adams Gorge
Dublin, NH

One of the most scenic spots on the Monadnock-Sunapee Greenway is just a short hike from busy route 101 in Dublin. The Eliza Adams Gorge, a mini version of Chesterfield Gorge, is well worth a visit.

The trail crosses the highway just west of the Howe Reservoir. At that point the trail is really a dirt road, and there is a sign reading Monadnock Wilderness Girl Scout Campsite. Parking is a problem. There is some space along the highway on its north side (westbound), and it is possible to pull over on the south shoulder (eastbound) and park along the dirt road that leads quickly to a gate – but don't block the gate. If you don't mind adding to your walk, you could park at the rest area on the north side of the highway where it crosses the reservoir, just east of the trail crossing.

From 101, follow the white blazes of the MSG. The trail begins with a steep but very short climb and then levels out for a while. As stated above, the trail is really a road as it leaves the highway, and it is very easy to follow. You do have to watch for the trail markers, though, because there are other woods roads and trails that intersect with the Greenway. There's also a powerline to cross under. Although the Howe Reservoir is close by, you won't see it till you are fairly near the gorge. There is also a side trail with blue blazes about a mile from the highway which leads to the Leighton State Forest Campsite. The campsite is a tent platform and pit toilet a few yards west of the trail. Not long past the campsite side trail, the water comes into view and the trail begins to go downhill. There's a sharp left turn and the trail, which is just a trail at that point, descends by switchbacks to the gorge.

The gorge is just below the dam at the northern end of the Howe

Reservoir. In early September of this very dry summer, there was only a small stream of water exiting the reservoir and flowing through the gorge. However, it certainly wasn't dry, and the sound of moving water was a nice contrast to the sound of cars on 101 which is what you hear for the first half-mile or so.

The walls of the gorge are rocky and quite steep. There is a rugged, two part footbridge, built by volunteers from the Monadnock-Sunapee Greenway Trail Club. At this time of year, the bridge is several feet above the water, but in spring or following heavy rains, the water may be almost up to the bridge, and crossing it can be dangerous.

The gorge is a cool and shady place, and that makes it especially attractive on a hot summer day. On the other hand, I'm sure it's vjust as attractive in the fall foliage season and in winter with snow and ice coating the ledges. Threre are short paths on either bank of the stream that allow you to enjoy several perspectives of the gorge, but since the path passes through private property, hikers have to stay close to the treadway.

I continued north on the trail for about a third of a mile to the intersection with Brown Road. Going that far from 101 makes the roundtrip about three miles. It also allows you to encounter the gorge coming from the north on your way back and see it from another angle. Some hikers don't like out-and-back walks and prefer to use two cars, one at either end of the hike; they are the ones who are trying to complete an entire trail such as the Greenway from one end to the other. If that's your goal, you might feel it is a waste of time to re-trace your steps. I've found that it isn't. For one thing, a trail walked in the opposite direction is really a different trail in its feel and look. For another, it gives you a second chance to enjoy the highpoints of the trip. You can also recover that water bottle you forgot when you stopped for lunch!

After another pause at the gorge, I was soon back within sound of the highway traffic. I crossed the road – easily the part of the whole trip that requires the most caution – and was finished. Including two pauses at the gorge, the whole hike took just two hours.

If you are looking for an easy, two or three mile walk in the woods to a very beautiful destination, Eliza Adams Gorge is a real winner.

October 2002

4
Wapack Trail
Cabot Skyline
Sharon, NH

The Wapack Trail is a twenty-one mile hiking trail that runs along the ridges from Mt. Watatic in northern Massachusetts to North Pack Monadnock Mountain in Greenfield, New Hampshire. Although the whole trail is doable in one very strenuous day, most people like to take it a portion at a time or even hike the same sections over and over.

The Cabot Skyline part of the trail in Sharon is named for Thomas Cabot, and it passes through the Avelinda Forest which Mr. Cabot established many years ago. The forest occupies much of the high lands from Sharon through Temple and into Peterborough. It's not all in one piece, being interrupted by Temple Mountain Ski Area, Miller State Park and private holdings. Mr. Cabot was a true conservationist who wanted others to enjoy the beauty of the Wapack. He granted an easement for the Wapack Trail to pass through the Avelinda Forest. You might notice one of the small, silver metal signs that bear the name of the forest on a tree trunk as you walk along the trail or walk up the auto road to Miller State Park.

I often hike the section of the Wapack that includes the Cabot Skyline, beginning at the small parking area off Temple Road in Sharon. Temple Road can be reached from route 123 not far from the Sharon Art Center. There is room for only a few cars at the parking area, but it is seldom filled. On the other side of Temple Road, the bright yellow triangles that mark the Wapack lead into the woods.

The first part of the trail going north from Temple Road is wide and pretty steep. A few yards from the road is a large sign and map of the Wapack Trail and a trail log. Right after that there is an old frame building just off the trail on the right. It's a two story structure that may have been a house or cottage although the guide calls it a shed. There's still some plaster clinging to the first floor ceiling, but the ceiling itself has mostly fallen. I know many hikers have taken shelter there from storms, but it's surely not safe.

The trail gets narrower past the house, and before long there is a nice view to the east. From that point the trail continues upward steeply until you reach another outlook to the right of the path. That is the start of the Sharon ledges part of the trail, and there is a sign identifying the Cabot Skyline as the next 2.2 miles. Although there are plenty of bare rocks and ledges, the area is not without vegetation. The trees are spaced more, and many are rather small. There are lots of blueberries and several cairns to show the way in winter. At this point the trail is almost level, but there is still a gradual rise as the ridge leads to Burton Peak.

After about three quarters of a mile, the woods become more dense. A stone wall parallels the trail on the right at this point, and it is in really good shape. It's a reminder of the days when the ridges and hills in the area were open pasture land, free of trees for the most part. The path takes a few dips and rises, still going mainly up, and at a about a mile and a half from the road a sign announces the junction with the Berry Pasture Trail which comes up from near the Sharon Art Center.

From the trail sign for the Berry Pasture Trail, it's a short but steep climb to Burton Peak, 2020 feet high. It's one of the two bumps you can see on Temple Mountain when you are approaching from the west on route 101. The other one is Holt Peak which is slightly higher. The top of the ski area overlooking 101 is actually lower than Holt Peak.

Burton Peak is a good place to rest or have lunch. The summit is tree-covered, but there is a good view to the east right at the top, and there is another view to the west on some ledges just a few feet north of the summit.

The Cabot Skyline portion of the Wapack ends just beyond Burton Peak, but I walked a little farther north to a nice rocky viewpoint just before the final climb to Holt Peak. There's a good view all the way to the Green Mountains from that spot. It's just about two and

CABOT SKYLINE

a half miles from Temple Road, so turning around there gives me a five mile hike for the day. If you continue north from that point, over Holt Peak and through the ski area to the highway, it's about four and a half miles, but you'll need another car waiting for you.

The Wapack Trail is a fine hiking path, and it is maintained by volunteers from the Friends of the Wapack. They do a great job keeping the trail open, well-marked and clean. Their address is Friends of the Wapack, PO Box 115, W. Peterborough, NH 03468.

October 2002

5
Off Season
Greenfield State Park
Greenfield, NH

In summer, Greenfield State Park is a busy place. Most of its 252 campsites are usually occupied, and day visitors crowd the beach on Otter Lake. Cars, bicycles and pedestrians swarm the network of roads and paths. It is a sizable community of happy people temporarily living the simple life of campfires and sleeping bags.

After Labor Day the crowds decrease, and the park closes for the season on Columbus Day. The office is shut down; the water lines are drained, and the staff is dismissed until spring. However, the park remains open for day use all year. The campground roads are great for walking or biking. When the snow arrives, cross-country skiing, snowshoeing and snowmobiling become popular. If the snow is plentiful, in fact, the park can get pretty busy on weekends. For most of the off season, though, it's a very quiet place and there are very few visitors.

I spent the morning of the first Monday in November walking in the park, and the peacefulness and lack of visitors made it easier to appreciate the natural features. Of course the picnic tables, roads and toilet buildings were still there, and I could almost hear the summer hum of voices and radios, but only almost. Most of my walk was either in the woods or along the beach anyway.

I began on the main road into the campground. The roads are blocked off to cars, but there is a small parking area near the camper dumping station. From there I walked by the front of the large A frame which is the park headquarters and took the footpath leading to Hogback Pond. If you've only been to the beach and picnic area on Otter Lake, you might not know there are three small ponds within the park itself. Hogback can be reached only by foot, and it is a good fishing spot, stocked with brook trout. There are no campsites or picnic tables on the pond, but there is a path around it which passes under some very tall pines.

After walking around Hogback, I took the footpath that parallels the Bennington Road which borders that section of the park. Except for a mild climb up from the pond, the path is mainly level and very easy walking. It passes close to the main campground, but the sites are not visible. In summer the noise of the campers would be evident in some spots, but in November there was no sign of being so close to so many campsites.

The highlight of the trip happened as I was on that section of trail. I came around a bend in the path and saw a barred owl perched on a pine limb about twelve feet above the path. I stopped, quite close to the owl, but he only stared at me with his dark eyes. He didn't seem the least bit frightened and must have been used to campground visitors. After a minute or two, I walked directly under him, but he still didn't move other than to twist his head around and give me another stare.

I stopped again to watch the owl, wishing I had remembered to bring my camera. Then I noticed first a pair of chickadees, then a nuthatch on a trunk, then several titmice, and finally a blue jay. One of the chickadees flew onto a small branch just inches from me. I hadn't seen or heard any other birds for the first minutes I was watching the owl. I wondered if they had been keeping still and quiet for fear of me or for fear of the owl. It was a Disneyland experience, and I half expected to hear music from *Bambi.*

I watched the owl and the small birds for another minute or so and then headed down the trail. It soon joined the campground at the extreme northern end of the park. I followed the campground road around the outside of the main camping loop. The road was covered with leaves, and that helped me to forget how many cars travel it during the camping season. I couldn't ignore all the empty sites with their tables and fireplaces, but they didn't spoil the beauty. The sites actually create a nice openness to that portion of the park. I walked the road until I reached site 162 where a path leads to the beach.

The beach area is always lovely, no matter what time of year.

I'm sure the woods along the far shore of the lake were striking a few weeks ago, but plenty of color remained. There were the pines in the picnic area, the sandy beach and the water. The marsh behind the center part of the beach even had bright bunches of orange winterberries to accent the prevailing tans and grays. I took advantage of one of the picnic tables to rest and admire the lake for awhile, and then I walked up the beach road to my car.

This winter, when there's snow and the ponds are iced over, I plan to return to Greenfield State Park with my snowshoes. I plan to bring my camera, too.

November 2002

SUNRISE ON PACK MONADNOCK

6

Sunrise on Pack Monadnock Peterborough NH

The winter solstice came around eight o'clock on Saturday evening, December 21st, this year, and I decided the next morning would be a good time to see the sun rise and begin its trip to the north. It's the solar new year. The days are getting longer now, but the cold is still intensifying. As the saying goes: "As the days get longer, the cold gets stronger." Still, it is nice to have increasing rather than decreasing daylight.

To get a good view of the sunrise, I thought I would walk up the Miller State Park auto road to the summit of Pack Monadnock Mountain in Peterborough. I pulled into the parking lot off route 101, just opposite Temple Mountain Ski Area, at about 6:30 Sunday morning and started up the road, which is gated and not maintained in the winter. It was still pretty dark, but light enough to walk without a flashlight. The road surface was covered with a thin layer of packed snow and ice. Many footprints were frozen into the surface, showing that even in winter the park gets visitors.

The road is steep right from the start; it's one of the steepest paved roads in the state. That, combined with the ice, made for fairly tough going. The temperature wasn't very cold, just a bit below freezing, and the uphill climb soon made me feel pretty warm. I couldn't see it in the weak light, but just before the first hairpin turn there is an inscription on a roadside rock that identifies the company of the Civilian Conservation Corps that improved the road and helped develop the state park back in the 1930's. There is also a sign at the summit area giving the CCC credit.

About a half a mile from the base there are two hairpin turns on a very steep stretch of the road. Just past the second turn there is a nice lookout to the south and east. When I reached that point, the sky was showing a narrow strip of red above the horizon, about where Boston can be seen on a clear day. To the south from that point I could see the nearby ski slopes on Temple Mountain and the whole Wapack Ridge leading to Mt. Watatic in Ashby, Massachusetts. Beyond Watatic, the ski slopes on Mt. Wachusett, near Worcester, were also clearly visible.

I enjoyed the view for a few minutes and then continued up the road. For a quarter mile or so past the lookout the road is fairly level, compared to the rest, and there is a nice view toward the west and Mt. Monadnock. The local cable TV installation is located just west of the road in this section, but it isn't noticeable from the road. On the other hand, there are a number of towers and structures lining the road for the last, very steep stretch to the summit.

At the summit, the road makes a one-way circle and widens into the parking lot for the main picnic area of Miller State Park. There are wonderful views to all points of the compass from the summit area, but to get a 360 view, one has to climb the tower at the center of the parking area. For many years the tower was capped with a fire lookout cab which was manned until the 1980's. The cab is gone now, and the tower is just a platform for a number of antennae. The little fire lookout's cabin that was nestled in the trees just below the summit is gone also (moved to Forest Park in Greenfield), and in its place there is a very large tower. There were some objections to that tower, but there it is.

Since it was the sunrise I wanted to see, instead of using the old tower I walked over to the picnic tables that sit on a ledge just behind the park storage shed. There is a great view to the east from that point. When I got there, it was just about time for the sunrise, and the horizon was glowing red. All of it that is except several cloud-covered miles right where the sun would rise. I never saw the sun itself that morning, but I knew it rose, right on time. Clouds can hide the sun, but they can't hold it back.

I sat on a picnic table for awhile, watching the light grow stronger, despite the clouds. Then I started to feel a bit chilly; a strong west wind was blowing, and I started back down the road to the parking lot.

January 2003

7

Little Monadnock Mountain Fitzwilliam NH

On the Monday before New Year's, I decided to do some snowshoeing on the still-fresh snow that fell on Christmas. I thought I would drive to Rhododendron State Park in Fitzwilliam and hike from the park to the summit of Little Monadnock Mountain. I hadn't been to the park for several years, and I had never been there in the winter, so it seemed like a good choice.

It turned out to be a very good choice, especially for the beauty of the day. The drive over to Fitzwilliam was lovely. Poole and Pearly ponds in Rindge were frozen and snow-covered, and they simply glowed beneath the brilliant blue sky. The common in Fitzwilliam with its grand old houses was another treat on the way to the park. The park is easy to find, located on Rhododendron Road, which joins Route 119 just beyond the common. There are plenty of signs to guide you.

The entrance to the park was blocked by a huge snow bank, but there was enough cleared space to park two or three cars safely off the road. The snow on the road which leads past the park and continues to the north wasn't plowed, but it was pretty well-packed, so I carried my snowshoes until I got into the park itself. There were plenty of tracks: boots, skis, and snowmobiles. When, after only a few yards, I turned into the parking lot area, I noticed a sign that said the park trails were off-limits to all mechanized vehicles. There were no snowmobile tracks beyond that point.

I stopped at the entrance to the trail that loops around the rhododendron grove and put on my snowshoes. There are two tall stone pillars marking the beginning of the path that make quite a dramatic entranceway to the dense grove of rhododendrons that are the park's main attraction. They bloom in July, of course, but the thick coating of white snow that crowned the dark green leaves when I snowshoed along the path rivaled the flowers of summer. The leaves themselves hung down in pendulous clusters which resembled miniature folded umbrellas or bunches of freshly dipped green candles. They arch over the trail so that it is almost like walking through a tunnel at times.

After about a quarter mile, a sign marked the beginning of the trail to the top of Little Monadnock, one and a half miles from that point. The rhododendrons thinned out quickly and the woods opened up so that the sky was visible. Some cross- country skiers had used the trail since the last snow, and I followed their tracks upward, gradually at first and then a bit steeper. I probably could have done without the snowshoes and walked on the ski tracks, but I didn't want to post hole the tracks. Modern snowshoes are so easy to use anyway that I found it easier to keep them on, and I knew there would be plenty of places on the trail where I would really need them.

The skiers had given up about half way to the summit when the trail reached a fairly long, steep section.Their tracks ended, but one set of boot tracks kept going up the trail. There were also plenty of deer and squirrel tracks in the snow, but I didn't see a deer or squirrel all morning. It was quiet, and there was very little wind. I was really the main source of noise as I made my way up the trail .

About a quarter of a mile from the summit, the boot tracks reversed themselves and started back down the mountain. From that point on to the top of the mountain, only animal tracks had broken the surface of the snow cover. There were a few more steep spots, and I had to steady myself a number of times by grabbing onto tree trunks, but really it wasn't very difficult. I did get pretty warm and a little sweaty.

The park trail ended at the junction with the Metacomet/ Monadnock Trail, a tenth of a mile below the summit. There's a sign at that point which points to a vista just south of the junction, and it also shows the way to the actual top of the mountain. I went on to the forested summit first, where another sign marks the 1800′ peak of the mountain, and then I doubled back to the junction and down the ridge to the vista. There's a really great view from that point. To the west, the ski areas of southern Vermont were clearly

MOUNT MONADNOCK FROM LITTLE MONADNOCK

visible, and to the east Mount Monadnock dominated everything else.

The trip down was easier, but it was also more slippery. I found myself on my rear several times, but the snow cushioned my little falls. It would have been easier without the snowshoes, but I knew the steep spots would soon give way to the more gradual pitch of most of the trail. I was back at my car in an hour.

January 2003

8
The Wheeler Trail On Snowshoes Peterborough NH

The deep snow and mild temperatures of the day following the big Presidents' Day storm were perfect for snowshoeing. I wanted to do just that, but I had only part of the day available. The solution was easy; I decided to visit the Wheeler Trail in Peterborough. It was an easy decision because the trail is less than a mile long and less than a mile from my house.

To get to the trail, I walked to Cheney Avenue with my snowshoes under my arm. It was nice to leave the car at home. About a quarter of a mile up Cheney, I put on my snowshoes and started across the large open area that lies between the road and the forested area that includes most of the trail. The town owns the field, and one of its features is a small pond that is used by skaters. No one was skating as I crossed the field because the pond was covered with nearly two feet of new snow.

For the first part of my little trip, I had to break trail. The snow was not only deep but very fluffy, and I sank to my knees at each step. Before long I came to the trail of another snowshoer, and that made the going much easier. I soon reached the section of the trail which goes along the edge of the field and followed it to where it goes back into the forest. I was beginning the trail at the point farthest from the actual trailhead, which is on route 101. The small parking lot there is buried in snow and hidden by the huge snowbanks on the highway.

Once in the woods, I was impressed, as always, by the beauty of the little trail. It mostly follows a small brook and crosses it several times on small footbridges. There is a nice mixture of mature pines, hemlocks, beeches and birches. The lower branches of the smaller hemlocks were laden with the fresh snow, and as I went along I set off small cascades of snow. White and gray were the dominant colors with the many shadows playing on the new snow. There was also the deep green provided by the hemlock branches, but it was the tree trunks themselves that offered the most interesting contrast with the whiteness. Not only was there the great variety of bark texture, but there was also a variety of colors. Sometimes we may think of tree trunks as just black or brown, but really there is a great range of shades including the nearly chocolate brown of the large hemlocks to the pale olive smoothness of the beech trees. The pure light of the winter day helped make the subtle colors more noticeable than usual.

The little stream, Wallace Brook, was completely covered with snow and it was silent. In spring and summer its clear, moving water is the real focus of the trail. Most of the trail goes along its banks, and it is at the center of the main loop. I followed it to the trailhead next to the highway. There is a mailbox there with trail maps and a small notebook for visitor comments. At that point, the sound of traffic on 101 was inescapable, but the huge snowbanks kept the cars hidden.

From the trailhead, I started back to the field, crossing the first bridge in order to complete the loop. When I reached the field, I followed the short spur trail which leads down to the little pond. The field itself is lovely, and the few scattered pines and birches give an almost landscaped aspect to the area. Viewed against the unbroken snow they suggested a very large Japanese garden.

From the pond, I retraced my tracks back to Cheney Avenue. A few minutes later I was walking back down my street. I count myself very fortunate to have such as beautiful little trail so close to home, but all of us who live in the Monadnock Region are fortunate in that there are so many lovely roads, paths and trails close at hand. We just have to take those first steps outside.

March 2003

9
Skatutakee and Thumb Mountains Harris Center Hancock NH

Since I recently became a member of the Harris Center, I thought it would be a good idea to take a late winter hike on some of their trails. The trail map shows it is possible to make a four mile loop from the center which includes the summits of both Skatutakee and Thumb mountains, and on a mid-March morning I set out to do just that.

The first thing I noticed upon arriving at the center, located on King's Highway in Hancock, was that there is a major renovation going on to the buildings. In fact, the office is temporarily located in Jaffrey. I don't know what the buildings looked like before, but they are certainly going to be impressive after the renovations.

I parked in the small lot just below the center and walked a short distance to the beginning of the Harriskat Trail, which leads to the top of Skatutakee. I was carrying my snowshoes, thinking I would strap them on once I was on the trail. When I started the trail itself, I quickly decided snowshoes wouldn't be needed because the path was solidly packed and as easy to walk on as in summer. I carried the snowshoes back to my car and started over.

The summit of Skatutakee is 660 feet above the Harris Center, but as the trail map states, the climb on the Harriskat Trail is quite gentle. The trail goes through a mixed forest of hardwoods and evergreens. One of the first features I noticed was a number of large boulders near the trail. They were all topped with a smooth coating of snow, and only patches of the gray stone were visible. About a half mile from the road, the yellow blazes of the Thumbs Down Trail lead off to the right. My plan was to return by that route, and I kept on the Harriskat Trail to the top of the mountain.

As it nears the summit, the path goes through a grove of very tall pines and then a stand of spruce. I noticed several large trees that must have fallen this winter and are now hung up above the walkway. The last section of the trail has some steeper parts, but it is really an easy hike. The summit is marked by a cairn, and there is a fine 180 degree view that includes Crotched Mountain, the Packs, and Mt. Monadnock. The view of Monadnock from the north is much different than the better-known views from east and west. With its snow cover, it is an impressive sight.

From the top of Skatutakee, I followed the Thumbs Up Trail toward Thumb Mountain. Thumb is just about the same height as Skatutakee, but the first part of the trail goes down quite a bit, so there is a climb to the top of Thumb. The Thumbs Up Trail meets the Thumbs Down Trail a quarter mile from the summit. The last stretch starts with a steep climb, but most of the final quarter mile is easy. The view from Thumb is not as grand as that from Skatutakee, but Mt. Monadnock, being the main attraction, seems larger.

Although it wasn't particularly cold, especially for this winter, there was a stiff southerly breeze blowing across the summit, and I soon started back down. When I got back to the junction with the Thumbs Down Trail, I followed it in order to complete the loop I had planned. Halfway down, the trail passes Jack's Pond. The snow-covered pond, with the shoulder of Skatutakee looming behind it, was the highlight of that section of my hike.

I hadn't seen any wildlife to that point, although I had heard some chickadees and a woodpecker pounding away in the distance. Then I saw and heard a fairly large bird flying away among the trees. A little while later I came to a large, dead tree next to the path which had two, large rectangular excavations – the work of the pileated woodpecker, which was probably the bird I saw and heard. The snow beneath the tree was littered with bark and wood chips; he must have been working really hard.

Not long after that, the trail reached its junction with the Harriskat Trail. I followed that back to the Harris Center and my car. It was a pleasant hike, and I look forward to doing it again in summer. There are other trails within the center's 7,000 acres that I plan to walk, and there is canoeing on Spoonwood Pond. If you are interested in finding out more about the Harris Center, its address is 83 King's Highway, Hancock, NH 03449. There is also a website: www.harriscenter.org.

March 2003

10
Hiking in April

April may not be "the cruellest month" as T.S. Eliot wrote, but it might be the teasingest month. There will be sunny, warm days and blooming flowers this month, but there will also be gray days with sleet and snow. In "Two Tramps in Mud Time," another poet, Robert Frost, had it right:

You know how it is with an April day
When the sun is out and the wind is still,
You're one month on in the middle of May.
But if you so much as dare to speak,
A cloud comes over the sunlit arch,
A wind comes off a frozen peak,
And you're two months back in the middle of March.

Last April was a perfect example of its teasing nature. You probably remember that last winter was mild, and the snow was gone in March. Then we had some really warm weather in April. Wednesday, the seventeenth of April, had temperatures in the nineties. Trees were blossoming early, and so were many wildflowers. It was summer!

Four days later, my brother, Kye ,and I were beginning a four-day backpacking trip on the Appalachian Trail from Cheshire, Massachusetts, to route 9 in Vermont. By that time the weather had turned much cooler and there was the possibility of snow flurries.

It was sunny and fairly mild when we started up Mt. Greylock, but by the time we reached the summit there was ice forming on puddles, and a cold wind blowing. That night there was even a bit of sleet, and we found ourselves hiking through rain and sleet showers all the next day.

We stopped for a warm meal in North Adams, and then began the climb into Vermont where the Long Trail joins the AT. There are good viewpoints along the trail near the Vermont/Massachusetts border, but all we could see were clouds. It wasn't raining constantly, though, and it wasn't cold. Actually, since hiking along with a forty-pound pack generates plenty of heat, the temperature was quite pleasant.

That night we camped at the Seth Warner Shelter in southern Vermont, and by nightfall the temperature was dropping, and there were snowflakes mixing with the sleet. We left a candle burning in the front of the three-sided shelter, and when I woke in the middle of the night I could see heavy snow falling. In the morning there were about four inches of new snow covering the picnic table in front of the shelter.

We were not unprepared for such weather, and both of us had waterproof parkas, warm hats, gloves and gaiters. On the other hand, things were getting damp and it was too cold to sit still for long, so we decided to get an early start and hike all the way to route 9 that day instead of stopping for another night at the Congdon Shelter.

Soon after we started that morning, my hands got very cold. My gloves had gotten wet during the night, and they had lost their insulating value. When I realized my hands were getting numb, I knew I had to find a way to get them warm again quickly or suffer frostbite. We stopped on the trail, and my brother dug out his camping stove and lit it. I warmed my hands over its flame, and then I made mittens out of an extra pair of socks. They worked well, and in a few minutes my hands were warm again. I was glad my brother was there, because my fingers were probably too cold to allow me to light my own stove. I won't be caught without an extra pair of gloves in winter or early spring again.

The rest of the hike was enjoyable; the clouds broke up, and we could see some blue sky. We followed a bear's tracks for several miles, and we wondered if he was asking himself what happened to the summer weather of a few days earlier. We lost his trail on a rocky ridge, and we thought he might have gone back to his den to wait for April to make up its mind.

April 2003

11
Mount Grace
Warwick, Mass.

On a sunny, warm day near the end of April, I decided to drive into Massachusetts and hike Mt. Grace. It's a modest mountain, about 1600 feet high, surrounded by state forest. To get there, I took route 78 south from Winchester. Before it gets to the border, the highway runs through open farmland, but as soon as the road enters Massachusetts the country changes to hilly woodland. I was looking for a parking spot where the Metacomet-Monadnock Trail crosses the road, but I missed it on my first try and drove into the little town of Warwick where I turned around to try again.

It's easy to miss the trail because the road is narrow and winds through the forest. However, I had noticed what looked like a trail on my first pass, and it turned out to be the MM crossing. There had been a woman riding a horse toward the road from the woods when I went by the first time, and I could see that she had crossed the highway and headed north on the trail. There is a parking spot well off the road on the east side, and I left my car there, crossed the highway and started up the trail to the summit of Mt. Grace.

Just beyond the crossing, a side path leads to the south and the picnic area of the state forest, and there is the wreckage of an old dam on Mountain Brook. Beyond that point, the broad trail started a gentle climb up the mountain, and I was soon at the three-sided shelter building which is available to hikers. It sits on the banks of a small stream which provides water for overnighters at the shelter. There is another trail from the south which joins the MM at that point, and it would be easy to take it for the main trail, which

HIKERS ENJOYING THE MONADNOCK REGION

curves around the front of the shelter and is somewhat narrower as it resumes the climb.

The path climbs steadily through a mixed forest of hardwoods, hemlocks and pines. Some of the trees are quite tall. The trail is never very steep, and the first part of it is on an old woods road. Near the summit the path follows what was once a ski trail, and there is a slightly steeper stretch just before the top. From the road to the summit is about a mile and a half. It's good exercise, but not difficult.

The summit area is wooded, and there is a tall fire tower which is not in use but can be climbed to just below the cab. From the tower there are fine views into Massachusetts, Vermont and New Hampshire. It was hazy when I was there, but I could see Mt. Monadnock, Stratton Mountain in Vermont, and a portion of the Quabbin Reservoir to the south. In the small clearing below the tower, there is a large boulder with a rectangular indentation that clearly once held a plaque. I wonder if it was removed for repair or by vandals. Just below the tower there is an active radio tower and its building which is reached by an unpaved access road.

Instead of returning to route 78 the way I had come, I decided to continue down the south side of the mountain to where a side trail leads toward Warwick and the state forest. From the summit, the trail to the south follows a telephone line, and it goes down rather steeply for a quarter of a mile where it enters a clearing and meets the side trail.

I followed the blue marks of the side trail downhill on another woods road for about another quarter mile before it reached a large open picnic area next to route 78. A man was walking his dog on the field, and he was the only person I met on the trail that day. The path skirts the edge of the field and then re-enters the woods. I could see the hoof prints of the horse I had seen earlier in the morning. I followed them through the picnic area that is in the woods along the highway.

The state forest appears to have been a more popular spot years ago. There are sturdy stone fireplaces scattered about in open areas, but they don't seem to have been used for some time, and there are no tables. I passed the remains of a building that contained what had been the engine for a ski tow. The slope is covered with trees now, but the old building with its ancient six-cylinder motor is a reminder of an active past.

When I reached the shelter building, it was only a few minutes walk back to the highway and my car. On another day, I plan to hike to the same spot from where the MM Trail enters New Hampshire.

April 2003

12
Fremont Conservation Land
Peterborough NH

I was headed toward Peterborough on the Old Jaffrey Road on a cool, drizzly May morning when I saw the sign for the Fremont Conservation Land, and I decided to stop and go for a walk on its mile-long trail. I had been meaning to explore the area for some time, and since the rain seemed to be letting up for at least a while, it seemed like a good time to do it.

The area is one of twelve described in the Peterborough Trail Guide, which is sponsored by the Peterborough Conservation Commission. The 172 acres include a large field, two beaver ponds and forest; it's a great variety for a fairly small area. The trail begins in the field, and there is a mail box containing information about the trail and the area's history and wildlife.

The path leads first to a low part of the field, near a beaver pond, and then climbs toward a power line and the woods beyond. From the field there is a good view of Pack Monadnock Mountain. The top half of the mountain was hidden by the rain clouds when I was there, but that only made a more atmospheric picture. The rain had stopped, and the air was clear and fresh, but I was sure more showers would arrive. It was a nice time to be outside.

After the field, the trail crosses the power line and follows an old woods road that leads uphill through the forest. It passes a huge boulder left by a glacier and, near the top of the hill, a very old cellar hole which dates back to the early nineteenth century. The trail ends where it meets Wilder Road, but that road can be followed to another beaver pond. There are a number of side paths and woods roads that intersect the trail, and the trail map indicates that some will be improved and incorporated into the main trail system.

The cellar hole is a reminder of the early settlers who farmed and kept sheep. Their stone walls are still in evidence, but their fields and pastures are all woods now. The cellar and the walls are from a time that is remote to us, but it is the boulder that is the real time machine; it has occupied its present spot since being deposited by a glacier over a hundred centuries ago.

Glacial erratics, like The Rock, as it is known, are not uncommon in our region. There is another large one in the Shieling Forest, for example, just a few miles from the Fremont Land. They are even seen on some lawns. It's fascinating to think how many changes their surroundings have gone through while they have sat unchanged through the centuries. How many different forests have grown up and disappeared around them? How many generations of animals have used their cracks and crevices for shelter? How many people have sat against their steep sides to find shelter from the winter wind or the summer sun?

Although many glacial erratics can still be found in New England, many others are long gone, pulverized and paved over by the growth of our towns and cities. Perhaps a hundred years from now The Rock that stands on the Fremont Conservation Land will also have disappeared, replaced by an apartment building or a parking lot. I prefer to think that it will still be there, maybe the center piece of a park, maybe even once again surrounded by fields or pasture.

I passed by the boulder for a second time on my way back to the field and my car. The rain had held off for just about the whole trip, and not until I was re-crossing the open field, only a quarter of a mile from the trailhead, did the first drops of another shower arrive. Time was on my side that day. If you have some time, even an hour or two, the Fremont Conservation Land is a good place to spend it.

May 2003

13
The MM Trail: Falls Brook
Richmond, NH

On a sunny day in early June, I hiked a section of the Metacomet-Monadnock Trail from Greenwoods Road in Richmond down into Massachusetts. From the guide book, I knew the trail followed Falls Brook to a point just above a waterfall, but the beauty of the path along the stream and the size of the waterfall surprised me.

To get to the trailhead, I drove south on route 32 from the junction with 119 for about a mile and a half and then turned left onto Greenwoods Road. The MM Trail crosses the gravel road about a mile from the highway and just beyond a pond. I parked on the left of the road in a space large enough for two cars.

I left my car, crossed the road, and headed south on the white-blazed trail. The first part of my hike was along the shore of a pond, dense with hemlocks and mountain laurel. I soon noticed trees partially gnawed by beaver, and then I reached a point where the path was underwater. The beaver had built a large dam on the brook and flooded a section of the trail.

I made a small detour and was soon back on the trail which went uphill for a bit and moved away from the stream. Before long, though, the path was right on the bank of the brook again. Falls Brook moves through a narrow gorge, and the surrounding forest, mostly hemlock, is dense. Although it was a bright day, only a few rays of sun made it to the ground or the water. Nearly everything was gray, green, or brown. Even the water, when it wasn't white from motion, was brown, dyed by the tannin from the hemlocks.

About three quarters of a mile from the trailhead, I came to a small water fall with a large, nearly round pond beneath it. The rocky streambed began to show the effects of the moving water. There were potholes and large boulders carved by the water. Most impressive were a large, perfectly formed arch and a huge boulder with a concave depression across the stream from the arch. By the time I reached the arch, I was probably in Massachusetts, but I didn't notice any sign or marker.

As I neared the point where the MM Trail fords the brook, yellow blazes appeared along with the familiar white ones. They marked the Tully Trail, which is an eighteen mile loop starting from the campground on Tully Lake in Royalston, Massachusetts.
The white and yellow blazes also lead from the ford up a few yards to the lip of the major waterfall on the aptly named Falls Brook. From the ford itself, I couldn't see the falls, but it was really very near. There was a safety railing of steel cables and then the water plunged about forty feet. I followed the yellow blazes downstream to get a good look at the waterfall from that perspective. It was certainly worth the hike.

The Tully Trail goes south along the stream for another half mile or so and then follows a woods road for another two miles before crossing route 68. It would be easy for a hiker to follow the white and yellow blazes up the top of the falls and then follow the yellow blazes south. In fact, if a hiker isn't looking for the ford across the brook above the waterfall, he or she could end up following the Tully Trail for a long time before realizing the need to return to the waterfall and the ford above it.

I crossed the ford, stepping from rock to rock, and climbed the steep bank. The path became an old road, leveled out and reached route 32 just south of the Newton Cemetery. There were two picnic tables, space for several cars and a large, glassed-in signboard with a map of the Tully Trail, which runs along with the MM Trail for several more miles as they both head west along the Massachusetts-New Hampshire border.

I sat at one of the tables for a while, and then I decided to visit the old cemetery. Some of the headstones dated back to the early 1800's, and I was reminded that the countryside around Falls Brook was once more heavily settled farmland. I wondered if, in life, those buried there had picnicked by the waterfall so near their resting place. I wished them well and headed back down the trail to the ford and New Hampshire.

June 2003

14
The Raymond Trail Peterborough NH

The Marion Davis Trail and the Wapack Trail are the most popular paths to the summit of Pack Monadnock, but the nearby Raymond Trail is a good alternative. The trailhead is on East Mountain Road in Peterborough, less than a mile from route 101. There isn't much parking space, just enough for three cars. The trail was cut by Boy Scout Troop 808 back in the 1980's, and it is now maintained by the Peterborough Conservation Commission.

I hiked up the 1.6 mile long trail on a morning after a day of rain. There was still mist in the air, and each puff of wind caused a new little shower as the leaves let go their burden of water. It was also refreshingly cool for hiking.

The trail passes through a mixed forest of softwoods and hardwoods. Near the beginning there are some pines among the birches, maples, and oaks, but as the trail gets higher spruce trees dominate. Not far from the trailhead the path goes downhill to a muddy area and then begins a climb that is gentle for about a mile. The trail crosses a couple of little streams, the first of which was already just about dry in mid-July. It also crosses two stone walls built in the days when the mountainside was mainly clear of trees and used for pasture. The walking was easy on that stretch; there were few rocks on the path, and it was padded with fallen needles and leaves.

Then, a little over a mile from the trailhead, the path turned rocky and steep. Since everything was wet from the recent rain, I had to be careful on the slippery rocks. The steepest portion led to an opening that I knew had a good view to the west, but the persistent mist kept me from seeing more than a few yards. A nice rock for sitting and a wide clear spot indicated it was a popular resting place.

From the viewpoint on, the trail continued to climb fairly steeply, but with easier stretches. By that point the spruces were the main vegetation. When I was approaching the end of the trail, just below the peak of Pack Monadnock, a ray of sunshine broke through the mist and showed that I was nearly finished with the climb.

The Raymond Trail ends near the most northerly cluster of picnic tables in Miller State Park. They are on a rocky point that has a tremendous view from Mt. Monadnock in the west around to the hills near the coast. When the air is clear and dry, Mt. Washington and other peaks in the White Mountains are visible to the north. Of course the nearby mountains, including North Pack, Crotched Mountain and Lyndeboro Mountain, can be seen on all but the most cloudy or hazy days.

Once at the park, I had several choices. To the right, a path led to the main picnic area and the auto road. In addition to the road, the Marion Davis Trail and the Wapack Trail both would have taken me to the main parking lot off route 101. From there, I could have walked a few yards west on the highway and then turned onto East Mountain Road and back to my car. I could have simply turned around and headed back down the Raymond Trail. The final choice was to turn left and follow the Wapack Trail toward North Pack Monadnock. That's what I did.

I had lunch on North Pack, and it was early afternoon when I climbed back up South Pack and returned to the Raymond Trail for the last section of my hike. By that time the sun had been out for hours, and when I reached the rocky viewpoint that had been socked in on my way up the mountain, I had a fine view of Cunningham Pond and Mt. Monadnock.

July 2003

15
The Wales Preserve
Sharon NH

Located on Spring Hill Road in Sharon, the Wales Preserve is 48 acres of hilly, dense forest that is bisected by the lovely little Gridley River. The area belongs to the Nature Conservancy and was donated by the late Ralph Wales. He had a home and tree farm just up the road. I spent the summer of 1964 working for him, mowing lawns, pruning shrubs and tending the gardens. It was a beautiful place, and I felt privileged to spend so many hours there. Many paths wound about the trees and ponds of the estate. One of them led down a steep, wooded hill to a small stream. I didn't know its name then, but it was the Gridley River. Mr. Wales donated the land along the river to the Conservancy before his death in 1967.

In the preserve, the Brookside Trail follows the north bank of the river for nearly a mile. I followed it late in the afternoon of one of the last days in July. Although the sun had several hours left to shine, the dense forest, mostly hemlock, kept most of the path in shadow. When beams of sunlight did manage to hit the surface of the swiftly moving, tannin stained water, it looked like a frothy ale.

For the first half mile of the trail, the river is narrow and there are a number of small waterfalls. Overall, according to the Nature Conservancy's handout, the stream falls a total of 120 feet within the preserve. Beneath each of the falls there was a pool, and nearly every pool had a flat ledge protruding into it. They were all fine places to sit and enjoy the busy water. The sound of the water tumbling over the many falls and rocks was constant and soothing.

At about the half mile point, a second trail, The Woodland Trail, led off to the right, but I kept on the river trail. Just past the trail junction, the river turned from its westward course to the north. It also split in two to pass around a couple of fair-sized islands. The eastward branches of the river, which the path followed, were much smaller than the main stream. They were also nearly dry and mostly just strips of mossy rocks. The far side of the river also became steep at that point, cutting a channel beneath a hill. The river had grown wider and was flowing much more slowly by then. Just as I noticed the hillside on the far bank had lowered again, I heard a loud splash ahead of me. I saw a large deer bounding out of the water into the woods across the river.

Shortly after that, I reached a sign marking the second junction with the Woodland Trail. The Brookside Trail and the preserve ended just a few yards from that point. I decided to take the other trail on the way back. It led away from the river and up a hill. It passed among and under huge trees, mostly hemlocks at first with a few maples and birches, and then some tall pines. The music of the river soon disappeared, but it was a windy day, and the sound of the great trees being pushed around by the breeze was as lovely, if less constant.

The most remarkable feature of the trail, other than the trees, was a field of large boulders. Some of them were over seven feet high. They loomed in the shadows, mossy and gray.

The Woodland Trail is only about a half mile long, and I was soon back at the river and the Brookside Trail. I retraced my steps back to the road. Before leaving the preserve, I logged my name into the record book that is enclosed in a foldout stand along with the preserve handouts.

I spent most of my time in the preserve walking, but it really isn't necessary to walk more than a few yards down to the Gridley River. Sitting by one of the falls is probably the best way to experience the place. The beauty of the Wales Preserve encourages contemplation more than exercise. I left there with renewed reverence for the natural world and with appreciation for Ralph Wales and the Nature Conservancy.

August 2003

16
Between the Packs
Peterborough NH

The ridge between Pack Monadnock and North Pack Monadnock mountains provides some of the best hiking in the area. Fortunately, the land is well protected from development. Much of it is in the Wapack National Wildlife Refuge. Another portion is part of the new Joanne Bass Bross Preserve of the Nature Conservancy, and Miller State Park includes a good portion of the northern slope of Pack Monadnock itself.

On one of the nicer days of this summer, I hiked between the packs from Miller over to North Pack and back. I've done the hike many times, most of them while I was manager of the state park for over twenty years. Some of the walks I made on the trail during those years were in search of hikers reported lost. Usually that meant they had gotten to North Pack and then headed down the wrong side of that mountain and ended up on Old Mountain Road. I often found lost hikers on their way back to the park, nearing the end of a walk that was turning out to be much longer than they had planned. Well, I haven't worked at the park for years, but I still like to make the hike.

I followed the yellow triangles of the Wapack Trail on my recent hike down the steep mountainside to the low spot between the two summits. That part of the trail is the most difficult, especially on the way back. The pathway is mostly rock and can be slippery in wet conditions. Not far from the bottom of the climb, I noticed the handsome new sign that marks the Bross Preserve. I had also noticed, on the way down, one of the remaining metal tree markers identifying the Avelinda Forest, the forest preserve created by the late Thomas Cabot.

Once I passed the low point of the trip, I started up the first of two "saddles" that divide the climb to North Pack into easy steps. Years ago a person standing on the parking lot at the summit picnic area on Pack Monadnock could see hikers on their way north as they crossed the higher of the two saddles. The hikers, in turn, could look back and wave at the old fire tower. Now the woods have grown up so that the trees block the view. Boys from Brantwood Camp used to camp out at that point on the trail as one of their activities. They haven't done that for years, and all traces of their old campsites are gone.

Not far past the saddle, I came to the point where the Cliff Trail goes off to the right and then climbs steeply up the side of the rugged cliffs that are visible from the state park. I decided to take it to the summit of North Pack. It added a little over a half mile to my trip, but I wanted to enjoy the views from the top of the cliff. I wasn't in a hurry, either. The Cliff Trail begins by going downhill for a while. It's pretty rocky, too. Then it crosses a little stream and goes nearly straight up for a hundred yards or so. I had to scramble over some ledges, but I was soon sitting above the cliffs and looking back at Pack Monadnock and Temple Mountain.

The rest of the Cliff Trail is a more gradual climb over rocks and through a couple of spruce groves to the peak of North Pack. The summit area is rocky and there are great views to the north, west and east. When I was there the blueberries weren't ripe, but I could see they were getting close. Many people climb to the summit from Old Mountain Road to pick the berries. Actually, some of the best picking is just below the summit. A friend of mine claims to have been picking from a large bush one day when she discovered a bear eating from the other side. Evidently it was as frightened as she was and ran away.

I had a bit of lunch at the top and listened to a towhee make its *drink your tea* call. After that I headed down the Wapack toward Miller. For the first few yards the trail was a deep grove in the bare rock. It was steep, but not for long. Soon I was walking among some tall trees, and the path was broad and easy. I passed the junction with the Cliff Trail and was back on the section I had already walked.

The hike back to the park was more difficult once I passed the low point between the packs and started up the long, steep climb to the summit of Pack Monadnock. It made a tough ending to my hike, and I was glad to reach the picnic tables once again.

August 2003

17

Monadnock-Sunapee Greenway Pitcher Mountain to Jackson Hill Stoddard NH

As usual, there were a few clear, cool and dry days in late August. On one of them I hiked the Monadnock-Sunapee Greenway from Pitcher Mountain to just past Jackson Hill and back. It was a hike that covered what I consider one of the nicest sections of the Greenway, and it included a mix of narrow paths, ATV trails, and dirt roads. The route wasn't hard, but there were two good climbs each way.

I took route 123 from Peterborough through Hancock and Stoddard and parked at the small lot next to the highway, about half a mile from the summit of Pitcher. The drive was pleasant, and it would make a good route for foliage viewing this fall. One of the more interesting moments of my day came on that ride when a flock of turkeys slowly crossed the road in front of me. That happened less than half a mile from the center of Hancock. Sometimes it's hard to understand how any turkeys survive hunting season.

For the first part of my hike, the Greenway followed the access road to the fire tower. At the summit the trail crossed over the rocks directly below the tower and entered the berry fields on the north side. There was, of course, a fine view from the top of the mountain. The trail guide warns hikers to be careful crossing the open areas on Pitcher and Hubbard Hill because there are many side paths among the blueberry bushes. However, I found the white blazes of the Greenway easy to follow. The MSG Trail Club does a fine job of maintaining the path. I've walked just about all of it at one time or another, and I truly appreciate the job they do.

The extensive blueberry fields on Pitcher Mountain and Hubbard Hill are all within the Andorra Forest. In fact, my whole hike that day was within the forest. It is privately owned, and the owners have protected 11,000 acres of it forever by giving the development rights to the Society for the Protection of New Hampshire Forests. The owners have also designated a portion of the forest as a wildlife refuge in which hunting is not allowed.

The trail crossed the dirt road that leads to Hubbard Hill from the parking lot off route 123 and then entered the woods for a stretch. Before long it hit the road again and joined it for over a mile through the berry fields to the top of Hubbard. Just as I turned onto the road, I noticed another flock of turkeys a few yards down the road in the opposite direction. I counted twenty-two birds. One large tom kept his eye on me for a while as I watched the flock cross the road and go into the trees. They had come out of the section that is off limits to hunters. Maybe they know to stay there in hunting season.

Just beyond Hubbard Hill, the trail entered deep woods and went downhill toward Fox Brook. There were two small streams at the bottom of those woods, and there was a campsite on the first one, just a few yards from the trail. I'm not sure which one was Fox Brook. Once I crossed the brooks, the trail began its climb to the summit of Jackson Hill. Part way up the hill I came to what appeared to be an old house site. There was what looked like a cellar hole, and a couple of old apple trees were still bearing fruit.

At that point an ATV trail joined the Greenway for the ascent to the top of the hill. From there to the summit the trail was wide and smooth. The top of Jackson Hill was mainly open, with low bushes and large rocks. There were good views in every direction, and I could see Stratton Mountain to the west, Monadnock to the south, Pack Monadnock to the east, and many hills to the north. I could also see the white church in Marlow.

Since it was too early for lunch, I followed the trail down the north side of the hill to a large beaver pond. The ATV trail continued to follow the Greenway for most of that distance, until just before the pond. I walked past the pond for a few minutes and then decided it was time to head back up to the top of Jackson Hill for a rest and a snack.

I had my little lunch, enjoyed the view for a few minutes, and then headed back to Pitcher Mountain. *September 2003*

18
Mount Watatic
Ashburnham Mass.

On a gray and showery day in late September, I hiked the Wapack Trail from route 119 in Ashburnham, Massachusetts, up and over Mt. Watatic to the New Hampshire border and back. Despite the clouds and rain, which obliterated the distant views from the hilltops, it was a pleasant and scenic walk.

To get to the trailhead, which is the southern end of the Wapack, I drove east on 119 from its junction with 202 in Rindge. There is an ample parking lot on the north side of the road, just past a sign for the Mid-State Trail, which joins the Wapack from 119 to the state line. I haven't hiked south on the Mid-State Trail yet, but I intend to walk some of it soon. It goes all the way to Rhode Island, and that means a hiker could follow one trail from North Pack Monadnock to the Ocean State.

The first part of my hike to the Granite State followed a broad woods road past a marshy area. The trail soon left the old road and went into the woods on the right. The road, the State Line Trail, continues on to the border by a much more direct route, and it can be used as part of a loop. Just beyond the junction, the trail passed between the halves of a large split boulder and began a fairly steep climb toward the summit. The forest at that point consisted mainly of large old hemlocks, and there was little undergrowth. There were a few small oaks growing in patches where there was ledge, but the hemlocks dominated.

I came to a level spot not far below the summit, and just beyond that stood a decaying shelter. The open-sided structure was missing

THE SUMMIT OF MOUNT WATATIC

half of its floor and all but a few shingles. The remains of a recent fire in a stone ring in front of the shelter showed that it still gets some use.

When I reached the summit, the clouds were showing some bright areas, and I was hoping that the forecasters prediction of sunny breaks would prove accurate and I would have a view on my return trip. I walked about the top of the mountain a bit and looked at the cement footings that mark the site of the old fire tower. That tower is gone now, and the ski area has been out of business for years. A few years ago developers almost built a large radio tower and a number of houses on the mountain, but a group of concerned people, The Campaign for Watatic, was formed and successfully blocked the construction. The area is not completely out of danger, however. Anyone interested in preserving it may donate to the Campaign at PO Box 144, Ashby, MA 01431.

From the summit, I followed the trail north. For a short distance it paralleled the gravel road that once served the ski area, but it soon left the roadside and entered a deep wood. That section of the trail, leading to Nutting Hill, was the best part of my hike. The forest there was a mix of hardwoods and evergreens with quite a bit of low growth. There were a few stone walls among the trees, but they were so old and moss covered that they seemed nearly as natural as the trees.

The trail didn't lose very much altitude before it began an easy climb to the top of Nutting Hill. The summit was mostly open ledge and surely offered good views, but when I got there even the few brighter areas of cloud had given way to an ever-darkening, solid gray.

On the north side of Nutting Hill, the trail joined an old cart road, Nutting Hill Road. At that point one could turn left and reach the State Line Trail and follow it back to 119. I followed the Wapack Trail for another half mile to the New Hampshire border. There is a stone wall along the border, and a side path leads left to the granite Borden Survey Monument of 1834. Just beyond the monument is another, taller granite marker showing both the Massachusetts/ New Hampshire line and the Ashby/Ashburnham line. Embedded in the wall at that point is a third marker for the end of the Mid-State Trail. From there one could also follow the State Line Trail, which was formerly part of the Mid-State Trail, back to the highway.

It was the turn-around point on my hike. I headed back down the trail toward Mt. Watatic and route 119. A light rain began to fall as I walked over Nutting Hill, and it was pouring when I reached the summit of Watatic. It didn't dampen my spirits, however, and I reached the shelter of the trees below the summit without getting very wet.

October 2003

19
The Birchtoft Trail
Mount Monadnock
Jaffrey NH

As everyone knows, Mount Monadnock is one of the most climbed mountains in the world. That means crowds of hikers, especially on beautiful, sunny fall days. However, even on busy days it's possible to hike on the mountain and encounter few if any other hikers. One way is to take one of the less-traveled routes to the summit such as the Pumpelly Trail or the Metacomet Trail. Of course there will still be many people at the top. Another way is to take a hike on the mountain, following one or more of the many side trails and not climbing to the summit at all. There are miles and miles of side trails on Monadnock that provide plenty of exercise, offer great views, and are almost never busy.

On the twentieth of October, a nearly perfect fall day, I took one of those trails, the Birchtoft Trail. Actually, it's probably one of the more popular side trails since it begins at the Gilson Pond Picnic Area off Dublin Road. There were only three other cars in the parking lot. I saw two people heading off to the path around the pond, and a young man and woman were right behind me as I headed down the access road to the trailhead. Just as I was leaving the picnic area, a man who had evidently just finished a hike got into the third car and drove away. There was certainly not a crowd.

The first part of the trail followed the shoreline of Gilson Pond, and I stopped for a moment to take in the view of the water, the still colorful trees on the far shore, and the looming mountain. I also wanted to give the young couple a chance to get ahead. I had noticed they were walking fast, probably going to the summit. I could see them for a short time after I started walking again, but they were soon out of sight. I didn't see another hiker on the Birchtoft Trail.

After it leaves the pond, the trail begins a steady climb up the mountain. There are some pretty steep stretches, but mostly it's an easy ascent. The path goes through a thick hardwood forest, and there are many old walls, almost a maze of walls at times. One of the steeper pitches leads to a nice rock outcropping, and the path crosses a number of ravines or hollows. The Birchtoft Trail ends at its junction with the Cascade Link, just over two miles from the Gilson Pond picnic area. The pond is about 1200 feet above sea level, and the junction is about 2000 feet. That means there is nearly another 1000 feet to climb to reach the summit. If I had wanted to go to the summit that day, I could have followed the Cascade Link upwards to the Spellman Trail and hiked that trail to its junction with the Pumpelly Trail and on to the summit.

Instead, I took the Cascade Link downward. That trail is very rocky, but many of the rocks are large and flat – almost like stairs. I soon came to the little brook that is the main cascade on the link. The trail followed it for quite awhile, and there were several spots with large, flat rocks near the water that would make fine rest stops. About three quarters of a mile from the junction, I came to the Harling Trail, which goes east toward the Dublin Road and has a junction with the Hinkley Trail, which begins on Poole Road, the entrance road to the park.

I could have taken the Harling-Hinkley trail and probably not seen another hiker until I was at the park headquarters, but I wanted to see how busy the park was, so I followed the Cascade Link to where it met the White Dot Trail, probably the busiest on the mountain.

Long before I reached that trail, I could hear the hikers heading up and down. Once I was following the white dots, I had plenty of company. There were large groups of school kids and plenty of smaller parties hiking that day. When I reached the main park, there was a crowd in front of the store, and the parking lot was more than half full. It was a real contrast with the Gilson Pond parking area.

There are many other side trails on Monadnock that I want to hike. Next time I think I'll try the Mossy Brook Trail, The Monte Rosa Trail, and maybe the Side Foot Trail. None of them lead to the summit, but then the summit is the smallest part of the mountain.

October 2003

20
Bald Rock
Mount Monadnock
Jaffrey NH

The last Monday in November had mid-October weather; it was sunny with calm winds and temperatures in the fifties. I decided to take advantage of the fine day and hike more of the side trails on Monadnock. My plan was to start at the Old Toll Road parking lot and hike to Bald Rock using part of the Side Foot Trail and the Hedgehog Trail. To return, I intended to go down the Cliff Walk Trail to the Lost Farm Trail and follow it around to its junction with the Parker Trail, which would lead me back to the Old Toll Road.

I arrived at the parking lot a little after ten that morning, and by 10:15 I was hiking up the Old Halfway House Trail, which parallels the Old Toll Road. The *olds* are there because the Halfway House is long gone and there is no longer a toll on the road. Also, I suppose, "Old" works better than "Former." It was a steady but easy climb to the Halfway House site, and much of it was through a hardwood forest, mostly oak. The trail was covered with fallen oak leaves, and the bare trees allowed the sun and blue sky to brighten the day. Just before I reached the Halfway House site, I could see a huge building on the Old Toll Road. Much of it looked new, and I suppose it is private property.

The White Arrow trail leads from the Halfway House site to the summit, and the Side Foot Trail branches off to the right. I took it and immediately passed the beginning of the Do Drop Trail, which leads to the Cliff Walk Trail. As you have probably gathered, the

KIASTICUTICUS PEAK, BALD ROCK, MOUNT MONADNOCK

portion of the mountain I was on is the nexus of many trails. A glance at the trail map provided by the park shows the Halfway House site as the focus of a dozen paths.

Staying on the Side Foot Trail, I passed the sign for the Noble Trail and quickly came to the one for the Hedgehog Trail, which leads to Bald Rock. There was an old set of stone block steps at the start of the trail, and I imagine it was a popular route for people staying at the Halfway House. Beyond those two steps, the trail followed a rocky, narrow gully, which must be full of water in the spring, steeply upward. There were few, if any, markers, but the trail was very easy to follow. At least it was easy to follow until I reached a large tree that had fallen across the path. I ducked under its trunk where there was space enough, and once beyond the tree I wasn't sure of the trail. I knew I had to keep going up, and I could see Bald Rock from that point. I moved a bit to the right, looking for the trail, and I soon came to one.

I followed that trail upward, and in a few minutes I reached a junction with the Cliff Walk Trail. It was that trail's junction with the Noble Trail. I had gotten on to it after losing the Hedgehog. It was no problem, of course, and I continued up the Cliff Walk Trail.

After some scrambling over rocks and ledges, I arrived at the top of Bald Rock. There was a good view that day. It was a bit hazy in the distance, but there was more than enough to see. To my right, I saw Stratton Mountain; Perkins Pond and Gap Mountain were directly in front, and around to my left Pack Monadnock and the Contoocook River Valley lay. The most dominant feature of the view, though, was the summit of Monadnock.

I rested for a while on the rock and had lunch. Before starting down the Cliff Walk Trail, I looked at an inscription carved into the flat face of a large rock just below the top of Bald Rock. In block letters, it read KIASTICUTICUS PEAK. I'm curious about its significance. Just below the rock, another sign pointed to an old graphite mine site.

The Cliff Walk Trail is well named because it passes over and around a number of large rocks and ledges. It's quite steep in many places, but I was in no hurry and enjoyed going down it.

I followed that trail past the Noble Trail, The Do Drop Trail, and the Thoreau Trail to the Lost Farm Trail. I followed that trail along the steep side of the mountain for about a mile to its junction with the Parker Trail. At that point I was near the park headquarters. The Parker Trail, much of it fine, level walking, led me to the Old Toll Road, and from there it was only a half mile back to my car.

December 2003

21
Goose Pond
Keene NH

On one of the few relatively mild days in January, I took a walk around Goose Pond in Keene. Actually, it was pretty cold, about twenty degrees, but compared to the many days of the month when the temperature stayed in the single numbers, it felt almost balmy. It was a pretty day as well, and I enjoyed my walk through the woods around the pond.

I had wanted to visit the area since last summer when I noticed the sign at the parking lot off East Surry Road. That's the road which leads from Court Street in Keene to the Bretwood Golf Course. I stopped at the parking area while on a bike ride and decided to come back for a walk. It took me a while, but I really enjoyed the visit, and I plan to return.

Although there was still plenty of snow on the path when I took my recent walk, it was so packed down and frozen that there was no need for snowshoes. In fact, the many footprints showed that the path gets plenty of winter use. The first portion of the trail goes uphill from the parking lot, making use of a number of log steps. The main trail, marked in white, goes straight to the pond and then circles it. There are also three side trails: green, blue and red.

When I reached the snow and ice covered pond, I turned right and soon came to where the path crosses the spillway from the pond. There was about an inch of water going over the spillway, but that was no problem for my waterproof boots. I could see that several people had simply walked across the pond above the dam, and there were footprints and ski tracks to be seen on much of the pond's frozen surface. Since there is no swimming allowed at the pond in the summer, winter is the time for people to get out on the lake.

I followed the path along the scalloped shore of the pond. Hemlocks and pines dominated the woods, but there were some hardwood trees as well. The path was easy walking with only a few icy spots, including a few small steam crossings. At times the path was right on the pond, but in some sports it crossed the bases of projections or little peninsulas and was some distance from the water. I could see unmarked paths that clearly led to the water at those spots.

I walked over the second portion of the dam, just an embankment, and came to where a steep hill comes down to the pond. The trail hugged the edge of the pond at that point. Just beyond that portion, the forest leveled off a bit, and I stopped to look around. Just a few yards in front of me, a barred owl was looking down from a tree branch, about fifteen feet above the path. We looked at each other for a few seconds, and I said "hello, owl." At that, he turned his back, either because he didn't want to fly my way or just in disdain, spread his enormous wings, and flew to another tree about a hundred yards away. It's remarkable how the owl appeared rather small while perched and so large while flying.

I continued my walk around the pond and crossed a pretty large stream leading into it. It was completely frozen over, but the water could be seen and heard moving rapidly under the ice. There was a small bridge in the woods nearby that had evidently been moved from its regular location for winter.

The final portion of the trail was wide and smooth, and I was soon back to where the path led away from the pond toward the parking lot. I hadn't seen another person on my walk, despite the many tracks that showed how popular the area is. One of the advantages of being semi-retired is the freedom to go places on weekdays when most people are working.

After walking for almost an hour, probably a mile and a half, I was back at the parking lot. I stopped to read some of the information posted at the kiosk there. There was a history of Goose Pond, which explained that it was a source of water to Keene for many years. There were also maps of the trails and of other natural attractions in Keene. Goose Pond is certainly one of the nicest, and I am eager to see what it's like in spring and summer.

February 2004

22
Granite Town Rail-Trail
Milford NH

The conversion of old railroad beds to trails is one of the best recycling plans. There are many rail-trails in the Monadnock region, including several around Keene. Rindge, Jaffrey, Peterborough, Hancock and Bennington have all converted parts of the former railroad bed that once led from Massachusetts to Concord. Another rail trail goes from Greenville through Mason part of the way to Fitchburg, Mass. I have walked and biked on all those trails, some of them frequently.

Recently, I walked another rail-trail just a few miles east of our region in Milford. The Granite Town Rail-Trail follows the former Milford-Brookline rail bed south from the public works building on South Street in Milford for about three miles to the Brookline town line. Except for one hill and one scramble up to a road crossing, the trail is level. Although it passes through a well-settled area, much of the trail is wooded and out of sight of houses.

The trail was snow-covered when I walked it, but it was old snow and well-packed down, so there was no need for snowshoes or skis. Just after a fresh snow, it would be good for cross-country skiing. No motorized vehicles are allowed on the trail except for the last mile, south of Melendy Road.

From the unpaved parking lot adjacent to the public works building, the path skirts the fenced in yard and then crosses Great Brook, which flows at the center of a marshy area. It follows the stream for quite a while, with some houses visible on the west side, and the marshy stream on the east. At about the half mile point, the trail crosses a road, then another bridge over the brook, and finally passes through a tunnel (really a six and a half foot high culvert for possible overflow from the brook) under route 101.

South of route 101, there is a mix of woods and fields with a few houses nearby. Then, a little over a mile from the trailhead, the trail leaves the railroad bed for a detour of nearly a half a mile. At that point there is a huge trailer park, and the rail-trail becomes a footpath, which climbs a wooded hill and then drops back to the railroad bed south of the development. It's a pretty steep climb, and would be a bit of a problem for skiing or biking, but it's the only real hill on the whole trail.

Once back on the railroad bed, I walked through a fairly wooded section and passed Compressor Pond on my left. Then, a little more than two miles into the trail, I scrambled up the embankment to Melendy Road. There was an underpass at that point, but it has been filled in, so climbing up to the road and back down to the railroad bed is the second "hill" on the trail. Motorized traffic is allowed from that point south, and I noticed the tracks of a four-wheeled ATV, but they were the only ones I saw on my walk, and they followed the trail for only a hundred yards.

The last section of the trail is probably the most scenic. Just south of Melendy Road there is large marshy area on the western side of the trail. It was frozen and snow-covered, but small trees, brown marsh grass, and a number of large, snow-topped boulders made a nice picture. Not far beyond the marsh, another small pond appeared on the opposite side of the trail.

The Granite Town Rail-Trail ends about a half a mile south of the marsh, just before a power line crosses the railroad bed. The Milford/Brookline town line is just north of the power line, 2.95 miles from the public works building on South Street.

I continued walking for a few minutes, past the power line and into Brookline. The trail was wide and straight at that point, and it appeared to continue for quite a distance. It may go into Massachusetts, and I thought of exploring it farther on my mountain bike sometime in summer. Having made that plan, I turned about and walked back to the South Street trailhead.

February 2004

23
The Midstate Trail
Ashburnham Mass.

The last time I climbed Mt. Watatic, I thought about the Midstate Trail, which starts at the Rhode Island border and goes north through Massachusetts to the New Hampshire line just north of Mt. Watatic. For most of the last section, the Midstate Trail joins the Wapack Trail, which begins at route 119 in Ashburnham, Massachusetts. While on that hike, I decided to someday walk south on the Midstate Trail from route 119.

So, on a cloudy but rain free Monday morning in mid April, I drove east from Rindge and parked at the large lot at the base of Watatic. The parking area is less than two miles into Ashburnham from the New Hampshire line.

It was 10:15 when I began my hike by crossing the highway and following the yellow plastic triangles of the Midstate Trail south. The first half mile or so was on a paved road that led uphill toward a wooded ridge. There were a few newly built houses on the first part of the road, and as soon as I passed them, the road surface became broken and eroded. The land to the right of the road belongs to the Fitchburg Sportsmen Club, part of their Swallow Hill complex, but I suppose there might soon be more houses built on the left side of the road.

When I had walked about ten minutes, the road turned to the right, and the trail went straight into the woods. It was still uphill, but not very steep, and the path was in good shape. It was certainly well marked and easy to follow. Most of the way to the top of the hill was through a mixed forest, mainly hardwoods, but near the top there was a large stand of red pine trees. I reached the top of the hill after walking a little over a half an hour, so I estimated I had come about one and a half miles from 119.

The hilltop was wooded, mostly pine, and rocky. There were several tall stone walls that crossed there, and the remains of two campfires. It was a pleasant spot, with grass growing among the pines, but it wasn't a good place for having a fire. Since it was wooded, there wasn't much of a view, but I could make out some distant hills through the tree limbs.

From that hilltop, I walked downhill and passed a rocky outcrop. The forest was mixed again, and I noticed many mountain laurel bushes growing among the trees. Soon I began climbing another hill. It was a short and easy climb, and I was on its pine- covered summit in a few minutes. The trees were really thick on that hilltop, but the pines were replaced with hardwoods on the southern side, and as I started down that side, I caught a glimpse of Mt. Wachusett in the distance, its ski slopes still white with snow.

Part way down the hillside, I heard what sounded like a large animal moving through the woods. I stopped, thinking I might see a deer, but instead a woman riding a white horse appeared below me on the rocky trail. The horse was a bit surprised to see a hiker, but a few words from the rider calmed it, and we exchanged greetings as she rode by.

At the bottom of that hill, there were several larger trails intersecting the Midstate Trail, and it looked like a popular place for horseback riding. I'm sure there is also much snowmobile activity in the winter. I also crossed two small streams, and there were the remains of a lashed together bridge over one of them.

Just beyond the bridge, I saw a new electric fence to the right of the trail and then the roofs of several buildings. In a moment I came to Massachusetts route 101, the road that runs north from the center of Ashburnham and joins route 119 east of Mt. Watatic. The trail turns right at that point and follows the highway south. There is a large camp there, Camp Winnekeag, named for the nearby lake. It was 11:30, and I had walked close to three miles. I decided it was time to head back.

On the return trip, I stopped on the hilltop with the old campfires and had lunch. By one o'clock I was driving back toward Rindge. As I passed the Swallow Hill area, I saw six herons standing in the pond near the road. They were the first I saw this year, and they made a good ending to a nice trip. *April 2004*

24
A Short Walk on The Long Trail Rutland Vt.

Over the last few years I have been hiking portions of Vermont's Long Trail, and on the first day of summer I walked from route 103 south to Bear Mountain. It was a moderately difficult hike with many interesting features, and the weather was great.

The day began with clear skies and cool temperatures, and the drive into central Vermont, although nearly two hours long, was pleasant. I took route 12 north from Keene to the bridge over the Connecticut River in Walpole, and then I drove up the interstate to Rockingham, where I got onto Vermont 103. I followed that road north through Ludlow and parked at the trailhead for the Appalachian and Long Trails, a few miles east of Rutland.

I decided on hiking from that point partly because I had hiked all of the Long Trail from Massachusetts to route 140 in Wallingford and thought it would be nice to add a new section. I have some ambition to hike the entire trail, eventually. Mainly, though, on the trail map it just looked like a good walk. It was a little after eight o'clock when I started walking.

The most unusual feature of the hike was also the first one I reached. A short distance from the parking lot I crossed the suspension bridge over the Clarendon Gorge on the Mill River. The narrow bridge is high above the rushing water, and it swayed a bit as I crossed. It made me think of scenes from action movics such as the Indiana Jones films, and images of breaking ropes and crocodile-filled water came to mind.

THE MINERVA HINCHEY SHELTER

South of the gorge, the trail began a steep climb to a ridge that would lead me first to the Minerva Hinchey Shelter and then to route 140, five and a half miles away. Once I reached the top of the ridge, the trail became nearly level and was broad and smooth. There was a great view to the west, overlooking the Rutland Airport. On that part of the trail, the first of several north-bound hikers passed me. As is always the case on the Appalachian Trail, they all had friendly greetings. I figured they had spent the night at the shelter I was approaching.

Not far from the airport lookout, a small power line appeared on the right, and the trail ran parallel with it for nearly a half a mile before crossing it. Soon after that, the trail went downhill a bit and I arrived at the shelter. It was empty at that time of day - too late for hikers from the night before and too early for hikers stopping for lunch. The Minerva Hinchey Shelter proved to be a typical open structure, plain and clean. Hikers do a good job of cleaning up after themselves, and it's only when shelters are close enough to roads to get used by non hikers that they tend to get trashed at all. After a quick look at the shelter, I continued my southward hike. It was only a little after ten o'clock, and I planned to stop at the shelter on my return trip for lunch.

I crossed another power line and came to a sign that described a relocation of the next portion of the trail. I had expected to follow the woods road that becomes Bear Mountain Road and leads to route 140, but the new location of the trail was to the west of the old and went over the top of Bear Mountain itself. I decided the summit would be a good turn around point for my hike. It meant I would have a nine mile hike rather than the eleven miles I had planned, but I felt that would be plenty and a mountain top made a good destination.

The trail from that point followed a woods road for about a half a mile, and it was easy walking. I crossed a series of wooden snowmobile bridges, and then the footpath narrowed and began the climb to the top of Bear Mountain. It was a little steep going up, but there were a number of switchbacks, and it wasn't that difficult. When I reached the tree-covered, viewless summit, another hiker arrived from the south. Speaking with an clearly British accent, he said, "Is this the top then?" He also asked if had heard the weather report. When I told him rain was due for the next day, followed by more good weather for a few days, he said that sounded fine and he would get to cool off for a spell. Then he headed north, and I sat down on a rock to take a break.

I rested there for a few minutes and then headed north myself. I stopped at the Miverva Hinchey Shelter for lunch at a quarter after eleven and crossed the Clarendon Gorge bridge again about an hour later.

June 2004

25

Horatio Colony Preserve Keene, NH

For a long time I had the Horatio Colony Preserve on my list of places to be visited. Actually, I had a desire to explore the wooded ridge that rises to the south of route nine long before I learned that the preserve was there, on West Hill. I learned of the preserve a few years ago, and I finally visited it on Tuesday morning in mid August.

It was very easy to get to Colony Preserve; I drove west on route nine and turned onto Daniel's Hill Road, which was the first left past Base Hill Road. Although it was one of the better days in that part of the summer, weatherwise, there were no other cars in the small parking lot when I arrived, just before ten.

From the parking lot, I walked up a dirt road into the preserve itself. The first obvious feature I came to was the old cabin built by Horatio Colony in the 1930's. It was locked, but a sign indicated that visitors may enter it at times. Not far beyond the cabin, I reached the kiosk at the trailhead for the three hiking trails in the preserve. There was a large trail map at the kiosk, and there were booklets explaining the twenty-one numbered sites of interest on the trails. From the map, I could see that the trails really linked together, but the first - the Red Diamond Trail - was a loop which could be taken separately. To get to the other two trails, a hiker has to walk at least half of the red diamond trail. Since the total length of the three trails was less than four miles, I decided to do all three and follow the numbered sites around the preserve.

The points of interest included both natural and man-made features. Each of the sites had a page in the booklet explaining its significance and history. The booklet was very well done, and the sites were all interesting. I had not walked very far up the Red Diamond Trail before I realized another outstanding aspect of the preserve: how well kept it is. There was no litter, and the sign posts for the sites were all well-maintained and clear. That proved to be the story for all of the trails. I didn't see one piece of paper or empty can anywhere in the preserve, and all of the numbered sites were in good shape. As one who worked for many years at a state park, I know how hard it is to keep up that level of maintenance.

Probably the most interesting site on the Red Diamond Trail was the cellar hole and foundation of the Colony family's Tip Top House. It was on the top of the hill, and there was a view of west Keene, including the high school. The booklet informed me that the hurricane of 1938 destroyed the old cabin.

Mid-way through the Red Diamond Trail, I reached the junction with the white-blazed Ridgeline Trail and followed it as it ran due south, mostly just below the summit of the ridge. One of the things I had hoped for on the hike was a view to the east, but there was none. I'm sure there are places above the trail from which one could see off to the east and Mount Monadnock, but not from the trail itself.

The beauty of the trails was not in what could be seen from them in the distance but in what was close at hand. The trail guide included a list, a partial list, of birds, mammals, amphibians, trees and other herbaceous growths visible in the preserve. There were forty-eight items on the list. Oddly, one of the most interesting trees in the preserve wasn't on the list but did have its own numbered site. At the southern end of the Ridgeline Trail, there is a tupelo or black gum tree, a type of tree normally found much farther south than the south end of that trail. Another intriguing site on the Ridgeline Trail was the old "black lead" or graphite mine. The site itself was simply a water-filled hole, but the story in the booklet was a reminder of a different time.

The third trail, the Slickenside Trail, was a short appendage to the Ridgeline Trail. Its blue markers led to a rocky cliff that marks a fault line in the earth. From the booklet I learned that rocks formed by the geological forces in such areas, burned and sanded by the shifting of continental plates, are called *slickensides.*

From the cliff face, I retraced my steps onto the Ridgeline Trail and back to the Red Diamond Trail. I followed the second part of that loop back to the trailhead. It was a good hike, and I figured that with the walk to and from the parking lot and several short side trails I had followed that I had walked about four miles. Most of it was either nearly level or up and down an easy grade. Only the first part of the Red Diamond Trail was very steep.

In short, the Horatio Colony Preserve is a good place to visit for an informative and pleasant walk in the woods.

September 2004

THE RUINS OF MADAME SHERRI'S CASTLE

26
Madame Sherri Forest
Chesterfield NH

The Madame Sherri Forest in Chesterfield is best known for the remains of Madame Sherri's "castle," but it is also the starting point for a number of good hiking trails. The trails are maintained by the Chesterfield Conservation Commission, which plans to incorporate them into a Wantastiquet-Monadnock Greenway.

I spent a good part of a fine September day hiking most of the trails that can be reached from the parking lot just below the castle site, and I found all of them to be enjoyable and easy to follow. I particularly liked the lovely views found on each trail - especially the spectacular ones from the rocky outcrops on Mine Ledge.

Getting to the forest was a little complicated, but not really difficult. I took route 9 west from Keene to route 63, where I turned left and drove through the center of Chesterfield. Just past the school and post office, I turned right onto Stage Road and then, almost immediately, left onto Castle Road. I followed that road to its intersection with Gulf Road, turned left again, and drove about a mile and a half to the small parking lot on the left side of the road. There's a large sign board there with pictures and information about Madame Sherri and her house, the remains of which are just a few yards up a dirt road from the parking lot.

I did stop for a look at the old stone steps and walls, but my main interest was the hiking paths. To get to the trailhead, I followed the old woods road that borders the pond formed by a stone dam that must have been part of Madame Sherri's estate. Beavers have evidently augmented the pond by blocking up the spillway of the old dam, and part of the road is now underwater, but the footpath skirts the wet parts of the road.

About a quarter of a mile from the parking lot, I reached the trailhead for one of the two main trails, the Ann Stokes Loop. There was a mailbox there with trail maps for that trail and several other trails, including the Daniels Mountain Loop, the Daniels Mountain Trail, and "unofficial trails" leading to Mine Ledge and the summit of Wantastiquet Mountain. The map showed me that the two loops connected and formed a rough figure eight, but the Mine Ledge Trail, which climbs a shoulder of Wantastiquet, split off from the Anne Stokes trail at Indian Pond.

I decided to take the arm of the Ann Stokes Loop that led directly to Indian Pond and then follow the unmarked trail to Mine Ledge and return to complete the Ann Stokes Loop and maybe walk the Daniels Mountain Loop as well. It was a good plan.

The hike up to the serene little pond took me along a ravine and across a small stream that came from the pond. Motorized vehicles are prohibited on the trails, but I did follow the tracks of one trailbike all the way to the pond. Those were the only such tracks I saw that day.

There was a nice open spot on the pond, which had wooded hillsides on three sides. It was clean and neat, and I thought people might fish from the bank. The trail to Mine Ledge led along the right side of the pond and quickly climbed to a large rock overlooking the pond. From that point, I had a good view over the pond and the wooded hill on its eastern shore. There was still some morning mist clinging to the hillside.

September 2004

27
Loverens Mill Cedar Swamp
Antrim NH

The Nature Conservancy's Loverens Mill Cedar Swamp is a 600 acre nature preserve in Antrim along the North Branch of the Contoocook River. In addition to the white cedar swamp itself, the preserve includes a three mile long hiking trail. I hiked the trail on a cold December morning and found it breathtaking -- from beauty, not difficulty.

The preserve is easy to reach; it is just north of route 9 on Loveren Mill Road, which is between the route 123 north and route 31 south intersections, a mile or so east of the Antrim/Stoddard line. The road begins with a bridge over the North Branch, and just beyond that there is a small parking lot on the right, with a large Fish and Game signboard, which displays maps of the preserve and information about the Nature Conservancy. The entrance to the preserve itself is on the opposite side of Loveren Mill Road, where there is another sign and an old woods road, blocked by a heavy metal bar.

I started down the old road a little after ten that morning. It was only twenty degrees; the sky was partly cloudy, and there were occasional snowflakes in the air. There was also an inch or so of snow covering the ground; it was crusty and crunched under my feet. The actual trail started a quarter of a mile down the old road, which ran a few feet above the rapidly flowing river. I saw the remains of the dam and mill buildings that, in one form or another, operated from 1798 until the 1920's. The water was roaring down from the pond above the old mill site, and it was obvious that plenty of power must have been available there.

Beyond the mill site, I came to the Loverens Trail, marked by a signpost with a small, folding desk containing a visitors' log and trail maps. As soon as I started on the trail, I was impressed by the lovely mixture of trees, including fir, spruce, pine and oak. The trail was narrow, and there were many small rocks to step on or over, but it was very well-marked and easy to follow.

I quickly reached the Cedar View side trail and followed it to a 200 foot long boardwalk that led me into the white cedar swamp. The swamp is noteworthy, not only for its undeniable beauty, but also because it is one of the best examples of a boreal cedar swamp in New England. I stepped carefully along the icy boardwalk into the swamp, and I felt I had entered an enchanted forest from a fairy tale. The cedars, with their distinctive bark, dominated the swamp, although there were also some spruces. The trees stood among pools of water, all covered with a thin layer of transparent ice. Through the ice, I could see the varied greens of sphagnum moss and other low growing vegetation. The pools were separated by rocks and higher points of ground, all snow-covered.

I stood at the end of the boardwalk for a few minutes, and then I walked back to the Loverens Trail and continued my walk around the preserve. I passed two huge boulders and then came to a fork in the trail. It was the beginning of a long loop that I followed for about two miles. There were two especially fine features of that portion of the trail. The first was a side trail that led me to a lookout over a marsh toward hills north of the preserve. The second was a long stretch along the river bank. The trail map mentioned moose are often seen in that section, but I saw no sign of any. I did see bear tracks crossing the trail and leading up a hill toward a stand of birches. In addition to the snow crunching under my boots and the rushing river, I could hear the traffic on route 9, which was above the far side of the river. That didn't spoil anything, however, and, as soon as the trail turned away from the water, the traffic noise vanished.

I walked up a small hill, down into a ravine, crossed a small stream and was soon back at the fork where I had begun the loop. From there it was only a half a mile back to my car. I had completely forgotten that it was the coldest day since last winter.

December 2004

28
Otter Brook Preserve
Sullivan NH

The Nature Conservancy's Otter Brook Preserve is located just north of route nine in Sullivan and Stoddard. There are over ten miles of trails in the preserve, which wander up and down the wooded hills, ford the many small streams, and lead to the shores of Bolster Pond and Ellis Reservoir. I walked about five miles on some of those trails early in January, and it was well worth the visit.

To get there, I turned off route nine in Sullivan onto Center Street, just opposite the general store on the highway. Almost immediately, I turned right onto Valley Road and drove a couple of miles on it to Bowlder Road. I drove on that road for about a half a mile to the Nature Conservancy's parking lot and trailhead. Just beyond the parking lot on Bowlder Road was a large auto salvage yard, where a backhoe was noisily working.

At first, the trail paralleled the salvage yard, and just a few yards along I came to a signpost with a folding desk, in which were trail maps and a visitors' log. The map showed I was on the Warren Hill Trail, one of five named trails in the preserve. It also showed the Warren Hill Trail ended at the Clarence Jewett Loop, which connected to the three other trails. I decided to do the loop and short sections of the Bolster View Trail and the Elllis Reservoir Trail.

The trail led me downhill to a small stream, and within a hundred yards or so the junkyard was out of view, if not hearing. The trail at that point seemed to have been a woods road not long ago, but beyond the tiny stream young hemlocks were growing, and they effectively narrowed the trail to a footpath. It looked to me like the young trees had been planted for that purpose. I followed the Warren Hill Trail up the eponymous hill, passing first through a hemlock grove and then mixed woods. The narrow trail became a woods road again, and that was the pattern for all the trails: sometimes narrow paths, other times broader roads. No matter the type, the trails were all easy to follow, well marked with the Conservancy's familiar green and yellow arrows. They were clean, as well, and I didn't see any litter.

There wasn't any snow on the ground that morning, either, even though it was January. However, a light snow began while I was walking, and by the time I returned to my car, the ground was lightly frosted.

At the top of the hill, I walked down a short side trail to the Warren Cellar Hole. More remarkable than the filled-in cellar hole was a decrepit wooden shack, which contained built in benches and a small table. A hole in the wall indicated a stove had once shared the tiny floor space with the benches. Later, I contacted Eric Aldrich of the Nature Conservancy, and he told me he thought the shack was once used by blueberry pickers. I didn't see any evidence of berries on my walk, but I did notice a great number of old stumps in the woods, leading me to think there must have also been some lumbering there at one time.

Just past the cellar hole location, the Warren Hill Trail ended at the Clarence Jewett Loop. I decided to follow it to the left, and in a few minutes I reached the trail junction with the Bolster View Trail. I walked down that trail just far enough to have a view over the frozen pond, and then returned to follow the loop around.

The trail followed and then crossed a stream that flowed from Bolster Pond, and I thought it must have been the headwaters of Otter Brook. I crossed the stream twice, and the second crossing had a sturdy green nylon rope to hang onto as I stepped from rock to rock. I stayed on the loop at the junction with the long Kendall Lane Trail - saving it for another time - and followed the Ellis Reservoir Trail from the loop just as far as the edge of that marshy body of water.

On the frozen water on the far side of the reservoir, I saw three otters walk hump-backed on the ice and then disappear into open water. After a short break, I walked back to the Jewett Loop, followed it around to the Warren Hill Trail, and walked down to my car. I'll be back.

January 2005

29
Fox Forest
Hillsborough NH

On one of the last days in March, I walked a few of the twenty-two miles of trails in the state's Fox Research Forest, which is located in Hillsborough. My visit to the nearly 1500 acres of forest caused me to once again consider how blessed our part of the world is with wonderful, open to the public, forests, sanctuaries, parks, and preserves.

That morning, I drove north from Peterborough on route 202, and then right into the center of Hillsborough. From there, I drove another mile or two west, first on School Street and then on Center Road. The Fox Forest Headquarters buildings are located on that road, just beyond two impressive farms.

I parked in the large lot and then picked up a forest guide and trail map at the kiosk by the headquarters. I studied the map for a few minutes and decided to walk mainly on the Ridge Trail, which circles most of the forest. I had my snowshoes in the car, but the part of the trail I could see was so packed down that I left them there. As it turned out, there were only a few short stretches of trail that still had enough soft snow on them to make snowshoes an advantage. The recent heavy rain, which had just tapered off to showers that morning, and the above freezing temperatures of the previous week had melted much of the snow. That made snowshoes unnecessary, but there were also many icy patches and several flooded parts of the trails I walked – real spring conditions.

I started down the Ridge Trail at about a quarter to eleven that morning. By then it had stopped raining completely, and there were even a few patches of blue sky. The temperature was in the forties, and it was a fine day for a hike.

In a few minutes I came to the junction where the short Mushroom Trail went off to the right. I followed that loop to where it rejoined the Ridge Trail. I didn't see any mushrooms, but they must have been lurking under the slushy snow.

I passed the junction with the Valley Road trail and started downhill toward Mud Pond. On the way, I crossed a noisy stream on a sturdy, wide footbridge. Just before I reached the trail down to the pond, I passed a sign that marked the beginning of the Virgin Forest, a two hundred year old stand of hemlocks. I followed the Ridge Trail uphill under those hemlocks, some of which were enormous. I planned on following the Ridge Trail to the Gould Pond Road, but my plans were thwarted when I came to a stream crossing that consisted of single logs which were slippery and partly under water. I turned around.

Back at the Mud Pond trail, I tried walking down it to the Mud Pond Road, which I could have followed back to the Ridge Trail beyond the crossing that had stopped me. However, I soon came to another flooded crossing and turned around again.

I walked all the way back to the junction with Valley Road and followed it uphill. It was really a trail, despite the name, but I'm sure it was a woods road at one time. It was pretty rocky and had many wet spots, but it was still easy walking. Up to that point, I had seen only people and dog tracks on the trials, but Valley Road also had many deer tracks. Another branch of the Ridge Trail joined Valley Road after a quarter mile, and the two ran together to Concord End Road, a wide gravel road with heavy tire tracks in its snow cover.

Just a few yards east of the junction with Concord End Road there was a small cemetery with several headstones from the mid nineteenth century. It was gated, and there was a sign identifying it as the Gearry Cemetery.

To return to the forest headquarters, I walked south on Concord End Road for a short distance and then followed the Ridge Trail again for a few yards to Spring Road, which brought me back to Center Road. From there it was only a few minutes back to the parking lot.

The spring thaw and recent rains made part of my walk a bit difficult, but I enjoyed it all. I spent about two hours on the trails and walked about four miles. That means there are 18 more miles of trails to explore. I'll be back.

March 2005

30
The Marlborough Trail
Mount Monadnock
Marlborough NH

I spent a few hours of a sunny day in early April hiking on Mount Monadnock. Most of my hike was on the Marlborough Trail, but I also walked a short distance on the Marian Trail, which is a side trail about two thirds of the way up the mountain. The Marlborough Trail was the trail I followed on my first trips up Monadnock many years ago, but I hadn't been on it for a long time, and I noticed a couple of changes.

The first change was in Shaker Road, which is the road that leads from route 124 to the trail. It is more developed, and there are many new houses along it. The parking area at the beginning of the trail has also been developed, and it is larger than it was. However, I wasn't able to park in that lot on my trip because Shaker Road is not maintained in winter.

It was a little after noon when I reached the one remaining snow bank that blocked the road and marked where the plows had turned around during the winter. Evidently winter visitors sometimes park their cars where they shouldn't, and several of the houses near the end of the maintained road had no parking signs. I left my car parked on the road, in front of that last snowbank. I walked from there, and the road was completely open the rest of the way.

The trail head was about a third of a mile along, and I was soon walking up the mountain itself. My goal wasn't to climb the mountain; I wanted only to hike on it for a few miles. I have reached a point at which I no longer feel it is necessary to climb to the very top of the mountain every time I visit it. I have decided that if I make reaching the summit my goal on every hike, I will make the trip into an exercise routine with a job requirement. Instead, I more often go for hikes part way up or sideways around part of the mountain. Since I have been doing that, I have gotten to know the mountain much better, and I appreciate it more.

The first part of my recent hike was a gradual ascent through a mostly hardwood forest, and a good portion of the trail was wet. In fact, part of it was more of a shallow brook than a path. It was spring and only to be expected, and there were plenty of rocks on the trail to use as stepping stones. I stayed in the middle of the trail in order to avoid needlessly broadening it, and it really wasn't a problem beyond getting my boots muddy.

After I had been walking a half mile or so, the trail grew much steeper, and I followed an S curve around boulders and reached an open ledge with good views to the south. Gap Mountain and Little Monadnock were prominent in the view, but it extended far into Massachusetts. From that point on, the trail alternated between open ledges and spruce stands. The shaded portions and the hollows between rocks still had plenty of snow, and there were a few icy spots that made my walk a bit difficult. The sun was warm enough, but some of the stretches of snow were more than a foot deep.

I reached the Marian Trail, which was marked with small stone cairns and went southward along the mountain side. It leads to Monte Rosa, a sub-peak on the mountain. I followed it for a short distance and then stopped for a rest on a ledge. I considered going farther, but the next part of the trail went steeply downhill and looked snowy and rugged. I decided to leave it for another time.

I walked back to the Marlborough Trail, and climbed a few minutes more to another open area with an even greater view. From that spot I could see not only far to the south but also west into Vermont. I counted seven still snow-covered ski slopes in the southern Green Mountains.

That was as far as I climbed that day. On my way back down the trail, I met another hiker, who was sitting on a rock eating a snack. He had walked over the Marian Trail from Monte Rosa, and reported that it was indeed very snowy there. He said he had slid down a part of it. I congratulated myself for being prudent.

April 2005

31
Warwick Preserve
Westmoreland NH

The Nature Conservancy's Warwick Preserve in Westmoreland is small (36 acres), but the three trails it contains allow visitors to see nearly all of it. The Partridge Brook Trail follows that lively stream up part of Butterfield Hill, and the May-December and Cave Loop trails explore the southwestern shoulder of that 1,000 foot high hill. The small parking lot for the preserve is on the eastern side of route 63, East Edge Road, between Westmoreland and Park Hill. It's easy to find, but, since it is located at the bottom of a hill on a sharp curve, visitors need to be careful.

I drove to the preserve on a gray, damp morning in mid-May and spent almost two hours walking the trails and enjoying the woods and rocky ledges. It wasn't the greatest day weatherwise, but it didn't rain, and the sky lightened enough to make for pleasant walking. There were a few steep, rocky spots that were slippery from the recent rain, but they were easy to navigate. One of the steepest had a heavy rope stretched between trees to form a hand rail.

The pamphlet for the preserve mentions the diversity of plant life there, including a fine mixture of hardwood and softwood trees and many wildflowers. The most impressive flowers I noticed were purple trilliums, which were blooming in a large cluster near the trailhead and along the brook. I also saw many violets along the trails.

Showy orchids, wintergreen and Dutchman's breeches are among the other flowers to be found in the preserve.

From the trailhead, I followed the Partridge Brook trail uphill along the falling water. The trail was well above the water for the most part, and that made for good views of the brook. I noticed veins of white rock - quartz, I thought - in the stream bed, and as I walked through the woods away from the stream, I saw many white rocks.

I came to the trail junction with the May-December Trail and followed it clockwise farther up the shoulder of Butterfield Hill. That trail led to the northern most corner of the preserve, and I could hear traffic on route 12. However, the dominant sound on my walk was the song of birds. I didn't see many, but their music was all around. I did see the great variety of trees mentioned in the Nature Conservancy's pamphlet, including a shagbark hickory.

From the high point, the May-December trail led me south and then west and downhill to the Cave Loop trail. That trail was the shortest but most interesting in the preserve. I followed it over the top of impressive ledges, one with a steep drop of at least forty feet. There was a pretty good view to the southwest. One part of the trail passed close to a sheer, narrow chute, and a sign pointed to an easier alternate route, which would probably be a good choice in winter.The trail dropped down and passed the bottom of the same outcrop. I didn't see a real cave, but there must have been at least one among the tumble of rock.

The Cave Loop Trail returned me to the Partridge Brook Trail, and I was soon back at the trailhead. I figured I had walked about two miles, very little of it on level ground.

The three trails were all well marked with the green and yellow arrows of the Nature Conservancy, and I didn't see one scrap of litter anywhere. The Warwick Preserve is well worth visiting. It is beautiful, and the short but rugged trails provide a nice workout.

If you go, be sure to stop at the great country store in Westmoreland for lunch or a snack after your hike.

May 2005

32
Black Mountain
Dummerston Vt.

The Nature Conservancy's Black Mountain Natural Area in Dummerston, Vermont, is a bit out of the way, but the hike up the little mountain is well worth the trip. Even the *trip* is worth going because the ride over to Vermont is always interesting, and the final stage of the trip through East Dummerston and along the West River is really fine.

I drove over to hike the mountain on a Friday in mid-May, taking route nine to the traffic circle in Brattleboro and then going north on route five for just about a mile. I left route five where the road to Dummerston, Middle Road, forks to the left. I followed it through the village of East Dummerston to the covered bridge over the West River where I made a sharp left onto Quarry Road, a gravel road along the river's edge. I drove south for about a mile and a half to an out of service bridge over the river. At that point the road became Rice Farm Road, and a half mile farther along I came to a parking area on the river bank opposite a narrow dirt road leading up the hillside. I nearly missed the area since I saw only one small sign for the conservancy's land on a tree off the road.

I walked a few yards up the dirt road to a gate and a sign for the Black Mountain Natural Area. A smaller sign lead me to the trailhead, and I began my hike up the mountain. The trail at that point was an old woods road, and after a short but steep climb it leveled off. That proved to be the norm for the hike: short steep stretches and then level portions or easy switchbacks.

There was quite a mix of trees, both pines and hardwoods, and the road narrowed to a path, which for a short distance was lined on both sides with a dense hedge of small pines. I noticed several old, large stumps and some aged downed trees among the newer growth, and it looked like there had been logging there years ago. My guide book, Larry Pletcher's *Hiking Vermont,* mentioned the area had been burned over and that it was especially known for pitch pine and scrub oak. I passed a small kiosk with a log book enclosed and then came to a boardwalk across a small wetland. Beyond that, the trail remained narrow and began to wind its way up the mountain in earnest.

There were many small oaks and also beeches along the trail for most of the climb, but there were a few very large and very old maple trees among them. The mountain side also became quite rocky, with large outcrops. One of the more level spots on the trail went through a nice stand of hemlocks, punctuated with massive boulders.

As I neared the top of the mountain, the rocks and ledges became more prevalent than the trees. I walked up a steep gully choked with budding mountain laurel just beneath the summit. By the time this article appears, in early June, they will probably be in bloom.

The summit itself was broad and flat. It was tree covered, but the trees were well spaced, and there were several views. The best was of Mount Monadnock to the east. In addition to more laurel, there were many blueberry bushes on the mountain top. There was also an old shed, which was probably connected to radio towers that once stood on the mountain.

It was warm and sunny on the mountain top, and I sat there and had a little lunch. Unfortunately, the black flies were also looking to dine. After fifteen or twenty minutes, I started down the trail. Just below the summit, I noticed the shadows of large birds moving across the trail. I looked up and saw two vultures cruising along just above the trees. I suppose they were using the updraft from the river valley to circle about the summit and look for *their* lunch.

It had taken me about an hour to hike up the mountain, but I got back to my car in considerably less time. The trail is described as less than two and a half miles round trip, but I thought it was closer to three miles, at least. It was a good hike, not too difficult, and the summit area was a rewarding goal.

June 2005

33
Mount Ascutney
Ascutney Vt.

Mount Ascutney, Vermont, is forty miles northwest of Monadnock, and it is a similar mountain of nearly the same height, just over 3,000 feet, and with a grand, 360 degree view from its summit. I hiked up the mountain on the last day of spring, taking the Weathersfield Trail, a three mile long trek that led through deep woods and past several cascading brooks to the viewing platform on top. It was a beautiful and sometimes demanding walk.

The trailhead was just off Vermont route 131, three miles west of interstate 91's exit 8. Signs led me onto first Cascade Falls Road and then High Meadow Road and the small parking lot, which had room for a half dozen cars. When I arrived a little before eight that morning, the lot was empty.

The first half of the trail alternated between steep climbs and easy stretches across the western shoulder of the mountain. Just a few minutes into the walk, I came to the first cascade. It was just a narrow brook, tumbling over rocks. From there the trail climbed to a steep-sided, narrow ravine or gorge from which the same brook emerged in a series of three foot high waterfalls. Higher falls were visible farther back in the shadowy gorge.

The trail climbed out of the gorge on a number of stone steps and then a wooden staircase attached to the rock. Once above the ravine, it began an easy downhill stretch, and after about a half a mile I reached Cascade Falls, where a larger stream descended from high on the mountain, crossed a rocky ledge and then disappeared over a lip of stone to fall 80 feet to the woods below. There were narrow paths leading very steeply down to the bottom of the falls, but I decided against trying them.

The trail followed along the hillside above the brook for another half a mile and then came down to the narrowing stream and crossed it. By then the sun had come out, and as I came down to the brook, I could see a radio tower rising from the mountain top.

A short distance past the crossing, I came to a sign reading Halfway Brooks that included the distance to the summit - 1.2 miles - and back to the parking lot - 1.6 miles. The 1.2 miles proved to be very steep, but the trail also passed several spots with great views to the northwest. Not far below the west peak of the mountain, I crossed the open ledges known as Gus's Lookout. A sign and a metal plaque identified Gus as Augustus Aldrich, to whom the lovely spot was dedicated. From there, I could make out Mount Monadnock.

A short climb from the lookout brought me to the west peak of the mountain. Another sign pointed me east to the main summit, another half mile away. That last part of the trail was very steep in spots, and it was joined for the last few yards by a trail leading up from the auto road parking lot, less than a mile below the top of the mountain.

I gathered my remaining energy and climbed the observation tower, which appeared to be the base of a former fire tower. It had a spectacular view of both the ski mountains in southern Vermont and much of western New Hampshire. On a really clear day, one could see all the way to the White Mountains.

Just before I started back down, three young men reached the summit from the auto road. They were the first people I met that day, but on the way down I passed three groups climbing, including a man carrying an infant on his back and accompanied by two large dogs, a family of three, and a single woman with a single dog. When I reached the parking lot, at one o'clock, two more hikers were about to start the climb, and the lot was nearly full.

June 2005

34
Crotched Mountain Town Forest
Francestown NH

The Crotched Mountain Town Forest is a 650 acre forest in Francestown, managed by the town's conservation commission. Within the forest are several trails, including one to the summit of Crotched Mountain, beaver ponds, a black gum swamp, and wildlife habitat improvement areas. The forest is multi use: hunting is allowed, and there are occasional logging operations. It is a very interesting place to visit.

The trailhead for the forest is located on route 136, just east of the Greenfield/Francestown line. I pulled into the parking lot there around 10:30 on a late June morning. Two cars were there before me, and there was room for several more. A map kiosk showed three short trails in the immediate area of the trailhead and a link trail through the woods to the beginning of the Summit Trail, Scot's Trail and the Joslin Loop Trail.

I began my hike by following one of the short trails, the Quarry Trail, which looped around through what must have been a very small granite quarry two hundred years or so ago. That path led me to the Link Trail, which I decided to follow to the main forest. I crossed a sturdy footbridge over a beaver pond and walked through a young forest with many large old stumps and lots of undergrowth. It was a warm day, and the bugs were plentiful. I was glad to have remembered to bring the repellent.

The Link Trail ended at Bullard Hill Road, a non-maintained town road that is evidently used by cross-country skiers in winter. Just beyond the road was the Summit Trail, and on the road signs for both Scot's Trail and the Joslin Loop pointed west.

The trail brochure told me that Scot's Trail was an older trail, a loop about four miles long, that would take me by a vernal pool, the black gum swamp and a large beaver pond. I decided to follow it and return another day for the Summit Trail.

Scot's Trail left Bullard Hill Road after a short distance and went into the woods. Although there were a few ups and downs on the trail, it was basically easy walking, and the outermost portion of its loop reached only to the base of the really steep climb up Crotched Mountain.

The vernal pool was still pretty wet, and a nice, new boardwalk led me into the center of the old swamp. The brochure told me that some of the black gum trees could be over 400 years old. Scot's Trail and the Summit Trail ran together for a short distance, and then the white-marked Scot's Trail left the yellow-marked Summit Trail to pass around the northern end of Beaver Meadow, which was really a shallow, marshy pond. There were lots of nice views over the pond, especially from the north end. A number of nesting boxes stood on poles above the lake, and there was plenty of evidence of beavers chewing away at trees in the woods along the shore.

The trail led me away from the pond to a large, grassy field. Along the edge of the field were a number of young crab apple trees, enclosed in metal fencing for protection against deer. A sign told me that the trees were intended to provide food for wild turkeys and other birds, and that the whole field was cleared as a wildlife habitat. On the far side of the field, next to the beaver pond and on the Summit Trail, was a small shelter provided for bird watching over the water.

Beyond the field, I soon closed the loop formed by Scot's Trail and was back at the link trail to the parking lot. I hadn't seen anyone on the trails, but the same two cars were still in the lot, and I supposed the drivers were up on the top of Crotched.

June 2005

35
Fall Mountain State Forest
Charlestown NH

On September 28th, the state will formally dedicate its newest state forest, a nearly one thousand acre tract on Fall Mountain, in Charlestown and Langdon, and adjacent to Fall Mountain Regional High School. The creation of the forest was due to outstanding cooperation among several private and public parties. Probably the most important participant was the Nature Conservancy, which raised funds to purchase the land from the New England Power Company. Contributors included the U.S. Fish and Wildlife Service, the Land and Community Heritage Investment Program (LCHIP), and private citizens.

After the purchase was complete, the Nature Conservancy donated the forest to the state once an easement was obtained to protect it from development. The state will allow recreational use of the forest, including hiking, hunting and fishing, snowmobiling and nature studies. Closely managed lumber operations that do not damage sensitive portions of the forest will be conducted. Also, the current educational and athletic uses of the forest by Fall Mountain Regional High School will continue. Included in the list of activities *not* allowed in the forest will be ATV and trail bike riding.

Perhaps the main reason for the Nature Conservancy's effort was to protect several ponds in the forest on which the Northeastern bulrush grows. The bulrush is on the federal list of endangered plants.

However, as I found out on a recent visit, the forest would be well worth protecting even if no Northeastern bulrushes grew on

SOME HIKERS GET A FREE RIDE

its ponds. The old logging roads and trails, the ponds and swamps, the hillside forests, and the many animals that live in the forest make it a fantastic place for any of the activities mentioned above.

I drove to the forest on a Monday morning, not quite sure where the entrance to the forest was located. I found it just north of the entrance to Fall Mountain Regional on route 12A. There was a sign at a narrow dirt road on the left of the highway, and a few yards up that road I found a parking area on the edge of a large field covered with milkweed, sumac and young pines.

The entrance road proved to be the main trail in the forest, and I walked on it for two miles or so until I reached a section submerged in a swamp. I could see that the road surfaced on the other side, but that was as far as I went. By the time I reached that point, however, I had seen and enjoyed a good portion of the forest.

Just after I crossed the field at the parking area, I came to a metal gate across the road. Since I noticed only one set of trail bike tracks that day, the gate must be working. In the vicinity of the gate, there were a number of trails that seemed to come from the nearby high school. The teachers and coaches there evidently make good use of the paths and roads in the forest. For example, I saw tubes running from maple trees, which must have been part of a maple sugaring operation.

The road climbed steadily uphill, and it became grassy and lined on each side by asters and goldenrod. The surrounding forest was a mixture of soft and hardwood trees, and I could see old stumps that were evidence of logging. After a mile or so, I came to a fork with a branch of the road going sharply left, but I continued straight ahead. The road climbed some more, and then I could see a large pond through the trees. I walked down a path to the pond, which I later learned was North Pond and one of the sites with Northeastern bulrushes. A duck rose from the pond as I approached, and a minute later I saw a heron land among the reeds. A short distance from the little clearing next to the water at the end of the path, I was surprised to see a tall shagbark hickory tree. It was a beautiful spot.

I walked back to the road and followed it up a steeper section to what seemed to be the top of the hill. I had hoped to get a view of the Connecticut River or over to Vermont, but the road did not go to the very summit, and the woods were dense. From there, the road went downhill to an extensive swampy area that had many tall and bare tree trunks rising from its water and a number of rocky little islands dotting its surface. That's where the road went underwater and I turned around.

Back home after my trip, I spoke with the Nature Conservancy's spokesman, Eric Aldrich, about the forest. He was the one who told me about North Pond, and he also told me that the road I walked amounted to only a fraction of the trails in the forest. That's a great reason for another visit.

September 2005

36
White Ledges
Temple Mountain
Temple NH

I made my first visit to the White Ledges in Temple on a dreary, drizzly day in early October, and both the quartz outcropping and the forest trail leading to it brightened my day. The ledges are on town land and overseen by the Temple Conservation Commission. The outcropping is more properly known as Kendall Ledge, after the Kendall family, who owned the property for nearly two hundred years. Abbie Kendall Fish gave the land to Temple in 1975.

Getting to the ledges was simple. First, I drove east on route 101, over Temple Mountain, and then turned right onto route 45. I stayed on 45 for only a short distance and turned left onto Howard Hill Road. Just a few yards down that gravel road, I came to a fork where Howard Hill Road went right and a narrow, grassy dirt road went straight ahead. The smaller road was the "trail" leading to the ledges.

I parked next to the narrow road, near an old open shed. At the time, I wasn't sure if there was another place to park farther along the road, but when I later obtained a trail map, I found I had parked exactly where I should have. It would be hard to park more than two cars without blocking the road.

I began walking down the trail at 8:30. There had been some drizzle earlier, but that had stopped. It was misty and cloudy, though, and I expected more rain. The temperature was in the mid fifties. Perfect walking weather.

The first part of the trail went slightly downhill. On my left were woods, but the right side of the trail was bordered by a large field, on which there was one house. Large stone walls lined the road on both sides. Within a few minutes, I had left the field behind and was walking under tall oak and maple trees. After about a third of a mile, I reached the lowest point on the trip and started to climb. The hardwood trees gave way to a mix of hemlock and pines, and I came to a green metal gate. I hesitated for a moment, but I decided it wasn't there to keep out pedestrians and stepped around it.

The trail continued to climb after that, and led me to a open hillside that showed signs of being recently cleared. At the crest of the hill, I saw a dome of white rock.

When I got a bit closer, I saw that the dome was the high point of a quartz outcropping that ran from left to right for over a hundred yards. The dome I had seen first was the most prominent portion, and it rose about fifteen feet from the ground. When I stood on the ledge itself, I saw that it was also over a hundred feet wide. The rock was broken in spots by grass and shrubs, and much of it was covered with lichen. It was certainly white, and even in the dim light of the dreary day, the ledge was luminous.

From the ledge, I could see the land dropping off to the east. I was certain there would be a great view over the Souhegan River Valley on a clear day. Even then, I could see a large number of wooded ridges, many with tatters of cloud streaming from them. I could also see a small section of route 101, on which was a steady stream of tiny cars, all with their headlights on against the mist.

I walked about the ledges for a while, listening to the birds and admiring the tall oaks and beeches that leaned over the center portion of the outcropping. Before heading back down the road, I promised myself to return on a sunny day with a picnic lunch.

October 2005

37
Erving State Forest
Erving Mass.

The Erving State Forest is located just north of route two where the Massachusetts towns of Erving, Warwick, and Orange come together. Most of the forest is, of course, in Erving, but half of Laurel Lake, which is the real center of the forest, is in Warwick. The forest is really a large park, with a day use area on the lake, a boat ramp, twenty to thirty tent sites, and miles of unpaved roads and hiking/snowmobile trails. Oddly enough, there are also a number of private cottages lining all of the northern shore of the lake and part of the southern shore.

The forest is really not far from Keene. From Winchester, one would drive south on route 78 through Warwick to route 2 in Massachusetts. An even closer Massachusetts forest on that road is the Mount Grace State Forest in Warwick. In fact, there are several Massachusetts state forests and reservations extending south from the New Hampshire border to the Quabbin Reservoir. North of the New Hampshire/Massachusetts line, other state and conservation lands reach northward to Mt. Sunapee, and there is a growing interest in adding to and protecting the whole area as a natural corridor.

When I visited the forest in late December, however, I traveled by a different route. First, I met up with my old hiking buddy, Bob Ganley, in Winchendon, and then we drove south on route 202 to route 2 and then west to Erving. Although the state forest headquarters is on route 2, we drove past the paper mill into the town and then turned right onto North Street. We followed that

THE ENTRANCE TO ERVING STATE FOREST

road to its intersection with Swamp Road, which took us into the forest. We knew when we were in the forest, for the road's surface abruptly became ice-covered because the forest roads are not maintained in winter. Bob said it was more of a bob sled run than a road.

We found a place to park at the junction of Swamp Road and Laurel Lake Road, where Dunham Brook and Keeup Brook met. There was an entrance sign there and a container of trail maps. The maps had a summer use side and a winter one, which showed that the paved and unpaved roads in the park, as well as the hiking trails, all became snowmobiling trails once snow arrived.

After studying the map, we decided to walk a loop that would take in the central portion of the forest, including the lake and the camping area. It was about nine o'clock when we started our walk, and the temperature was hovering around twenty degrees. We crossed over Keeup Brook on a bridge, which marked the beginning of Laurel Lake Road. It was also a sheet of ice, and we could have used crampons. However, Bob had ski poles, and I had a carbide-tipped walking staff, and by walking on the edges of the road where the ice wasn't so slick and taking careful steps, we managed.

The first stretch was uphill, and at the top of the hill another road led to the north. A four-wheel drive truck was parked there in the snow, but no one was around. We continued east on the road, through a mixed forest of pine, hemlock and hardwoods. There were also many hefty stands of mountain laurel along the road, which explained the name of the lake. We wondered how many Laurel Lakes there are in the northeastern United States.

Soon we were walking along the southern shore of the lake. We walked down to the boat ramp at the western end and looked over the water. It was frozen, but the absence of tracks in the thin snow cover showed that the ice was still unsafe. We could see the private cottages lining the northern shore, and we passed a few on the southern side before we reached the public area. There was a large concession building there and picnic tables in the lakeside trees.

For the return trip, we walked along Camp Road, which paralleled Laurel Lake Road higher up the hillside. There were twenty to thirty tent sites along the road, each with a table and fire place. The sites were small, and although they weren't far from the lake, the trees prevented any view of it. Three sets of double outhouses were also scattered along the road.

As we walked along, we commented on the absence of visible wildlife. We did see a few deer tracks, and there must have been many animals silently watching us go by, but they kept themselves scarce. Just when we reached the end of Camp Road and were back on Laurel Lake Road, we did meet another man, out walking with a small dog. We exchanged greetings, and he headed east along the lake. We continued west and quickly passed the spot where the white truck had been parked. It was gone, and we wondered how he had gotten down the icy hill on Laurel Lake Road to Swamp Road. A few minutes later we were driving, very slowly, down the latter, and we were happy to reach the forest border and dry pavement.

January 2006

38
Friedsam Town Forest
Chesterfield NH

The middle section of January was warm and often wet. As a result, the snow cover was mostly gone when I walked most of the trails of the Friedsam Town Forest in Chesterfield on the third Friday of the month. Although I did find a few patches of snow on the lower portions of the forest, I hiked without snowshoes, and the only problems I had were with icy spots and a few flooded stretches.

Before setting out, I printed out a trail map from the Chesterfield Conservation Commission's excellent web site, www.chesterfieldoutdoors.com. The commission can be proud of its work, for the trails in and around the Madame Sherri Forest as well as for the Friedsam Town Forest trails.

I drove west on route 9 from Keene, turned left onto route 63 in Chesterfield, and parked in the small lot just a few yards south of the intersection. There are two other parking spots for the forest: the upper lot on Twin Brook Road, near route 63, and the lower lot, also on Twin Brook Road, just south of route 9. My walk included the latter, and I found it to be a more spacious parking area with a picnic table. The next time I visit the forest, that's where I'll park.

There was one other car parked next to route 63 when I began my walk at 8:45 that morning. It was still there when I returned at 10:30, but I never saw its driver or anyone else on the trails that day.

The map showed I could make a loop of something over three miles by following first the newest trail, the Ancient Oaks Trail, across the northern end of the forest and then the main trail, the Sargent Trail, east and south to the Cemetery Trail, which would lead me back to the Ancient Oaks Trail. My walk would include all of the forest trails save Audrey's Meander and the southern end of the Sargent Trail.

From my car, I stepped carefully down the slippery bank from the road to the Ancient Oaks Trail and turned right. I followed the white diamond markers a short distance north to where the footpath joined a snowmobile trail and turned west. The two ran together for a quarter of a mile or so before the footpath split off to the left. As was the case for all but a few of the lower spots on my walk, the way was nearly clear of snow, with only a thin coating of ice in spots. The forest was of the typical mixed variety, dominated by hemlocks, but with plenty of pines and hardwoods as well. The old oaks began to appear near the end of the trail.

Midway along the Ancient Oaks Trail, I climbed down a narrow ravine and crossed a brook before climbing up the other side. It was one of several stream crossings I would make on my hike. Much of the trail was close to route 9, and I could hear the traffic passing, but the portion just beyond the brook was a bit more into the woods, and the sounds of water, wind and - once- birdsong replaced the road sounds. The only bird I saw all morning was a nuthatch or brown creeper climbing up a big hemlock.

Near the end of the trail, I began to see some really tall oaks, and, at a point where the trail was very close to the highway, I came to an old apple orchard. A sign there informed me that the trees were still growing, but because they were overshadowed with pines they no longer bore fruit. The sign also told me there are plans to restore the orchard to produce some fruit for wildlife. Beyond the apple trees, I came to the real gem of the forest - a three hundred year old red oak tree. From another sign, I learned that it had survived hundreds of years of farming by being on a stone wall between pastures.

Not far from the old oak, I came to the end of the Ancient Oaks Trail and the lower parking lot. From there, orange markers led me first east and then south on the Sargent Trail. It included more climbing then the first trial, and I found myself walking down into the ravine through which Twin Brook rushed. I crossed there on a handsome and very rugged bridge and walked along the opposite side of the ravine before climbing the hillside to the highest point in the forest.

FOOT BRIDGE AT FRIEDSAM TOWN FOREST

The trail then went downhill and met the Cemetery Trail, which forms a loop with the Sargent Trail and also reaches the Ancient Oaks Trail. I followed the Cemetery Trail northward, through a partially flooded area, and rejoined the Oaks trail just south of the parking lot where I had left my car.

Driving home, I thought about how well the Chesterfield Conservation Commission and those who helped it, including the Boy Scouts, had organized and developed the trails in the forest. It is a super place to visit.

January 2006

39
McCabe Forest
Antrim NH

On the day after the mid-February snowstorm, I snowshoed the two mile trail in the Society for the Protection of New Hampshire Forests' McCabe Forest in Antrim. There really wasn't a lot of new snow in Antrim; the deepest amounts fell to the east and south - Nashua got about a foot, but there was enough to justify the snowshoes. More important, there was more than enough fresh snow and blue sky to create a beautiful winter day.

I had driven by the signs for the forest along route 202 many times, and I knew from the SPNHF's website that there was a trail in the forest, but I had never stopped for a visit. I thought the parking for the forest was the small open area near the first sign, about a quarter of a mile from the center of town, but a drive by that area showed me it was unplowed. Therefore, I decided to park my car at the shopping center's lot in town and walk down to the forest, carrying my snowshoes.

I left the car a little before eleven that morning and trudged down the highway to the forest. That was the only dangerous part of my trip, for the shoulder of the road was narrow and snow-covered, and the traffic whizzed by me as I walked along. When I reached what I thought was the parking area and the beginning of the trail, I didn't see any sign of either. Elm Street intersects with route 202 at that point, and I could see that it ended at a large house a few yards into the forest. I decided to check at the next forest sign along route 202, just a short distance north. I put on my snowshoes and walked along the snowbanks to the sign. There, I found what looked like an old logging road leading into the forest, and I started down it. I soon saw yellow trail markers and knew I was on the forest trail.

There were the marks of one snowshoer and one cross-country skier on the trail, and I followed them through a hemlock stand toward the Contoocook River. The fresh snow was still clinging to the trees; the sun had raised the temperature to a comfortable level, and it was a gorgeous place to be.

As I walked , I noticed wooden numbers at various spots on the trail, which were descending in order - 15, 14, etc. From that, I figured I was following the trail in reverse, which made me wonder where it had begun. However, it didn't bother me that I was walking the trail backwards. I soon reached the low land near the river, and I found myself walking across sections that had been flooded during the winter and were still covered with ice. The water underneath had disappeared in many spots, and the layer of ice sometimes collapsed as I walked on it. I could see that the skier and snowshoer had also broken through. There was no danger, however, for the ice was only a few inches above the ground.

The best portion of the trail was the long stretch on the river's banks. The Contoocook makes a number of wide turns at that point, including one oxbow, and the trail stayed close. There were many tall hardwood trees next to the river and also on a number of small islands. Their bare trunks and limbs curved gracefully over the water.

It was when I was nearing the end of the trail that I had a real surprise. I had reached the number three marker, and I knew the beginning of the trail was approaching. Then I found my way blocked by No Name Brook, which runs through the forest. It was way over its usual banks, and the trail was flooded. Fortunately, I was able to cross the brook by detouring through the grounds of the old McCabe farm house, which is now owned by the SPNHF. That led me to the trailhead and a large, freshly plowed parking lot. If I had driven a few yards down the Elm Street extension from route 202, I would have found it. There was an elaborate sign and a mail box containing trail maps, as well. Next time, I'll know better.

February 2006

40
Kidder Mountain
Sharon NH

It was the last day in March, and, as advertised, the month was exiting as a real lamb. By a quarter to ten that morning, when I parked where the Wapack Trail comes down to Temple Road in Sharon, it was already fifty-eight degrees and headed for seventy. It was a great morning for a hike, and I was headed for Kidder Mountain.

Most of the six-mile hike would be on the Wapack Trail, and for the first half mile I followed the yellow triangles south on Temple Road to Nashua Road, where the trail entered the woods. For the next mile and a half, I walked uphill along an old woods road. The lower part of the road was so heavily eroded that it was more of a stream bed than a road, and the trail had been moved into the woods, first to the right and then to the left of the road. After about three-quarters of a mile, I passed a growing beaver pond where I remembered a small house or camp once stood. The water flowing from the pond nearly covered the trail. Not long after that, I came to the rustic, environment-friendly houses of the Wildcat Partnership. Another quarter mile brought me to where a power line crossed the trail, and a sign for Kidder Mountain pointed northeast.

The side trail was marked with blue triangles, and they led me along the south side of the power line for a few hundred yards before crossing to the north and re-entering the forest. It was a steady climb up Kidder Mountain from that point. The trail passed through beautiful groves of hemlocks, hardwoods and pines, but it also took me through a couple of logged areas where young evergreens were growing amid the stumps. As I neared the summit, open ledge and grass appeared.

THE SUMMIT OF KIDDER MOUNTAIN

A few spruce trees stood on the northern edge of the top of the little mountain, but most of the summit area was rock and grass. A stone wall crossed from north to south, and it was easy to imagine sheep or cows grazing there. A small sign along the wall showed the summit to be 1,814 feet high. There was a good view to the south and southwest, dominated by Barrett Mountain. The sky was a bit hazy, but I could see Mt. Watatic and even Mt. Wachusett, far into Massachusetts.

I sat by the old stone wall for a few minutes and then began the return trip. By then, it was almost noon, and it was really warm. Except for the absence of insects, it was like a summer day. I did see a few butterflies, and I heard lots of birds. I noticed signs of moose and coyote near the top of Kidder Mountain, but the animals all seemed to be holed up for the day. There was also an absence of people. I didn't see a single soul on my hike up the mountain, and I was almost back to my car before I noticed one man in the yard of one of the houses along Temple Road. That was mainly because it was a Friday, and people were either at work or school. Still, I knew I wasn't the only retired or semi-retired person around, and I wondered where all the other codgers were.

April 2006

41
The Woods of West Wilton NH

Within the forest that covers the hills of the western portion of Wilton are two natural areas that border one another and include miles of pathways. They are the Nature Conservancy's Sheldrick Forest and the Heald Tract, overseen by the Society for the Protection of New Hampshire Forests. On a day in late May, I enjoyed a five mile hike that included paths in both areas.

My walk began and ended at the Sheldrick Forest's small parking lot in West Wilton. To get there, I drove east on route 101 to Temple Road, near Gary's Harvest Restaurant, and followed that road through the tiny cluster of old homes that make up the charming center of West Wilton. Just beyond a bridge, I turned left onto Town Farm Road, and drove uphill past a few houses. Small signs on trees on the left side of the road showed the edge of the Nature Conservancy's land, and a large, wooden sign on the corner of a grassy field, three quarters of a mile from the bridge, marked the parking lot. It would be easy to miss.

I arrived at eleven that morning; it was seventy degrees and sunny - a great day. After studying the trail map, I followed Helen's Path across the field and into the woods. I intended to make a loop on several of the forest's trails and then walk over to the Heald Tract and hike a longer loop around Castor Pond. Helen's Path led me downhill to a stand of some of the large old hemlocks, pines and oaks for which Sheldrick Forest is known. In fact, the forest was purchased and protected in order to prevent the old trees from being cut down for a development.

In the midst of the huge hemlocks, I left Helen's Path and walked the Swift Way toward the Heald Connector. The path took me uphill, across little Morgan Brook and then an old woods road, lined with small stones. About a quarter of a mile from Helen's Path, the Swift Way reached the path connecting Sheldrick Forest and the Heald Tract. I turned left onto that path and walked through a young pine forest for another quarter of a mile to the boundary between the two forests.

I had a trail map for the paths in the Nature Conservancy's forest, which were marked with their green and yellow tree markers and with low wooden posts, which also identified a number of points of interest described in a separate guide. I had no map for the Heald Tract, although I had walked part of it a year or so ago. From the boundary of the Sheldrick Forest, orange plastic rectangles with blue centers led me further south. The connecting trail ended at the Castor Pond Trail, which ran both right and left from a cluster of large boulders known as The Rocks. At that point, the orange rectangles lost their blue centers. I could see the pond off to my right, and I was certain the paths would take me around it. I decided to go clockwise and was soon walking along a stream that seemed to be an outlet from the pond. In a short while the Castor Pond Trail ended at its junction with the blue-marked Camp Trail. The new trail went both left and right, but I knew I had to keep right if I was to circle Castor Pond, so I continued the clockwise motion.

The path continued in the right direction, and I soon could see the pond again. The trail climbed a hill above the water, and a sign identified the area as Heron Heights and cautioned visitors not to disturb the herons nesting on the pond. I could see two large nests on dead trees in the center of the pond, one much higher. As the name suggests, the pond is a beaver pond and most of it is flooded forest. The Camp Trail reached the Castor Pond Trail again at the north end of the pond. A few yards from the junction, a short side trail took me to another lookout, right on the shore of the pond and just above the beavers' large dam. It was identified by sign as Cabane Du Castor, the beaver lodge. I rested there for a while and got to see a heron land briefly on the higher nest. I think it dropped off some food, but it happened quickly, and the heron took off again.

I completed the loop around the pond and then walked back up the connecting trail to the Sheldrick Forest. I turned left onto the Swift Way and completed the loop back to my car *May 2006*

42
The Dublin Trail to Monte Rosa Mount Monadnock

On a fine day in early June, I hiked some of the less used trails on Mt. Monadnock, and I had a fine, although tiring, day. My route took me up the Dublin Trail to the summit and then over the Smith Summit Trail to Monte Rosa. For the return trip, I first made a long loop by following the Old Pasture Trail from Monte Rosa to the Marion Trail and then the Marlboro Trail. I walked up that trail to its junction with the Dublin Trail and then down to my car.

The Dublin Trail begins on Old Troy Road, about a mile from the Dublin Lake golf club on Old Marlboro Road. The small parking area was empty when I arrived just before a quarter to eight and began my hike. Unlike much of this spring, the weather was good; the skies were only partly cloudy, and the temperature was close to sixty.

The first part of the Dublin Trail was broad, rocky, and not very steep. However, once the trail crossed a small stream, it became narrower and began climbing more steeply up the mountain. It's one of the shorter, more direct trails to the summit, and it pretty much went straight up. I was walking slowly, but steadily, and after nearly an hour the mixed woods I was walking through began to be dominated by spruces, and the first open ledges appeared. I had to scramble up a couple of chute-like passages before reaching the tree-free summit area. Just below the top of the mountain, the Marlboro Trail joined the Dublin Trail for the last few yards. By that time, I could hear and see a group of high-school students and their leaders arriving on the summit from one of the trails that begin in

THE SUMMIT OF MONTE ROSA WITH THE WEATHER VANE

the state park. Another lone hiker stepped off the Smith Summit Trail a few feet ahead of me, and I followed him up to the summit.

I didn't stay on top for more than a minute; it was crowded and getting more so by the second. The man I had followed the last steps to the top told me he had come up the Halfway House Trail with a detour to Monte Rosa, which was at the 2400 foot level, about a half a mile away. He started back down right away, but I stopped a short way down the Smith Summit Trail for a rest. It was a little after ten thirty, and there was still some sun.

A few minutes later I was following the white circles of the Smith trail down the south side of the mountain. Before long, I could see the arrow-shaped weather vane which stands on the top of the little peak known as Monte Rosa. By asking the question online at Yahoo, I had learned the area was most likely named by visitors staying at the old Halfway House who noticed the peak often turned rosy in the late day sun. As I approached the little peak and could see the weather vane up close, I thought that although it was an obviously unnatural feature, it didn't spoil the scene. I liked it where it was, though, and I wouldn't want it on the actual summit.

From Monte Rosa, I followed the Old Pasture Trail down the west side of the mountain to its junction with the Mossy Brook and Marion Trails. As I went along, I wondered what sort of agile animals could have used the old pasture. They must have been goats, maybe mountain goats! At the end of that trail, the Mossy Brook Trail went off to my left toward the Halfway House Trail, and the Marion Trail headed north. I followed the latter, staying at the 2200 foot level, to the Marlboro Trail. The side trails were marked only with low cairns and wooden signs at the trail junctions. They were a bit hard to follow at times.

I hiked up the Marlboro trail to its junction with the Dublin Trail. It was only a little over a half a mile, but the trail climbed over seven hundred feet in that distance. I stopped several times and enjoyed the view to the west. Two older men passed me on their way down the mountain.

It was about one o'clock when I reached the Dublin Trail and began my descent to Old Troy Road. Gravity was on my side now, but I had to be very careful climbing down the steepest parts. On the hike up that morning, I hadn't seen another person on the Dublin Trail, but on my way down I passed three groups heading up. When I reached the parking lot, it was filled to capacity. That meant six cars in addition to mine. On a busy weekend, there must be cars parked along the road for many yards. No matter how busy, though, I doubt the Old Pasture Trail ever gets crowded.

June 2006

43
Ted's Trail on Pack Monadnock Greenfield NH

I had heard about Ted's Trail on the north side of North Pack Monadnock - had even read some reports about it, but until this June, I had never walked it. Now that I have, I can understand why hikers are so enthusiastic about it. Ted's Trail is super, and so is its side trail, Carolyn's Trail.

The trail is named for its creator, Ted Bonner, who lives nearby; Carolyn's Trail is named for his wife. Some of the lowest portion of the trail is on private land, but most of it is within the Wapack National Wildlife Refuge. In a telephone conversation, Mr. Bonner told me he tried to design the trail to make the most of the land, and he certainly did.

To get to the trailhead on Old Mountain Road in Greenfield, I drove out Sand Hill Road in Peterborough for about four miles to where it becomes Old Mountain Road, just beyond the intersection with East Mountain Road. Soon after that, I was in Greenfield and passing the entrance to Brantwood Camp on my left and then the Wapack Trail on my right. From there it was downhill for about a mile to the small parking lot, which had room for only two cars, and the little sign marking the start of Ted's Trail.

I arrived just before eight thirty on a sunny morning; it was one of the few good ones in the first half of June this year. A few moments later, I was following the yellow rectangles that mark the trail. The first few yards were level and muddy, and I quickly crossed a small stream on a wooden bridge. From there, the trail began an easy climb under tall trees, with plenty of sunshine filtering through. I noticed a stand of red pines, crossed a second bridge, and then came to a new looking bench next to the trail. The trail had begun to follow the stream up the mountain, and for a long while I walked to the pleasant sound of falling water. A third bridge crossed the stream between a group of large rocks, over which the water cascaded. It was a beautiful spot.

There was a sign pointing to Carolyn's Trail at that juncture, but I had decided to stay on Ted's Trail all the way and then follow Carolyn's Trail down. The total route would be about six and a half miles. I'm sure, though, that many hikers make a short loop by walking over to Carolyn's Trail at that spot and then taking it back down.

Eventually, the stream moved away from the trail, and I began to near the summit of North Pack. There began to be more open ledge, and most of the trees were spruces. Not far from the top, I had a great view to the north, the first of many. Ted's Trail ended when it reached the Cliff Trail, which connects the summit of North Pack with the south facing cliffs on the mountain.

I followed the blue triangles of the Cliff Trail to the right and soon reached the large cairn at the top of North Pack. I rested there for a while and enjoyed the view. There are lots of blueberry bushes on the summit, but it was much too early in the summer for berries.

From the top, I retraced my steps on the Cliff Trail to Ted's Trail and then turned left onto Carolyn's Trail. A few yards below the junction, I sat on an open ledge and had a light lunch. The view from there was dominated by Lyndeborough Mountain, but I could see the beginnings of the White Mountains far to the north and even the little mound of Mt. Agamenticus up in York, Maine. Carolyn's Trail didn't have the long stretch of stream side walking, but it did have a fifty yard boardwalk through a marsh. Another new bench sat by the trail in the middle of the marshy area.

About halfway down, I saw a sign pointing toward Ted's Trail, and I figured that was the connector that led to the bridge among the rocks. I stayed on Carolyn's Trail until it reached its junction with Ted's Trail, only a short distance from Old Mountain Road.

When I got back to my car, there was one other sharing the little lot. I hadn't seen another hiker, so I decided the passengers were climbing up Ted's Trail while I was coming down on Carolyn's. In a way, I hope that's as busy as the trail ever gets, but I'm sure there must be times when cars are parked along the road. I'm sure anyone who hikes Ted's Trail once will want to do it again.

June 2006

44
Pinnacle and Rose Mountains
Lyndeborough NH

The view of Lyndeborough from Miller State Park, on the top of Pack Monadnock Mountain, features what looks like one low mountain with three distinct bumps or peaks. Officially, each peak is a separate mountain: Winn, Rose, and Pinnacle. Rose and Pinnacle, from a distance, appears as a long, flat plateau with summits at either end - almost like a dog bone. I had read about the trails in Ted Bonner's, *Ted's Favorite Hikes in Southern New Hampshire* but had never walked them. Until recently, that is. On a fine weekday in mid-September, I hiked up Pinnacle Mountain and then walked over to Rose Mountain. When I completed the loop and was back at my car, I had hiked about four miles along narrow footpaths and wide snowmobile trails. It was all easy going, and I enjoyed the woods, the open peaks, and the fine views, which included both the skyline of Boston and the White Mountains.

I also enjoyed the drive to the trailhead because it took me through an interesting part of Lyndeborough that I had never visited. From Greenfield, I drove east on route 31 to South Lyndeborough and turned left onto Center Road. I stayed on that road for nearly two and a half miles and then made another left onto Mountain Road. Just past the highest point on that road, I found a small parking area on the left side of the road. There was really room for just one car, which is something to consider before making the trip. Yellow trail markers showed the beginning of the trail up Pinnacle Mountain. There was also a sign prohibiting trail bikes.

The sun was shining and the temperature was in the low fifties when I began my hike up the narrow trail. I had an easy climb for about five minutes, through a mostly hardwood forest, and then I came to a pine-covered ridge. Beyond that, the trail dipped a bit, and I stepped across a small stream. About ten minutes into my hike, I came to a split in the trail, where Helen's Trail came in on the right. I stayed on the main trail, and reached the top of Pinnacle Mountain at nine-thirty, less than a half hour into my walk.

It was a very clear morning, and I had a wide view from the summit. Fairly close-up, I could see Monadnock, Pack Monadnock and, to the northeast, the Uncanoonucs. Farther away, I made out the outlines of Mt. Kearsarge and Mt. Moosilauke. I could even see the Franconia Ridge and the peak of Mt. Washington.

From Pinnacle Mountain, I walked on the snowmobile trail over to Rose Mountain. The trail was wide, really a road, and went along the nearly flat ridge or plateau between Pinnacle and Rose. The only problem was there were no markers, and I came to several trail junctions. I kept to the right each time, and that worked out. Part way up the slope to Rose Mountain, there was an open area with a fine view back toward Pinnacle. A little later, I came to an open ledge on the left side of the trail which had a nice view of Monadnock. Just beneath the summit, the remains of an old truck, including the cab, engine block, and wheels - one with a tire - sat in the woods next to the trail. It was a good reminder of the days when farms operated on the hillsides.

The trail curved around to the right just beneath the summit, and another trail joined it. The top of the little mountain, just 1720 feet (17 feet higher than Pinnacle) was rocky with blueberry bushes and other low vegetation. The view was at least as grand as the one from Pinnacle, and I could just make out the Boston skyline. Thanks to the snowmobile/ATV trails, Rose probably gets many more visitors than its twin peak. One evidence of that was an unusual collection of stone artwork. The artist or artists had made a number of sculptures by piling rocks at a variety of angles. None of them were more than a few feet high, but they covered a wide area.

I walked back to Pinnacle Mountain and then took Helen's Trail down from the summit, completing the loop back to the main trail. The narrow trails on Pinnacle were definitely used only by hikers, in contrast with the multi-purpose trails leading up Rose Mountain. I was back at my car before noon, more refreshed than wearied by the neat little hike. *September 2006*

45
Cobb Hill Trail
Hancock NH

The Harris Center in Hancock has an extensive trail system, and most of the trails begin near the center's headquarters on King's Highway. The Cobb Hill Trail, however, is a few miles away on Jacquith Road. I hiked the trail on a cool, cloudy Tuesday in late October, and it brightened my day. What's more, just the ride over to the trailhead from King's Highway was an enjoyable outing. I had never been on Old Dublin Road or the western end of Jacquith Road, and I found the trip on the narrow, sparsely settled dirt roads to be beautiful. I was also glad I didn't meet up with any cars going in the opposite direction.

I had picked up a trail map at the Harris Center, and it directed me to turn right onto Jacquith Road and drive about a half a mile beyond the last house to where the trail went into the woods on the left. When I reached that last house, a structure built circa 1790, a closed gate ended my driving. A small sign on the gate announced foot travel only, and I parked in a very small space beneath a sign for the Sydney Williams Woods. Just before ten thirty, I stepped around the gate and began walking along the last stretch of Jacquith Road. Within a few yards, I was quite happy that I was walking and not driving, for the road was bumpy with large rocks and parts of it were soggy. Having it closed to auto traffic only added an enjoyable mile to my hike.

Half way to the trailhead, the road was flooded with water from a beaver pond. Several cut and chewed trees showed the beavers were active. The road climbed from that point, and a stream of water ran down a channel in the road that looked like it had been at least partly dug out by someone to keep most of the road dry.

A few minutes more brought me to the beginning of the Cobb Hill Trail itself. The trail map showed it was marked with white discs, and some of them were still to be seen, but new, yellow and black diamonds with the Harris Center's lynx logo led me up the wooded hill. Much, if not all, of the trail passes through the Williams Woods, and I was walking through a fine forest of mainly oak and beech trees. Some of them were quite old and tall. It was late enough in the fall for most of the leaves to be down, and the sunlight, which was finally breaking through the heavy clouds, lit up the woods.

It was a steady climb up Cobb Hill but never steep enough to require the use of hands. When I was approaching the summit of the hill, the trail met a woods road and turned left to follow it for a short distance. Then, about a half a mile from the trailhead, the trail left the road and climbed steeply toward the summit. A sign just above the road identified the last section of path, which was a little less than a quarter of a mile long, as the Jane Greene Trail. Still below the top of Cobb Hill, the trail turned to the left and ended at a lookout with a fine view of Monadnock and Lake Skatutakee. Before walking back down, I bushwhacked to the summit, which was crossed by a stone wall and thickly wooded.

I didn't see much wildlife on my little hike, but as I walked back on Jacquith Road, a flock of juncos flew along both sides of the road ahead of me for a hundred yards or more, landing for a few seconds and then taking off again as I grew closer. They seemed to be keeping me company.

I was back at my car a little before noon and decided to follow Jacquith Road all the way to route 137 instead of turning onto Old Dublin Road again. I had been on the lower portion of the road before, but the section just east of Old Dublin Road was new to me and surprisingly lovely, highlighted by a massive old red barn standing near the road between a broad, wet meadow and a series of rocky ledges. It was a nice way to finish my trip.

October 2006

46
Converse Meadows
Rindge NH

Converse Meadows in Rindge is a work in progress. The centerpiece of the natural area is a large beaver pond, its shores lined with a mix of hardwoods and evergreens. Since the town obtained the land a few years ago, the Conservation Commission has been working to make it more accessible and comfortable for visitors. One recent addition, a kiosk near the entrance, just off route 119 on Converseville Road, lists the names of many private citizens, businesses and corporations that have donated money and time to the development of the area. Improvements already finished include a number of granite benches, most with a view over the water, and a sturdy, two part bridge over the stream flowing from the pond.

The pond, of course, is the main attraction. When I visited Converse Meadows on a mild and sunny November day, I parked near the kiosk, walked the few yards down the access road to the dam, and was immediately impressed with the beauty of the pond.

One of the granite benches faced directly across the water, and I sat on it for several minutes, enjoying the view. The pond was longer than it was wide, and the far end looked to be about a mile away. The shores were tree lined, and the pond appeared to end in a grassy marsh. A shoulder of Temple Mountain was visible above the trees to the north.

A stone wall ran along most of the old beaver dam, and just beyond the right hand or east end of the dam, a sign marked the beginning of private property. I walked along the dam and crossed the outlet stream on the new bridge. The water was still high, and the stream was rushing along with lots of white water. On the other side of the bridge, a wide, grassy trail, really a road, followed the water's edge, and I decided to find out how far it went.

After only a few steps, I came to a fork in the road. The left branch went uphill, away from the water, so I followed the right branch. The road continued to be wide and level for over a half a mile, and I passed another bench, sitting right on the shore. There were also several paths leading from the road down to the water's edge. Eventually, though, the road narrowed, and I could see I was near the marsh on the northern end of the lake.

I thought I might be able to walk around the tip of the pond and maybe even make a loop around the little lake, but the trail nearly disappeared among the rocks and puddles in that section. What remained of the trail appeared to be moving away from the water, so I bushwacked until I reached a stream flowing into the pond. A rotting footbridge led me to an old camp or shack. I wasn't certain I was still on public land, so I returned to the original trail and followed it back to the fork.

At the fork, I turned right and walked up the hill for ten minutes or so. I thought it might lead to a view over the pond, but I didn't find one. There were many freshly trimmed pine branches piled along the road, and I thought people might have been getting it ready for snowmobile season. When the road began to go downhill and away from the pond, I turned around again and walked back to the dam.

November 2006

47
The Pinnacle
Fitzwilliam NH

Despite having lived in this part of the country for nearly fifty years, I am constantly reminded of how much I don't know about it. For example, recently a friend and resident of Fitzwilliam, Molly Haas, gave me a brochure from the Fitzwilliam Conservation Commission about the Pinnacle Hiking Trails near the center of town. The brochure showed me the parking area for the trails was on Richmond Road, just west of the Fitzwilliam Inn and informed me that in the winter the trails were primarily for cross-country skiing. Molly told me that years ago there had been a downhill ski area there. An on-line visit to Lost New Hampshire Ski Areas, the web site originated by Jeremy Davis, gave me a look at photos of the ski area, which operated from the late 1940's until the mid 1970's. By the time the area closed, it had several rope tows, a lift, a base lodge, and even some snow making. It was called the Fitzwilliam Ski Area, but the hill it was located on had been called the Pinnacle since the days of the first settlers.

I decided to drive over to Fitzwilliam on the second Monday in December and walk some of the trails. There was no snow, other than a thin patch or two left over from the flurries of a week before, so I didn't have to worry about messing up ski trails. Once the snow gets here, only skiers are allowed on the trails.

I drove west on route 119 from Rindge into Fitzwilliam. At the common, where 119 makes a left turn, I drove straight onto Richmond Road, passed the Fitzwilliam Inn, and stopped at the trailhead, less than a quarter of a mile from the inn. There was a chain across the entrance, and I parked in front of it, just off the

FITZWILLIAM STEEPLES FROM THE PINNACLE TRAIL

road. It was almost eleven o'clock on a cloudy, cool day. There had been a few sprinkles earlier, but it looked like the sun might come out at any time.

The first part of my walk was up an open, hillside field to a white mailbox that stood at the beginning of the woods covering the slopes of the Pinnacle. It contained one laminated trail map and a request to return the map after using it. The map was very useful, for there are many side trails that intersect the four loops that make up the trail system and very few trail markers. It would be easy to get off the loops and onto one of the side trails, some of which are on private land. In the winter, of course, ski tracks would make following the trails easy. Although the map was useful, I learned it is very awkward to carry a stiff, laminated map around on a hike.

From the mailbox, I walked on the Yellow Loop, going uphill or counterclockwise. It took me through a hardwood forest until I reached a fairly level area over halfway up the hill, where pines and spruces replaced the oaks and birches. After walking about twenty minutes, I reached the first intersection, where the Green Loop went straight ahead, and the Red Loop came down from the north and joined the Yellow Loop, which turned south. A short distance later, the Yellow Loop turned to the left, and I followed the Red Loop to the south. The Yellow, Red and Blue Loops are all a mile or more long, and the Green Loop, which is identified as the easiest for skiers, is only three quarters of a mile. I decided to walk around the Red Loop back to its junction with the Yellow Loop and then complete that loop.

The Red Loop took me close to where the old ski lift reached the top of the ski slope. I noticed the remains of the footing where the lift was anchored, but I was more interested by the smooth ledge that covered most of the surface of the area. It looked almost like poured concrete. I stopped for a moment at the highest point on the trail system, just below the summit. The trail did not go to the top of the Pinnacle, but at the high point and just before a ninety degree turn to the right, there was a large boulder, probably an erratic, identified in the brochure as Lunch Rock. I'm sure many hikers do stop for a break there.

Although I hadn't planned it that way, the last section of my walk was the most rewarding. There hadn't been any real views on the hike, due to the thick forest, but the trail ended at the old ski slope, which is still very clear. From it, I had a great view over the Fitzwilliam Common, and the white spires of the town hall and the Community Church rose out of the trees and were silhouetted against the distant, blue hills.

I returned the map to the mailbox and walked down the field to my car. My walk had taken about an hour and a half and covered about two and half miles of easy walking. Next time I visit, I hope it will be with my skis.

December 2006

48
Bruce Edes Trail
Bennington NH

Named for a respected local EMT and lover of the outdoors who died in 2004, the Bruce Edes Trail near the center of Bennington, New Hampshire, connects two of the dominant features of many Monadnock Region towns: the forest and the mill. The start and finish of the mile long trail follow the railroad that leads to the Monadnock Paper Mill, but the main portion loops through a hillside forest containing towering pines. The duality is reinforced by the Contoocook River, which lies between the little forest and the town, its natural flow interrupted by a series of dams.

Although I had read about the trail and its dedication to Mr. Edes, I hadn't walked it until a Monday afternoon in mid February, I parked in the lot next to the VFW building, just off route 31 in Bennington, and between the railroad and the river. It was just before noon, cool and cloudy when I began my little hike. There was a thin coating of snow on the ground, and a few flakes fell as I walked, but only boots were necessary. One reason I chose to walk the trail that day was the expected arrival of the first major snow storm of the year later in the week.

I stepped onto the railroad bed and followed the trail signs north. The markers were blue and white, featuring a Native American four winds symbol. In two tenths of a mile or so, the trail left the tracks and turned left into the woods. A few steps into the trees, I turned left again and began the only climb on the trail. The path followed a stone wall upward, through a mixed stand of trees with many hemlocks. The wall suggested the wooded hill was once a pasture, but the size of the trees indicated that must have been very long ago. Only the last few yards were steep, and the top of the little hill featured a view through the bare limbs of hardwood trees over the town to the humpback of Crotched Mountain. In summer, the view would be obscured, but it was certainly interesting, and I was glad to see it. The white steeple of one building was nicely framed by tree trunks, and the blue bulk of the mountain made a great background. The nearness of the buildings added to the notion of a juxtaposition of the natural and the man made.

From the hilltop, the trail circled through the woods and downward toward the river. It led me through a stand of enormous pines and over a completely frozen little stream. The Contoocook river appeared, its surface beneath the last of the dams broken by snow covered rocks. The mill itself rose on the far side of the water.

The path rejoined the railroad just before the tracks crossed the river on a wooden trestle to end at the mill. I walked south along the railroad toward the VFW building, stopping close to the end of the trail to enjoy the view over the river, which included the water flowing over one of the dams and a great perspective on the graceful arch of the stone bridge that leads to the center of town.

I finished my walk forty-five minutes after I began, but I was struck with the idea that in that short time I had passed through or viewed elements of several centuries of the New England experience.

Since it was noontime, I got my lunch from my car and sat on the bench by the water to eat it. Although it was late November, the temperature was near sixty, and it was great to be outside. As I ate, I could see a number of geese feeding at the far end of the pond.

February 2007

49
The Ledges Trails
Hancock NH

The system of winter trails for cross country skiing and snowshoeing at Boston University's Sargent Center is a great resource for area residents who enjoy self-propelled snow sports. First there has to be snow, however, and that necessary ingredient didn't arrive until mid-February. A week after the Valentine's Day storm, I drove up Windy Row from Peterborough to the center of the Center, just over the Hancock line on Sargent Camp Road, and signed in at the office. The Center welcomes visitors, but they wisely ask everyone to sign a waiver form on the first visit and sign in on each visit.

From the office, I drove west on Sargent Camp Road, passed the beach area on Halfmoon Pond, and parked in a small, plowed area at the beginning of the Peninsula Trail. That trail is named for the triangular thrust of land that nearly pinches off the western end of the pond, and it makes a nearly perfect equilateral triangle as it goes around the peninsula.

It was about 10:15 when I started snowshoeing; it was cloudy with a temperature slightly below freezing - too warm, if anything. Since my objective was the Ledges Trails, I walked only the base section of the Peninsula Trail, following the tracks of a cross country skier. In a few minutes I reached the point where the Peninsula Trail turned right and the outlet of the pond flowed under the road on its way to the Nubanusit River. I stepped onto the road and walked a few yards to the beginning of the Lower Ledges Trail, which followed the western edge of Halfmoon Pond to a three-way junction with the Bog, Boulder, and Upper Ledges Trails. All of those trails were marked for snowshoe use only, but I walked along the tracks of another skier until the junction. Until then, I was wondering why the trail was for snowshoes only. I had the answer when the link to the Upper Ledges Trail went to the left and steeply uphill. A sign proclaimed it to be "most difficult." There were no ski tracks going up - for that matter, there were no tracks at all, even though it was over a week after the snow storm. The ski tracks I had followed kept going north.

I took my time climbing up the hill, stopping just below the top where there was a view through the bare branches of hardwood trees over Halfmoon Pond to both North and South Pack Monadnock. From there, it was only a short trek to the very top of the hill, which I reached at about eleven o'clock. The hill was tree covered, mostly with hemlocks, but the outstanding feature was the ledges - piles of huge rocks scattered among the trees. There was also another trail junction where the West Ridge Trail went north, paralleling the Boulder Trail. I stayed on the Upper Ledges Trail, which dipped into a narrow ravine and then climbed again. Mine were still the only human tracks visible on the snow, but there plenty left by small animals.

Just after the trail began to head downhill, I came to the most impressive cluster of boulders. The largest was split in the middle, and a heavy wooden ladder leaned against it. Since the Sargent Center conducts classes in the woods, I guessed climbing the ladder to the top of the big rock was a regular activity.

The rest of the trip was a pleasant walk through the woods back to Sargent Camp Road. The Upper Ledges Trail ended a tenth of a mile or so west of where I began the Lower Ledges Trail, and I walked east on the road back to my car. At a quarter to twelve, my trip was over. On my next visit, if the snow holds up, I plan to follow a couple of the ski trails.

February 2007

50
Casalis State Forest
Peterborough NH

Casalis State Forest is located east of route 123 in Peterborough, near both the Sharon and Temple town lines. Its 228 acres include a large marsh and several small streams; the forest climbs part way up the western shoulder of Temple Mountain and gets quite close to route 101. An old woods road serves as a trail running from the parking area for the marsh on route 123 to Condy Road, which descends from route 101. A shorter trail leads south toward Town Line Brook.

I visited the forest on the Friday following the April nor'easter and walked the longer trail from the Sharon Road to Condy Road and back. Although there were still many patches of snow and lots of standing water, the weather was sunny and warm, and I enjoyed my nearly two hour walk.

The parking lot on the Sharon Road (route 123) can take up to a half dozen cars, but it was empty when I arrived a little after noon. I stepped around the gate and walked down to the marsh, about a quarter of a mile. The marsh is operated by the state as a water fowl study area, and it is a popular fishing spot. The trail crosses a dam on the south side of the pond that is the center of the marsh, and the water flows into a drain, much like one in a bathtub, before passing under the road on its way to join Town Line Brook. A number of nesting boxes were mounted on trees rising from the water on the far side of the pond. Closer to the road, a few dead trees rose out of the water, their bare branches making interesting patterns against the bright blue sky.

Beyond the pond, the trail was downhill for a short while before reaching a fork where the trail to Town Line Brook went downhill and the one to Condy Road went uphill to the left. I followed recent footprints of a person and a dog on the latter, an it took me through a mixed forest, climbing for only a short stretch at a time, and eventually into a stand of hemlock. There were still several inches of melting snow on much of the trail, and the ruts, which may have been very old, were filled with water. Other than those seasonal problems, it was an easy trail to walk. After walking about a mile, I passed a cellar hole just to the right of the trail and next to a small brook that flowed under a very old log bridge.

Not long after that, I came to another fork. I had no map, so I decided to follow the prints, which took the right hand road. Soon I could hear the traffic on route 101, and another trail entered from the left. (Later, I looked at a topo map of the area and saw that it was the same trail that had forked to the left earlier, rejoining the main trail.)

I passed just below two houses located near or on route 101, and then I reached Condy Road. The trail came out at the pond that can be seen when one looks down Condy Road from route 101. There was a house just above the pond, toward the highway, but the pond itself was undeveloped, and there was a great view of Pack Monadnock across the water. As I stood on the road enjoying the view, a rural mailman drove by and returned a minute later, so I knew that although the end of Condy Road was close, there was another house.

There was room for at least one car to park off the road where the trail reached it, so two people could leave a car at either end of the trail for a shorter walk. I,however, was happy to have another mile and a half of walking. The trip back, probably because some of it was downhill, went quickly, and I was surprised at how soon I reached the marsh. A few minutes later, just before two o'clock, I reached the parking lot, still empty but for my car.

April 2007

51
Beech Hill
Keene NH

A familiar sight in Keene is the wooded hill on its eastern edge. From the highways that enter the city from the east, west and south, the hill is hard to miss. A tall antenna rises from the top of the hill, and a couple of houses seem to cling to the southern ridge not far from the summit. The view from those houses has to be grand, and the sunsets often spectacular. Fortunately, one doesn't have to own one of those houses to enjoy the view, for there is a 180 acre preserve owned by the city and open to the public, which includes the lookout known as Sunset Rock and a loop trail through the woods.

The website of the Keene Recreation Department recommends entering the Beech Hill Preserve from Chapman Road, which can be reached by driving east on Roxbury Street and then Roxbury Road. There is a metal gate off Chapman Road and parking space along the eastern edge of the road. Only authorized vehicles are allowed to drive up the paved road that leads to the TV tower. A hundred yards or so north of the metal gate, there is a small kiosk that marks the beginning of a woods road that also leads to the hilltop.

I visited the preserve on a pleasant morning in early May and spent about an hour walking the road and paths and looking out over the city from Sunset Rock. It was a very pleasant outing and certainly one that is easily accessible to the people of Keene. I'm sure, in fact, that many residents manage to climb up the hill from the streets just below.

My visit began with a walk up the paved road, which took me past a large water tank and curved steeply up the hillside. I noticed a footpath going into the woods across from the water tank and a woods road leading to the right farther up. They proved to be part of the loop trail that ends at Sunset Rock.

When I reached the tower area, I walked past it and entered the woods to the south. There was a narrow path along the very top of the ridge, and it led me to the low foundation wall of what looked to have been a rather large building. Not far beyond that, I came to the same woods road that I had noticed on the way up. I turned left on it, and a moment later I was at the little clearing in front of the rocky lookout known as Sunset Rock. The city of Keene was spread out beneath me, and in west I could see the hills of Chesterfield and Westmoreland. In the distance, the mountains of southern Vermont were also visible. It was a wonderful view. The only sour note was the amount of litter - mostly cans and bottles, but even the remains of a couple of campfires - that lay on the ground around the lookout. I'm sure the recently melting snow uncovered much of it, and I know the city will soon take it away. It's too bad that people had to leave it there.

I took the woods road back to the paved road, which took me by some really beautiful beech trees, helping to explain the name of the hill. I followed the woods road to the paved road and took it down to the water tank. Then I walked the much narrower footpath that went south from the road. Apart from the great view, it was the nicest part of my trip. The path was very clean as it went through a mixed wood just below the top of the ridge. I could see the towers through the trees. After a quarter of a mile or so, I was back at Sunset Rock. Since I liked the path, I walked back on it instead of taking the woods road, which I had walked earlier anyway. The birds seemed to like the path, too. On the way up I heard and got very close to a thrush or veery, and on the return trip a barred owl flew low across the path just in front of me and then perched on a limb and stared back at me. Finally, a tiny brown creeper flew from tree to tree in front of me, moving on only when I got within a few feet of him.

May 2007

52
The Pumpelly Trail
Mount Monadnock
Dublin NH

The Pumpelly Trail is the longest trail on Monadnock, nearly four and a half miles from Dublin Lake to the summit. It is named for Raphael Pumpelly, a geologist and Dublin summer resident, who laid it out in 1884. Although the average grade is less than that of the other trails, the middle section is quite steep. The upper half of the trail is much gentler, and it is nearly all along open ledges with great views. The trail is much less popular than the ones beginning at the state park, and the nine mile round trip makes it a pretty demanding outing. However, anyone fit enough for that kind of a hike will find it very satisfying.

I hadn't hiked the trail for several years, so I thought it would be a good way to spend a nice mid June day. The trail begins on Lake Road in Dublin, just south of route 101. There is no real parking area, but there is a wide shoulder about fifty yards farther south that several cars can use. The trail goes into the woods across from one of the lakefront houses, and it's not very obvious.

Just as I began my hike at a quarter past eight that morning, another two hikers had arrived and were getting ready to start. I didn't see them again for over an hour.

The first part of the trail, over a mile long, goes through a mixed forest, and it climbs only gradually. The trail is easy to follow, and it's smooth walking. Then rocks appear, and the path begins its longest and steepest stretch. After I had been walking for about an hour, the trees had pretty much disappeared, and the view had opened to the north and east.

From then on, the trail followed the long ridge up to the top. At about ten o'clock, I passed the junction with the Cascade Link, which climbs up from the state park. Just beyond that, the trail skirted around a rocky nob, and I decided it would be a good place for a break. I stepped off the trail and up to the top of the outcropping, where I was treated to a fine view to the east. Just below the mountain, Thorndike and Gilson ponds broke up the sea of green.

While I was sitting there, the two hikers I had seen getting ready to hike passed by, talking cheerfully. They didn't notice me.

The last section of the trail, all above the trees, included several interesting features. Two more trails, leading from lower on the Cascade Link, joined it, first the Spellman Trail, and then the Red Spot Trail. The trail also passed by two well-known natural sites: Thoreau's Bog and the Sarcophagus. The latter is a large boulder that does resemble a coffin, a very big one.

I followed the stone cairns that mark the trail across the bare rock toward the summit, which was in view for most of the trail above the Spellman Trail junction. The people I could see on the top of the mountain gradually grew in size, and by a quarter after eleven I had joined them. There were about twenty hikers up there that morning, not very many for a fine June day.

After a brief rest, I began the walk back. At twelve-thirty, I stopped for lunch at the same spot I had used for a break on the way up the mountain. It was a pretty warm day, and I was glad I had brought plenty of water. I sat there for about a half hour and then hit the trail again. It was well after two when I reached Lake Road. Later that day, I checked a six year old entry about my earlier hike on the Pumpelly Trail, and I was a bit surprised to see that it had taken much less time. That bothered me for about a minute, and then I realized that I am now more concerned with how much time I can spend on a trail than how little.

June 2007

53
Trout - N - Bacon Trail
Stoddard NH

The Trout - N - Bacon Trail connects Bacon Ledge and Trout Pond, hence the name. It is located in the Charles L. Peirce Wildlife and Forest Reservation, a property of the Society for the Protection of New Hampshire Forests. I had read about the trail in the Monadnock-Sunapee Greenway Trail Guide and, more recently, Joe Adamowicz's *The New HIKING the Monadnock Region,* and I finally got around to walking on it this fall. It was a pleasant hike, not difficult, with great views from the top of Bacon Ledge.

Getting to the trail head was easy, although the last mile was on a narrow and often rocky dirt road. I drove nearly all the way from Peterborough on route 123, turning right at the Stoddard Fire Station, crossing a bridge, and then turning right again onto Old Antrim Road. The latter was the dirt road mentioned above. A little less than a mile down that road, another road, blocked by a gate with a sign for the reservation, forked to the left, and just beyond that I pulled into a small parking space on the left. Another sign for the Peirce Reservation and yellow blazes on trees showed where a foot trail went into the woods just above the parking space.

I started hiking at 9:15. It was sunny and pleasantly warm, a great early fall morning. The path quickly connected with the road I had passed earlier, and I followed that uphill through a mixed hardwood forest. There were a number of recently felled trees along both sides of the road, some of them cut up and stacked on the edge. After about three quarters of a mile, I came to a junction where a narrow foot trail went right and the woods road left. Both were marked with the yellow blazes, and two arrows pointing in opposite directions indicated I was at the base of loop in the trail and would return to that spot whichever direction I took.

Since the narrow path to my right appeared to be taking a more direct route to the ledges, which seemed to be looming not far ahead, I took it. By then, the hardwoods had mostly been replaced with pine and spruce, and the trail was a little steeper. Twenty minutes after taking the right fork, I was scrambling up the last few yards to the top of the ledge. That was the only really steep part of the hike, and, although I didn't notice it, I read in the guide later that there was a side trail for avoiding the top of the ledges in slippery conditions.

There was a fine view in all directions from Bacon Ledge, but I did have to move around a bit to see all of it due to the trees. There was a stone cairn at the highest point, and a survey medallion on a nearby rock. A number of chipmunks scurried about the ledge, and a large flock of Canada geese flew over while I taking in the view.

I knew that I could follow the trail markers north to Trout Pond and then follow a side trail to Shedd Hill and take it back into Stoddard, but I decided only to close the loop I had begun at the fork, and save the Trout part of the Trout - N - Bacon Trail for another time. I started down at 10:10.

After descending only a short distance, the trail leveled as it skirted Round Mountain. I knew I would be moving in a counterclockwise direction to get back to the first fork, and when I came to another trail junction, with signs pointing to the right for Trout Pond and Shedd Hill Road, I turned left in order to continue closing the loop. For a long while, however, over a mile, rather than looping, the path was very straight. Finally, I came to the junction where I had turned right to climb up to Bacon Ledge, and I turned right once more for the last section of the trip. I was back at my car at 11:05.

Later, at home, I checked in the Greenway guide and figured the loop from the top of Bacon Ledge back to the fork was two and a half miles. That made the total distance of the walk nearly four and a half miles. That was more than I had expected, but I was happy to have had a longer hike.

September 2007

54
Thoreau's Seat
Mount Monadnock

As many know, Henry David Thoreau, the great 19th century author and naturalist, made several trips to Mount Monadnock. Today, there are at least three features on the mountain named for him: Thoreau's Bog, the Thoreau Trail, and Thoreau's Seat. The latter is a rock formation on the Cliff Walk Trail, just below Bald Rock. No one is sure Thoreau ever sat on his seat, but we know it was on a route he followed on at least one of his trips.

Looking over the trail map for the mountain, I plotted a walk of about six miles that would take me by Thoreau's Seat, up to the top of Bald Rock, and then down Thoreau's Trail on my way back to the parking lot at the park headquarters. I thought the "seat" might be a good place for lunch.

It was a lovely mid October morning when I pulled into the state park a little after 8:30. There had been a touch of frost earlier, but the sun was shining, and the temperature was expected to reach the upper sixties by afternoon. There were only a few cars parked before me, but as I was walking across the lot toward the beginning of the Parker Trail, seven school buses pulled in, and I knew the main trails would be busy.

In fact, I could hear people starting up the mountain on the White Dot Trail as I walked around the bottom of Poole Reservoir. After a bit over a half mile, I turned right onto the Lost Farm Trail, which took me steadily uphill for another half a mile through a mainly hardwood forest, with many stately oaks. A still sturdy stone wall ran parallel with the trail as I climbed. Then the trail became more level, turned more to the west, and crossed the face of the mountain for more than a quarter of a mile. The forest became mostly spruce, and the rocks on the path became more numerous. Just before ten, there was a good view to the south and east, and five minutes later I reached the Cliff Walk Trail.

There were lots of ledges to scramble over on the trail for the rest of the way up to Bald Rock. I began looking for Thoreau's Seat, but found only a sign for the Thoreau Trail, which joined the Cliff Walk a short distance below the top of Bald Rock. I knew there were three "seats" near or on the path in that area: Thoreau's, Emerson's, and Ainsworth's, and I clambered over many large rocks which certainly offered places to sit, but I saw no ID's.

I stopped on Bald Rock to enjoy the great view over Perkins Pond and then started back down the trail. Two minutes later, I passed three hikers on their way up. They were the only people I encountered that day, except for those in the parking lot. After they passed, I wondered if they knew where Thoreau's Seat was. I thought it was probably near the junction with the trail of the same name, which I quickly reached. Sure enough, this time I noticed a sign attached to a spruce just below a large, but not very comfortable, rock right on the trail, a rock I had climbed over only a half hour earlier. Thoreau's Seat, the sign read. I don't know how I missed it on the way up, but there it was, and just below the Thoreau Trail.

Since the "seat" wasn't very comfortable, I decided to walk part way down the Thoreau Trail before resting on a less famous but nicely padded rock for a break. Maybe Thoreau actually used that one too. Then I walked down to where the Thoreau Trail, the Point Surprise Trail, and the Hello Rock Trail all came together, just east of the start of the White Arrow Trail, which links the Halfway House Trail to the summit. I followed the Hello Rock Trail, which took me back uphill for a spell, to its junction with the Cliff Walk Trail. Both of those trails were rocky and often steep. The last portion of the Cliff Walk Trail included a massive log ladder, leaning against a nearly perpendicular ledge.

Then I was back on the Parker Trail and only a little over a mile from the park headquarters. That trail is one of the most level in the park, and it has a pretty smooth surface. Anyone looking for an easy, but very attractive, walk on the mountain would do well to walk it. I was back at the parking lot a little before one o'clock. Oddly enough, the first of the students who arrived in the seven busses when I was starting my hike were emerging from the woods after completing theirs.

October 2007

55
Berry Pasture Trail
Sharon, NH

Last May, when I hiked up the Berry Pasture Trail from Mountain Road in Sharon to the Wapack Trail, I walked through a thick forest, with only the briefest view of Mount Monadnock on the way up. A few weeks after that, the trail was closed for the summer to allow the owners of the property, the New England Forestry Foundation, to clear cut a large portion of the forest through which the trail runs. The trail was opened again this fall, and I thought it would be interesting to see how it had changed.

Rather than hike straight up the Berry Pasture Trail, I decided to begin my walk at the Wapack Trail parking lot on Temple Road and follow the yellow triangles up the southern end of the long ridge that is Temple Mountain. When I reached the trail junction just below Burton Peak, I would walk down the Berry Pasture Trail to the newly cleared area.

I drove south on route 123, the Sharon Road, from Peterborough and turned onto Temple Road, which is the first left past the art center. I pulled into the little parking lot just after 8:30 on a cloudy, cool November morning. The Friends of the Wapack have recently improved the parking lot, expanding it and adding a couple of benches and a new kiosk. A couple of minutes into my hike, I was surprised to see the old shack that had stood next to the trail for who knows how many years had been torn down. Only a pile of old boards and shingles remained. The first section of the trail is pretty steep, but I soon reached the first of several lookout points on the eastern side of the trail. I was on top of the ridge before nine o'clock. That part of the Wapack Trail is known as the Cabot

Skyline. It extends to the Temple Ledges, and much of it crosses fairly open ledge with low shrubs and bushes. It's one of the most beautiful sections of the entire trail.

The trail junction appeared at about twenty minutes after nine, and I started down the Berry Pasture Trail. The trail is 1.7 miles long, and I walked over half a mile before noticing any change to the surrounding forest. Then I reached the logged area, and I was startled by its size. There were many acres on the west facing slope that were completely cleared of trees. The blue triangles marking the trail through the clearing were all painted on ten foot tall stumps that wandered through the open area like miniature telephone poles. Although barren now, the logged area is expected to provide habitat for many species as re-growth begins. I noticed new bird houses on metal poles at regular intervals on the periphery of the cleared area, an indication of the hope for an increase in wildlife.

The most impressive feature, however, was the fantastic view of not only Mount Monadnock, but nearly 100 degrees of countryside from far to the east of Mount Wachusett in Massachusetts to the hills on the Massachusetts/Vermont border. It was the view that farmers in the nineteenth century must have had. In fact, I was reminded of the clearings the first settlers made in the eighteenth century. Looking at it that way, I realized the view wasn't new at all. It was the old view restored.

Since I was already over halfway down the Berry Pasture Trail, I decided to continue all the way to Mountain Road and then follow it to route 123 and Temple Road. From the end of the trail, it was a mile and a half back to my car. The half mile or so along Mountain Road was very pleasant, and I passed only one house, which was far above the road. The stretch up the more populated Temple Road was one of the steepest climbs of the whole hike. I was back at the little parking lot at 10:30, after hiking about four and half miles.

November 2007

56
Joe English Reservation
Bedford NH

The Amherst Conservation Commission's Joe English Reservation contains nearly 600 acres of woods, ponds and streams on the southeastern slopes of Joe English Hill. Within the woods is a web of thirteen trails that total ten miles. All of the trails are great for hiking, most for cross-country skiing, and two - the Hemlock and Bicentennial - for mountain biking. No motorized vehicles, including snowmobiles, are allowed on any of the trails. Hunting is permitted in season, and several of the trails may be used on horseback. There is also a just completed building housing the Peabody Mill Environmental Center. It's a wonderful place.

Until recently, my only knowledge of the area was about Joe English Hill. Working on the top of Pack Monadnock Mountain for years, I became very familiar with the shape of the hill, which rises just south of the two Uncanoonuc Mountains. Its most noticeable feature was the bluff or cliff on its southern side. I knew there was a small air force installation in New Boston, close to the hill, and the late Ron Finan, who was the fire tower lookout on Pack Monadnock for many years, told me he had watched airplanes using the hill for bombing practice in the 1940s. I also learned the hill was named for an early eighteenth century Indian, who once tricked pursuers into running off the cliff to their deaths. A friend to the white man, Joe English was later killed by Indians while serving as a scout.

I increased my understanding of the area by visiting the Joe English Reservation on a cool and cloudy Monday in November and walking about half of the trails. It was easy to find. I drove east from Peterborough on route 101, turning left onto Horace Greeley Road, not far south of the Bedford line. Then I took the second left,

Brook Road, and followed it for about a mile to the reservation parking lot. I began hiking at 8:30, wearing a lot of bright orange because it was the middle of deer season, but the only people I saw in the reservation were a small group visiting the environmental center. I had the trails to myself.

I walked part or all of six trails in the central portion of the reservation: Old Brook Road, Ledge, Bacon, Highland, Pine, Timber and Hammond Brook. The junction of the Ledge and Bacon trails was on the edge of very pretty Beaver Pond. One of a number of attractive foot bridges I saw in the reservation crossed the stream below the pond. The Bacon Trail took me well up the side of the hill and along the boundary with the air force base. A line of large signs warned visitors of unexploded ordnance, reminding me of Roy Finan's account of watching planes dropping bombs, some of which may still be there, unexploded.

The Ledge Trail included a restful spot with a very comfortable bench on the massive ledge it crosses. From the Highland Trail, I looked into a steep ravine with a brook running through it. The Timber Trail wound through a large stand of Mountain Laurel. All of the trails I followed were clean and very well marked. They were color coded, with blue, yellow or red blazes, and each intersection was numbered and identified with inscribed signs and a plastic covered copy of the trail map.

The only slight disappointment I had was that none of the trails I walked took me to the top of the hill. I'm sure that was because the air force land includes the summit, and there is nothing the Amherst Conservation Commission can do about that. What they have done is develop a very nice system of trails that make the most of the six hundred acres of the reservation. I hope to walk the rest of them soon, perhaps on snowshoes.

November 2007

57
Temple Mountain
Peterborough NH

When I climbed up Temple Mountain on the Wapack Trail over a year ago, it still looked like a ski area, even though it had been closed for some time. Hiking up this November, I saw remnants of the old business, but they were ghostlike and disappearing into thickets of new growth. The mountain is returning to its original form. In an effort to ensure it will stay undeveloped, the state and citizen groups are trying to make it a new state park. Anyone interested in helping that happen should contact the Monadnock Conservancy, P.O. Box 337, Keene, NH 03431.

I began my recent walk up Temple on the morning of the last Wednesday in November. It was partly cloudy and cool when I parked in the Miller State Park lot at 8:30. There were several cars parked there before me, but the passengers must have gone up Pack Monadnock, because I saw no one else on the trail up Temple. The only dangerous part of the walk was crossing 101 to get to the Temple Mountain side. From there, the Wapack Trail's yellow triangles led me across one of the old parking lots and then up the most westerly of the old slopes. Back when the area was operational, the trail stayed in the woods to the right of the slope for much of the way to the summit, but now it mostly keeps to the old ski slope. It would be impossible to ski that slope now, for where scores of skiers could be seen cruising downhill there are now thousands of young birch trees. Mother Nature has taken over grooming the trails, and she is letting them grow very hairy indeed.

The upper portion of the trail followed the rough access road, which is still used to get to the US Cellular tower. I was surprised by how wet much of the land on and near the upper slopes was, and many of the rocky stretches of the road had a thin coating of ice. When I stepped off the road to look at the remains of one of the old buildings, my feet sank into a partially frozen mixture of low shrubs and water.

There were several buildings still standing, including one that was at the very top of the main lift. Others were just piles of rubble. Here and there, water pipes, electrical conduits and boxes, and miscellaneous debris marked the edge of the old slopes. I saw one large spotlight, still attached to a tree trunk, probably high enough to have escaped removal. One of the largest remaining items was the terminal for the lift that went up the western slope. It stood in the middle of a thickening stand of young trees.

The trail now enters the woods just before the buildings at the top of the mountain. I remember it used to go in right behind the buildings, where a large sign warned cross- country skiers to be careful on the Wapack Trail. The buildings for the cell phone tower are enclosed by a heavy fence and, of course, still functioning. The nearby ski area buildings, however, are unprotected and quickly eroding. One is just a pile of boards, and the other is mostly a shell.

After looking at the buildings and admiring the great view of Pack Monadnock, I started back down. Just as I left, the generator in the cell phone installation turned itself on, sounding like the low growl of a big animal and startling me for a moment.

When I was nearly back to the highway, two dogs, wearing brightly colored vests for hunting season, came running toward me. Despite the distant whistles of their master, who appeared in the parking lot, they kept coming. Both were friendly, and after being petted they ran back down the hill. A few minutes later, I carefully crossed the highway again and found myself back on the familiar ground of Miller State Park. The two mile round trip had taken about an hour. It was good exercise, with great views and no lift fees.

December 2007

Part Two
Paddling

58
Mud Pond
Dublin NH

If you're looking for a gentle but interesting kayak or canoe ride where you are apt to be quite alone, Mud Pond in Dublin is a good choice. The pond is the marshy area visible from route 101 just east of Bond's Corner. It's a shallow pond with lots of vegetation, winding channels and a few broader open areas. There's a place to put in just off 101, but it's a bit steep and rocky. An easier launching place is on route 137, just a mile south of the intersection at Bond's Corner.

I recently put my kayak in at the route 137 site and spent a couple of hours on the pond. I had to wait for a family of geese to swim out of the way before I could start paddling the narrow stream that winds from the launch area toward the more open parts of the pond. They were the only geese I saw that day, but a cormorant lead me on for a while, landing and taking off several times, and I saw a heron flying away with an angry squawk. There were many red-winged blackbirds and a few ducks, too.

The dominant feature of the pond is the vegetation. Lily pads, wild roses and pickerel weed were things I could identify, but I'm no botanist and certainly there is a profusion of aquatic plant life on and about the pond.

There are fish, too, of course, and I saw a few jump in some of the more open places. I imagine fishermen have some problems with all the weeds, but some of the deeper spots must be popular.

Whenever I paddle on the pond I am reminded of the old classic movie, *The African Queen.* In that film there's a famous scene where Humphrey Bogart has to wade in weed-choked stream and pull the boat toward Lake Victoria. Nothing that severe happens on Mud Pond, but it is easy to forget the busy highways just a few minutes away and imagine yourself in a green and watery wilderness.

I paddled north from the launch area, and after a quarter mile of winding, narrow channel, the pond opens up quite a bit. There's a fine view of Mt. Monadnock's eastern face and of many lower hills. There are also a few houses visible on the shores, mainly along route 137, but I've almost never encountered another person on the pond, in a boat or otherwise. I'm sure that's because I haven't been there during evening or early morning hours when people are more likely to be fishing. There are several duck blinds on islands in the pond, some still in good shape, so hunters must use the pond in season.

Going north, the trip ends at route 101. Much of the pond along the highway is very shallow and weedy, and many geese can often be seen there. Going south from the launch area, the stream which flows into the pond quickly narrows and passes through two large culverts under a side road. Usually a kayak or canoe can pass through these culverts and continue up the stream for another hundred yards or so. Paddling this section of the stream puts you very close to route 137 and a little below it. It seems very odd to be so close to the occasional car passing on the road, and I wonder if the drivers ever notice the paddler. On my recent trip the stream was blocked with a fallen tree just a bit beyond the culverts, but I have often gone a surprising distance before having to turn around and paddle back to the pond itself.

When I got back to the launch area, the geese were still gone, my car was still alone in the small parking area, and only a few deer flies kept me company as I loaded the kayak back on the car.

August 2002

59
Contoocook River
Bennington NH

For my first kayak ride of the season, I drove over to the state's Powder Mill Dam recreation area in Greenfield. It's off Forest Road, just east of the covered bridge and the Hancock town line. Although the area is primarily a boat launch, its forested setting on a broad section of the river makes it a good place to fish or just sit and enjoy the scenery, which includes a nice view of the old bridge.

I unloaded my kayak by the water and then parked my car in the large lot. It was a weekday morning, and mine was the only car there. I had a swarm of flies around me as I got into the boat and pushed off, but once I was out on the water the flies disappeared.

Downstream from the launch area, the river soon opens up and forms the pond held back by the dam in Bennington. Upstream, once past the broad, marshy area near the launch, the river narrows and winds between tree-lined banks back to the dam in north Peterborough. I decided to paddle upstream. At first, the main channel of the river is a little hard to find since there are several coves or inlets and a number of small islands to maneuver around. There are a few duck blinds located in this area, and I saw a pair of orioles flying about one of them.

Just beyond the marshy area, as the river narrows, the railroad bed is right on the western bank. There is a pond on the other side of the railroad bed, and its outlet has a small bridge over it. The concrete bridge abutment is a popular fishing spot. The railroad bed is now the railtrail from Peterborough to Bennington, and I saw several people running along it on my trip.

The trail, of course, runs straight, but the river has many twists and turns, so the trail is not always right along the riverbank. There are a number of houses near the river on the eastern side, but only a couple of them are visible. As is the case with many streams which pass through well-settled areas, from the water the river appears to be flowing through a near wilderness.

As I paddled along, I noticed several turtles resting on the limbs of downed trees caught along the banks. I also saw a few ducks, many other birds, and one large water snake weaving across the river with only its head raised above the water. The river was very high that day, so the sandy edges which often reveal the prints of raccoons and other small animals were underwater.

The high water also covered many of the large rocks which clutter the river north of the old Cavender Road bridge. The bridge is closed to autos now, but it is open to pedestrians and bicyclists, and it is another popular fishing spot. I paddled under it and continued upstream for another half mile or so. The current was pretty strong, and when I reached what I figured was about two miles from the launch area, I had been paddling for seventy minutes.

Not far beyond the point where I stopped, the river narrows more and there is a fairly tricky place to paddle past near the Peterborough recycling center. Beyond that, the river passes near route 202 for a short stretch and then winds its way to the dam at the junction of routes 202 and 136. There is a boat launching site on the Greenfield road, route 136, just below the dam, and many people paddle from there to either the Powder Mill area where I started or all the way to the Powder Mill Dam itself.

I turned around at that point and headed downstream toward the covered bridge and my car. Although I hadn't really been struggling upstream, the ease with which I now moved along downstream was really noticeable. I could have just used my paddle to steer around the rocks and keep away from the trees all the way back to the boat launch area, but I wanted the exercise of paddling. The trip back took only half as long.

My whole trip that day took only two hours, but it would be easy to spend the whole day on the river. For one thing, there are a number of inlets and small streams which empty into the river that could be explored. For another, there is good fishing. I plan to bring my fishing equipment with me next time.

June 2003

60
MacDowell Lake
West Peterborough

Since I do most of my kayaking on ponds and flat-water rivers, I decided to buy a smaller, lighter kayak that would be easier to load on my car. I drove over to Pelletier's Sport Shop in Jaffrey and bought a ten-foot boat that weighs about forty pounds. The boat's decks are nearly flat, so I can put it on my car upside down like a canoe, and I don't need to use my kayak racks at all.

To test my new boat, I went to MacDowell Lake in West Peterborough. I drove out Windy Row to Spring Road and then down Richardson Road to the boat launch. It is also possible to put in small boats next to the swimming area just before the dam. To use that site, you would take the main dam road off Union Street in West Peterborough.

Unloading the little kayak was really easy, and I was soon out on the lake. There are two types of paddling available at the lake: the main, broad pond and two narrow channels that lead to the streams that feed the lake. I began by paddling across the widest part of the lake and heading toward the dam itself. The lake is shallow, and there were lots of water lilies and pickerelweeds still in bloom. As usual when I don't have my fishing rod, I saw several fish jump clear out of the water. Also as usual, I saw a heron flapping its way across the pond to a new fishing spot not spoiled by people in boats.

I paddled down the lake to the swimming area. There were no people on the beach or at the picnic tables. It was one of the many cloudy, humid days we had in early August, and I guess no one felt like a swim or a picnic. I turned around and headed back toward the launch area. Going in that direction, north, there is usually a fine view of the hills in Hancock, but I could see only clouds and haze.

I paddled past the launch area and followed the channel that parallels the access road. The stream narrowed quickly and made several twists and turns. The banks were covered with high grass and small shrubs. I noticed Joe Pye weed and the fuzzy white globes of buttonbush. That channel lead to the main source of the lake, Nubanusit Brook. There was a small waterfall where the brook entered the lake, and there was a small, rocky pool. The shade and the sound of the water as it tumbled a total of three feet made it a pleasant place to stop for a while.

I paddled back to the main lake and turned right toward the other channel. A few red floats marked where it joined the main lake. The area between the two channels is really a large marsh with small islands of trees and bushes. The second, or western, channel is formed by Bush Brook and Stanley Brook. It's longer than the Nubanusit channel, and there are lots of curves. I saw several small paths leading from the grass to the water that must have been made by small animals. I paddled around several of the bends, but I didn't go as far as I have on other trips. The channel eventually becomes too narrow to follow.

When the banks were not much farther apart than the length of my kayak, I turned around and headed back to the lake and the boat launch. My legs were feeling a little cramped by that time, and I discovered that I could paddle across the still water sitting cross-legged. The little boat was very stable. When I got to the main lake, I put my legs back into the boat and my feet back on the pegs for the last stretch to the launch area.

It was a good test of my new kayak. I was pleased with how easily it maneuvered. I was also very happy with how easily I picked it up and put it back onto my car.

August 2003

61
Hubbard Pond
Rindge NH

Hubbard Pond in Rindge is a fine place for a kayak or canoe ride. It's not very large, about a mile from one end to the other, and it's not very deep, but except for a boy scout camp the entire shoreline is free of development. The nearly pristine shoreline and the lack of motorboat activity due to the shallowness make it great for paddling.

The pond is also nearby, and that makes it a good place to paddle when time is limited. I had a couple of hours to spare on the morning of the Friday before Columbus Day, and I decided to spend them on Hubbard.

I drove east on route 119 to Cathedral Road and followed it toward Annett State Forest and Hubbard Pond. It was mid-morning, almost ten, but there was still quite a bit of fog and mist. Despite the lack of sun, the colors of the trees along the road glowed brightly. Just before the entrance to the roadside park at Annett, I turned right onto the narrow dirt road that leads down to the dam at the north end of the pond. It's a good road, but it has some rough spots and probably isn't suitable for cars with little clearance.

I parked next to the dam and unloaded my kayak. There are several good spots to launch a small boat in that area, and it obviously get some use, but there's no picnic area and very little litter. People come there mainly to fish or paddle, and the roughness of the road helps keep the number of visitors down.

Before I paddled off, I thought back to my first trip to Hubbard. I had won a handmade, canvas canoe in a friendly poker game, and my old friend Andy Pelletier (He's now the owner of Andy's Cellar

Sale in Jaffrey.) had brought me to the pond to try out the boat. He gave the canoe a push, and I paddled onto the pond. Actually, I paddled *into* the pond, for the little boat went down faster than it went out. As I was sinking, Andy was laughing so hard tears had started down his cheeks. Between guffaws, he was making that oogah sound we've all heard in submarine movies and shouting, "Dive! Dive!"

Well, the kayak I have now is watertight, and I wasn't worried about sinking as I paddled through the narrow channel that leads to the wide portion of the pond. There is one broad section, but there are many inlets and coves on Hubbard. There are many tiny islands as well, often just a few rocks and bushes. Once I was out on the main pond, I sat for a while and enjoyed the foliage that flamed on the shore. The bright oranges and reds of the leafed trees and deep red of the blueberry bushes contrasted nicely with the many evergreens of the forest that encircles the pond. By that time the sun had begun to burn through the persistent mist, and it was becoming a picture-perfect fall day.

As I neared the scout camp, vacant until next summer, I watched a huge flock of geese swimming across the pond in front of me. I counted over sixty birds in the main group and another two or three dozen in smaller clusters. I think hunting season for waterfowl had begun, but I didn't see any hunters. I did see a flock of ducks when I reached the eastern shore of the pond, not as large as the great fleet of geese, but there were about thirty birds.

Those ducks were in one of the many shallow inlets of the pond. I paddled a short way into the inlet, but my paddle was soon hitting bottom, so I returned to the deeper water. If there had been just a bit more water, I could have gone far into that inlet and some of the others. It would be easy to spend many hours exploring all the nooks and crannies of the shoreline.

I didn't have that much time on that day, however, and I paddled along the eastern shore back to the dam and my car. It had been a lovely two hours, and my boat hadn't sunk at all.

October 2003

62
Halfmoon Pond
Hancock NH

On the last day of April, I enjoyed a peaceful kayak ride on Halfmoon Pond in Hancock. The pond is at the center of Boston University's Sargent Center, and several buildings and a swimming beach are on the eastern shore of the pond. The rest of the shoreline is undeveloped.

There is a small public boat launch area on the southern shore, reached by taking Camp Sargent Road, which connects Windy Row with route 137 and passes through the main part of the Sargent Center.

The day I paddled the lake was warm and sunny, and I thought there might be a number of boats on the water. As I pulled up to the launch area, a motor boat with two people with fishing equipment was headed out, but that was the only other boat I saw. Once the Sargent Center becomes busy, I'm sure there will be quite a bit of canoe and kayak activity as well as swimmers on the beach.

From the launch area, I paddled along the eastern shore and passed the swimming beach and the few cabins that sit next to the water. I was headed for the most unusual feature of the pond: the spillway that extends from the pond like a narrow, slightly curved handle. It is nearly a quarter of a mile long and passes under Windy Row. I was told by a helpful ranger at the MacDowell Dam in Peterborough, Jason Tremblay, that the spillway is a part of the flood control system connected to the dam. He told me that the spillway last had water spilling out of it in 1987, when there was a "100 year" flood.

I had often looked over the spillway from the bridge on Windy Row, but I had never been on the water there before. I paddled right up to the dam which holds back the water and looked over the open slope beyond. The water was only a few inches below the lip of the dam, but I'm sure it would take a lot of rain to raise the level that last bit.

I paddled back along the spillway to the northern shore of the pond itself. One of the many cross-country ski trails that radiate out from the Sargent Center's headquarters runs along the wooded bank, from Windy Row to where the spillway joins the main pond. The northern shore is at first marshy, with thick brush and many narrow inlets. Gradually, the land next to the water becomes higher and more open, with large trees. As I paddled along, I noticed several widely scattered signs placed near the water. They had short, cryptic messages that I assumed were meant for the participants in some of the programs operated by the Sargent Center.

A stubby peninsula of land juts out into the pond from the southern shore, just west of the boat launch. The pond narrows at that point and then broadens out again into a small bay. I paddled into it and followed the shoreline to where the pond's outlet flows under the road and eventually joins Nubanusit Brook, which flows into MacDowell Lake. The two people in the motor boat I had seen earlier were fishing in that section of the pond. I didn't see them catch anything, but since it's a shallow lake, I imagine there are bass.

It had gotten windy, but I hadn't noticed until I was paddling back toward the main part of the pond. It wasn't enough wind to be a problem, though, and I was soon around the tip of the peninsula and approaching the road and launch area.

A few minutes later, I had my kayak loaded on my car and was ready to leave. Before I drove away, I sat and enjoyed the view over Halfmoon Pond. It had been a very relaxing little trip. It's a good place for anyone looking for an easy, pleasant paddle - especially in the off season.

May 2004

63
The Kensan Devan Sanctuary Marlborough NH

The Audubon Society of New Hampshire's Kensan Devan Sanctuary in Marlborough is a good place to go for a peaceful paddle around Meetinghouse Pond or a quiet walk on the paths in the woods around the pond. The 579-acre sanctuary is located a half a mile north of route 124 in Marlborough, at the end of Underwood Road, an unpaved road that meets route 124 about two and a half miles east of the junction of 124 and 101 in Marlborough.

I spent a couple of hours at the sanctuary on one of the many cloudy mornings in mid-July, and I enjoyed both a kayak ride and a short hike.

There is a large gravel lot next to the dam on the pond, and it is the first part of the sanctuary I saw as I drove down Underwood Road. There was no one there that morning, but the empty bait containers I saw in a trash container near the dam showed that it is a fairly popular fishing spot. There was a nice grove of hemlocks on a small knoll next to the dam, and it looked like a nice picnic spot, spoiled only by a spray-painted rock

After investigating the dam area, I got back in my car and drove the rest of the way down Underwood Road to the boat launch. There were no other cars when I pulled in, and in a few minutes I had unloaded my kayak and was paddling on the pond.

From the launch area, I followed the edge of the pond counterclockwise along the eastern and northern shores. Pickerelweed, lily pads and a few rocks broke the surface of the water. The shore line was totally undeveloped, and trees came down to the water. From a point on the far side of the pond, I could see the top of Monadnock over the trees near the boat launch.

The most unusual feature of the little pond is a floating bog near the western edge of the pond. The mat of vegetation formed an island, but the narrow strip of water between it and the shore looked too shallow and obstructed with tree branches to navigate, so I paddled along the outer edge. The information about the sanctuary on the Audubon's web site mentions a great variety of plants growing on the floating mass, but my poor knowledge of botany allowed me to identify only pickerel weed, lilies and blueberries. There were also some very small spruce trees growing amid the bushes.

I also noticed a muskrat lodge amid the bog's vegetation, but I didn't see any muskrats. I did see at least two kingfishers, a kingbird, and red-winged blackbirds. By that time there was a little sun, and I saw several turtles perched on rocks and tree branches above the water. One of them allowed me to paddle close enough to get a photo before it slid into the water.

After circumnavigating the little pond, I returned to the boat launch area where another car was parked next to mine. I didn't see any people, though. I loaded my kayak back onto my car, and then I decided to take a hike on one of the paths in the sanctuary.

There was a mail box for trail guides at the beginning of the trails, just a few feet east of the boat launch, but it was empty. I saw yellow blazes marking one trail, and I could see it at least began by hugging the shore. I decided to follow it, and I hoped it would lead me around the pond. It did take me along the water, but only about halfway around the pond. At that point it climbed a ridge and turned away from the water. It appeared to be making a loop that would take me back to the launch area, so I stayed on it. Eventually the path reached a woods road, turned right onto it and reached Underwood Road again in about a quarter of a mile.

For part of the walk back, the yellow trail was joined by another trail with red blazes and a sign reading "Lee's Loop." I thought it might reach the far side of the pond, but I saved it for another day. It was a good walk, and I liked the variety: shoreline, hillside and woods road. I thought I had walked well over a mile, and when I consulted the web site description I found it was a mile and a half long. I also learned that the long trail is named the Rocky Ridge Trail. The site also described the half mile long Winterberry Trail and the even shorter Beaver Pond Trail. There was no mention of "Lee's Loop," which remains an inviting mystery. *July 2004*

64
Nubanusit Lake and Spoonwood Pond Hancock NH

Paddling from the boat launch on Nubanusit Lake to the much smaller Spoonwood Pond is one of the best kayak or canoe trips in our region. It's a popular activity, but when my good friend, Steve Forte, and I did it on a recent Monday morning, we were the only boats on Spoonwood Pond.

To get to the boat launch on Nubanusit, we drove north from Peterborough on route 123, went through Hancock, and turned onto King's Highway for the last mile to the launch area. There isn't much parking at the boat launch, and when we arrived two cars with boat trailers were taking up much of the available space. There was more than enough for us, however, but I know it would be hard to find a parking spot on a weekend.

From the launch area, we paddled north on the narrow arm of Nubanusit, which curves around to the west and the dam where Spoonwood Pond meets the big lake. When we started out, there was a stiff wind blowing across the main body of the lake, and the water was choppy. By the time we reached the northern end and rounded the curve toward Spoonwood, the lake was much calmer. We heard a loon at that point, and noticed floats near the eastern shore which seemed to mark a protection area for the birds.

I had paddled the route years ago, and I knew that Spoonwood was the higher lake, but as we approached the dam, it looked like we were coming to a point where the water dropped off sharply, as if we were on the higher lake. When we got a bit closer, we saw the dam itself and pulled into the take- out spot to the right of the dam.

The last time I had made the trip, the dam was about to be repaired, and the water in Spoonwood was low. Now the dam is in great shape, and a set of rugged steps has been added to aid in carrying boats up to the put- in point.

Before getting back into our kayaks, Steve and I stood on the dam and admired the clear water in the pond. We also admired two huge water snakes curled up near the water. They were the largest I've seen, but they didn't seem at all impressed by our presence.

Spoonwood is completely undeveloped, and the land around the pond is protected. The Harris Center controls the northern and western shores, and Keene State College's Cabot Preserve in on the southern side. That keeps the pond nearly pristine. he Harris Center does have a few campsites on the pond, and as we paddled counterclockwise around the lake, we could see some of the sites in the trees near the water.

Both Nubanusit and Spoonwood have clear, cold water, but Spoonwood seemed a bit clearer. The bottom was rocky, and some boulders rose above the water along the shoreline. I have heard that there is good fishing in the pond, but we didn't see anglers that morning. We did see a large bird that might have been an Osprey flying high over the water.

Halfway around, we came to the portage where one can carry a boat across the narrow neck of land to Nubanusit's eastern end. I have done that in the past, and it is interesting to paddle the length of the big lake back to the boat launch, but we decided to complete our circumnavigation of Spoonwood and then return to the boat launch the way we had come.

Before long we were back at the dam, where we carried our boats down the steps to Nubanusit and launched them again. On the return trip we saw two more powerboats and one canoe in the distance, hugging the shore of Cabot Island.

When we got to the broad part of the lake, opposite the boat launch, the water was choppy again. As we neared the launch area, the wind was behind us, and it was almost like riding ocean surf into the ramp.

As we were getting out of the water, a man was preparing to back his trailer into the water and unload a large speedboat. He asked us how we had done, and we answered, "Great."

September 2004

65
Howe Reservoir
Dublin NH

The Howe Reservoir is a place that, despite being located on a major highway and close to several towns, allows a paddler on its waters to feel he is crossing a lake in the north country, far from civilization. That illusion, of course, is easier to maintain when one is paddling away from route 101 and the small cluster of houses on the southern end of the reservoir.

I visited the Howe Reservoir on a near perfect early fall day and paddled its shoreline from the put-in on 101 to the dam at the northern end and back. It was a weekday, and even though the weather was great, I was the only person on the water that morning. That factor only added to the sense of being on a more remote body of water.

I entered the water from the small parking area on the south side of the highway, which looks over the small section of the reservoir which is separated from the main body by route 101. The parking area is in Dublin, just east of the Marlborough town line. To get to the main portion of the reservoir, I paddled under the highway bridge. From the highway itself, motorists hardly notice they are crossing the narrow channel that connects the shallow southern end of the reservoir with the main body of water north of the highway.

Although the sky was mainly clear with only a few puffy clouds, there was a stiff breeze blowing from the north that morning, and I was glad I was in my kayak and not my canoe as I paddled across the open water. I decided to keep to the eastern side of the reservoir as I paddled toward the dam above the Eliza Adams Gorge, and as I crossed the wide portion of the water, the wind was hitting my boat broadside. However, one of the virtues of kayaks is that wind bothers them much less than it does canoes, which ride higher.

I was quickly past the cluster of houses on the southwest shore of the reservoir, and the sound of cars on the highway began to diminish as I paddled along the tree-lined shore. There were several small inlets or bays on that side, and I paddled into each one on my way north. As I approached one of them, a heron rose from the water where it had been hidden by tree limbs and flew across the reservoir just a few yards in front of my boat. It was never more that a yard above the water as it headed toward a spot where there was no pesky kayak to bother its fishing.

When I saw the steel towers of the power line that crosses the reservoir near its northern end, I knew I was not far from the dam. The reservoir narrows as it nears the dam, and once I had paddled under the power line, I could see where the water came to an abrupt end. Within a few minutes, I could see the concrete portion of the dam, and it was only a few yards from shore to shore.

From the dam, I paddled back toward the highway along the western side of the lake. From the northern end, I had a wonderful view of Mt. Monadnock, rising above the hills south of the reservoir. Although fall had just begun, there was already some color among the trees on the lake shore, and the trees, the water, the brilliant sky and the mountain combined to create a nearly stereotypical, calendar-style picture.

Just as on the opposite side, there were a few inlets along the western shore, and I paddled into them. One was quite extensive, and as I neared its end, a kingfisher flew from its perch across the water. It was a good morning for seeing birds.

October 2004

66
Silver Lake
Harrisville and Nelson NH

Silver Lake, in Harrisville and Nelson, can be pretty busy when all the houses and cottages along its shores are occupied and summer vacations are in full swing. However, when I paddled its clear waters on a weekday morning in early June, I met only one other boat on the lake, and the many homes on the lake's edge were quiet except for repair work going on at a few of the cottages. It was one of the first really warm days of the year, too.

I put my kayak in at the Harrisville boat landing on Breed Road, on the southern end of the pond. There was a paved parking lot across the bottom of the lake, next to the boat launch, and a man and woman were fishing from the bank, looking comfortable in lawn chairs. I decided to paddle along the eastern shore to the north end of the lake and then come back along the western edge. As I paddled away from the launch area, I was impressed by the clarity and calmness of the water. I could see the rocky bottom, which was rapidly falling away. The lake is pretty deep in spots, and it is designated a lake trout/salmon lake by the fish and game department.

I passed some impressive houses on the water, especially close to the southern end of the lake. As I got closer to the north end, I noticed the houses were smaller and the hillside came steeply down to the lake. By the time I reached the top of the lake, which is in Nelson, there were some tent frames mixed in with small cottages along the edge of the water.

The lake narrowed at its northern tip, and I pulled into a little beach on the west bank. There was a pine grove there with what looked like campsites. I thought the area was probably part of Brantwood Camp, which is located off Lead Mine Road in Nelson.

I started my return down the western side of the lake, and until I was about half way back to the landing, I had a splendid view of Mt. Monadnock. I saw only a few houses until I was again close to the southern end. About a quarter of a mile from the northern tip of the lake, I paddled by a camp and came to the mouth of Sucker Brook Cove. Not long ago, I had walked the trails of the Audubon Society's wildlife sanctuary that surrounds it. I turned my kayak into the mouth of the narrow cove, steering around the many rocks that jutted from the water. It was by far the most natural portion of the lake, and I let the boat drift up to its end, just above where Sucker Brook itself enters Silver Lake. Low bushes lined the shore, and grasses waved in the shallows. I saw one turtle sunning itself on a log and, just beyond that, the top portion of a snapper's shell, which slowly disappeared under the water as I grew close.

Sucker Brook Cove was the highlight of my trip, but the rest of my cruise down the western shore was also interesting. I saw the only other boat on the water that morning, an aluminum fishing boat trolling for trout on the deepest portion of the lake. I also passed between a tree-covered, rocky sided island and another nice inlet.

As I neared the Harrisville boat landing, the number of homes on the water increased again, and the sound of power saws and hammers were a sign of preparations for the coming summer. I landed my boat, and by the time I had it on my shoulder, the man who had been trolling on the lake had also returned. "Looks like summer's finally here," he said.

June 2005

67
The Gridley River
New Ipswich NH

The Gridley River is a short and narrow stream with a split personality. It begins in New Ipswich, just east of where routes 123 and 124 split, and then it flows into the forbiddingly named Tophet Swamp, south of route 124. From the swamp, it emerges to cross under 123 in Sharon, just west of the New Ipswich line. That section of the river, coming out of the swamp and crossed by the busy highway, is surely the most familiar section to area residents. Until a sign was erected in the marsh grass a few feet from the road, I'm sure few motorists knew the name of the little river.

As it passes through Sharon toward its confluence with the Contoocook River in Peterborough, the Gridley River changes from a slowly moving, twisting channel of water surrounded by marsh grasses and swamp maples to a briskly moving, tannin dyed stream that falls over a hundred feet in less than a mile.

Much of the river flows through conservation land. Most of the last, swift section is in the Nature Conservancy's Wales Preserve, but several other groups help protect the river's course. Unpaved Swamp Road runs close to a good portion of the marshy part of the river and crosses it on a sturdy steel bridge.

On a recent morning, I decided to see how far I could kayak south and north on the Gridley from where it passes under route

124. I remembered doing the southern stretch in a canoe close to twenty years ago, but not very well. As I was preparing to paddle away, a car passed, and the driver made a u-turn and pulled over. He asked me if there were fish in the river, and I told him, honestly, I wasn't sure. I also made it clear that I didn't know exactly where the river began, and that I thought there was a beaver dam across it not very far to the south. Before leaving, he said he planned to try putting a flat-bottom boat in and seeing if there were fish.

As I paddled south, I passed three beaver lodges, and after maybe a third of a mile I came to the dam. When I saw the low structure, I knew it was just as it had been on my first trip.

I paddled back to the road and, only by lying flat in the cockpit of my kayak, went under the bridge. From the road, the north side of the stream appeared to head for a channel through the weeds and shrubs. From being on Swamp Road, I knew there was at least some open water that could be paddled, but I wasn't sure if I could get to it. I quickly discovered another dam just a few yards from the road. I gave up on exploring by boat.

A few days later, I drove along Swamp Road and stood on the little bridge for while, admiring the calm water meandering through the marsh. There were lots of wild flowers along the shores, and it was a very pretty spot. Unfortunately, the flowers were outnumbered by the mosquitoes and deer flies.

I followed the course of the stream by driving to Jarmany Hill Road and then Mill Road. A short stretch of the water was visible from the latter, and it was moving much faster. However, the river slowed again and crossed under Mill Road into another, very small, marshy area before starting its descent to the Contoocook.

The Wales Preserve is located on Spring Hill Road, just north of its junction with Mill Road. I parked there and followed the preserve's Brook Trail down to the water. The swiftly flowing stream, cascading in little falls over its rocky bed, and passing under towering hemlocks, bore little resemblance to the Gridley River that emerged from Tophet Swamp.

July 2005

68
Spirit Falls
Royalston, Mass.

A couple of years ago, I was hiking the Metacomet-Monadnock Trail south from Richmond to Royalston Falls and accidently got on another trail just below the falls. It was the Tully Trail, and I soon learned it was an eighteen mile loop that began at the Tully Lake recreation area in Royalston, Massachusetts. Since then, I have hiked a portion of that trail and paddled my kayak on the lake and the river that feeds it. Most recently, on a Saturday in early November that was more like a day in summer, my old buddy, Bob Ganley, and I paddled up the Tully River to Long Pond and then hiked through the woods to Spirit Falls.

To get to Tully Lake, I drove south from Richmond on route 32 for about ten miles and then turned left onto Stewart Road, which led me to the canoe launch on Tully River, just beyond the campground. I pulled into the launch area at nine o'clock; there were no other cars. It was cloudy and cool, but the weather forecast called for clearing and sixty degrees. I hoped it was right.

A few minutes later, Bob showed up, and we launched our kayaks. We had to carry them a few yards to get above some debris that was blocking the narrow stream right at the main launch site. The engineers had been lowering the water in the lake since the recent flooding, but we could see how high the water had been because the undergrowth along the river was discolored with mud for several yards into the trees. In fact, the canoe launch area and a portion of the road leading to it had been underwater for a spell.

We paddled up the river, which went straight north with only one tricky curve that was partly blocked by beavers. Above that curve, the river was broader, and we had a good view of the hills just to the east of the stream. Since the banks of the river are in the flood control area, they are completely undeveloped, and we had the feeling of being in a much more remote place.

Just before we reached Long Pond, I saw a large splash near the left bank and thought at first it was a big fish. Then Bob noticed a beaver swimming across the stream in front of us. He lifted himself out of the water and used his wide tail to splash twice more as we paddled toward him. It was easy to see and hear how effective a warning that splashing could be to other beavers.

We beached our kayaks on the right side of the entrance to Long Pond and began our hike to Spirit Falls. We found orange blazes marking the mountain bike trail that begins at the campground and circles Long Pond and followed them along the lake shore to where a small stream came down the hillside and entered the pond through a marshy area. The stream was small but swiftly moving down the hill in steps of a foot or two high. We crossed it on a small wooden bridge and walked along the opposite side. Yellow blazes of the Tully Trail appeared, and we followed them up the steep side of Jacobs Hill toward the falls.

The trail stayed close to the water cascading down the gorge, and the little falls became higher and higher until we reached the two fifteen or twenty foot main falls. The path was close by the water, and although the trees pressed close to the falls, we had a good view. The stream itself is the outlet of Little Pond, which is close to Warwick Road, route 68, just west of Royalston Common. The Jacobs Hill Reservation includes the pond and the falls.

As we walked back down the trail, we met two women who had left their canoe on the shore of Long Pond and were looking for the falls. Then, back at our boats, we met a hiker, who was eating lunch by the water. He was named Emile, and he talked to us about his many hikes on the tallest mountains in the northeast, especially on Mt. Marcy in New York. We spoke with him for several minutes getting back into our kayaks.

As we paddled down the river to the launch area, we noticed that it had gotten quite warm. We met several kayaks coming up, and when we were back at the parking lot, it was nearly full.

As one of the other paddlers remarked, " Who would have thought we'd be doing this in November!" *November 2005*

69
Otter Lake
Greenfield NH

Otter Lake is best known for the beaches and picnic grounds of Greenfield State Park, but it is also a popular fishing spot and a good place for a peaceful kayak or canoe ride. Beyond the state beaches, it's relatively undeveloped, too, with only a few buildings on its shores. Visitors can launch their boats at the beach area - or rent a canoe or kayak at the park store. There's also a public boat launch off Forest Road, just west of the park's entrance. That site has two advantages: it's open at all hours, and there's no fee. Motor boats are allowed on the pond, but they must operate at slow speed.

I took my kayak to Otter Lake on a hot day at the end of July. I decided to get into the water at the state beach because I like launching at the sandy beach area and because old guys don't have to pay. However, that also meant I had to wait until after ten o'clock for the park to open.

I parked near the store and carried my boat the twenty yards or so to the water. It's ok to put in a boat on either side of the middle beach, as long as one is outside the float lines. The rental canoes and kayaks are stacked on the beach in front of the store, and that's where I launched.

I thought I would paddle around the nearly circular lake clockwise, and that meant I began by passing by the main, picnic area, beach and the boat launch, which is just beyond a fence marking the boundary of the park. There was a growing crowd on the beach, and I saw two cars with boat trailers parked at the launch area, which meant at least two fishing boats were out on the water.

Just past the boat launch, I paddled close to a half-submerged log that had ten young mallards sitting on it. They were spaced with military precision, and the patches of bright blue wing feathers that brightened their otherwise drab appearance also made them look like soldiers in uniform.

As I went along the tree-lined shore, I could see Crotched Mountain rising above the lake to the northeast. There were two shallow inlets on that part of the lake, and a man was fishing from a boat in one of them. I passed a lake side cottage and then came to the marshy area at the northern end of the pond. The second fishing boat, with two fishermen, was anchored there, and the men were casting into the reeds and water lilies, for bass, I suppose.

Beyond the marshy end, I followed the shore line around to the right, and soon I had a view of another mountain, North Pack Monadnock, looming over the woods of the park's campground. As I paddled along, I came up on another formation of mallards. This time it was eleven juveniles and two mature birds, all swimming in single file. I went slowly by them, and they turned away from me a little, but never broke ranks.

The southern end of the lake was the most developed. The park's beaches, of course, dominated the far shore, but I went by a two story house right on the water, which appeared to be vacant and undergoing repair, and then I came to the second major development on the lake. It included a dock, a beach, and several buildings. Years ago, it was Camp Union, a boys' camp, but now it is a private conference center. From there, I had only to paddle around the extreme southern end of the lake and then cross in front of the campers' beach to complete my circuit of Otter Lake. As I went along, I could see there was still a path on the shore from what was Camp Union. When I worked at the park, in the late sixties and early seventies, I remember the son of the camp's director, Wally Stone, used to work at the state park and walked around the lake to get to his job every morning.

I completed my trip about fifty minutes after I began it. As I was carrying my kayak back to my car, three people were setting out in one of the park's rental canoes, and two ladies with a small girl had just parked next to my car in a jeep with a canoe on top. Traffic was getting heavy on Otter Lake.

August 2006

70
The Connecticut River West Chesterfield

On the Wednesday at the very middle of August, two friends - Steve Forte and Bob Ganley - and I drove to the boat landing on River Road in West Chesterfield for a few hours of paddling. The Connecticut River is a wonderful place for a kayak or canoe ride, especially on a weekday morning when there's little, if any, motorboat traffic. It's even better when there are good companions to share the experience.

Just before we launched our kayaks at ten that morning, a man in a small motor boat went into the water and headed downstream. That was the last motorboat we saw or heard for over two hours. We turned right from the launch area and that meant upstream. However, although we were paddling against the current, we found it easy going. Once we had gone by the few houses just above the landing on the New Hampshire side, only trees and brush lined the banks on both sides of the river. I always find it amazing that the rivers in New England - even the Charles in Boston - often have so little development right on their shores. Of course, that's not true of the Merrimack and other rivers that pass through old mill cities, but it's certainly true of the Connecticut. It makes it easy to imagine one is paddling in an earlier, less populated time.

It was quiet, too, as we went along for the first half mile or so, but then we began to hear the auto traffic on the interstate in Vermont, and we caught glimpses of the highway itself. Closer to the river, sometimes right on its banks, were the railroad tracks. During our trip, one passenger train and one freight train went by, heading south. So there were sounds to remind us we were far from

THE CONNECTICUT RIVER FROM THE ROUTE 123 BRIDGE

the wilderness, but still it was quiet enough for us to converse in normal voices as we paddled up the river.

We stayed mainly on the Vermont side of the river, and after we had been out for about an hour we came to a boat landing. An apron of mud around the landing showed how the water in the river had receded in the last few weeks. We grounded our little boats in the soft mud and climbed the earthen steps to the grassy launch area. The area was deserted, but a sign showed us it was the Dummerston Landing. It was a bit surprising not to see anyone there; it looked like a good place to sit and watch the river. We did see another boat on the water in the vicinity of the landing - a one man scull being rowed downstream.

A few minutes later, we were back in our boats and paddling north again. In a short while we reached another landing on the Vermont side, which, I learned later, was the Putney Landing. That one had several sets of stone stairs, and there were two cars parked on it, one with an empty boat trailer. So we knew there were motorboats out there.

Not far north of the Putney Landing, we noticed a small stream entering the river on the Vermont side and a large stone arch bridge crossing it just before it joined the Connecticut. We paddled under the broad span, impressed with the stone work above our heads. As always, I found myself thinking about the physical labor that went into such structures. We went up the little stream for a few yards and then turned around and looked back through the tunnel formed by the bridge. We noticed the head of a fairly large animal swimming around in the water and saw it arch its body and dive out of sight. It looked like an otter, but it might have been a beaver.

We returned to the big river and paddled north for a few minutes more before turning around for the downstream run back to West Chesterfield. Just after our turn around, we were on the New Hampshire side, and we saw another swimming animal. It came much closer to our boats before diving - a beaver. It was just after noon when we went by the Putney Landing, and we saw that it had gotten busier, with people walking about or sitting near the water. A small motor boat was about to take off as well. That boat passed us a few minutes later, and when we went by the Dummerston Landing, there were people sitting on chairs looking over the river. Traffic was picking up!

Two more motor boats went by us before we made it back to the River Road boat launch. Along with the traffic, the temperature had also increased, and we were happy to back in the shade and cooling off after paddling for three hours.

August 2006

71
The Contoocook River
Peterborough NH

The Contoocook River flows right through the center of Peterborough, and it spills over three dams, all of which have ponds or broad sections of water just above them. The dam in north Peterborough, near the route 202 bridge, holds back an extensive and interesting pond, strewn with islands and beds of reeds. The whole area, although close to a busy highway and many homes, is surprisingly wild. I have seen otters and beaver in the river, and the work of the latter is evidenced by chewed tree stumps along the river's banks. However, until recently, I had only viewed that section of river from the roads and paths that border it. I've wanted to paddle on it, but since there is no public boat launch between the north dam and the dam just above Main Street, I never had. Then, on the last day of October, I decided to find a way to get into the river with my kayak.

I parked at the small lot next to the Peterborough Pathway on Summer Street and carried my little boat through the woods to the water. I had noticed where a small drainage ditch emptied into the river and made a reasonable launching spot, and that's where I began paddling. I really didn't have to paddle much at first because I was going downstream, and the current was swift. I quickly passed the several businesses along Concord Street (route 202) going out of town and was paddling by wooded shores on either side. The river twisted away from the road for a stretch, and I saw what looked like two cement abutments, one on the right bank, overgrown with vines, and the other in the water just off the opposite bank. They looked like they may have supported a narrow bridge, either for a railroad siding or a one lane road. Next, I reached the first of the several islands in the pond above the dam. The main channel of the river kept to the highway side, and the wide reach of the pond stretched out to my left. On one side, therefore, I could see only a wild and natural scene, but on the other the tops of speeding cars were visible.

An arm of the river branched off near an island with a large and old looking beaver lodge at its edge. I paddled down it for fifty yards or so and then returned to the main channel. Where the channel joined the pond, four geese were floating on the calmer water, and they rose, honking, and flew away as I approached. I paddled the much quieter water of the pond, amused by the view of two houses on Hunt Road, which was so different from their appearance from the road. The back of one house was right on the water, and it might as well have been the only house on a remote lake. I also had a different perspective on the bridge just below the dam, viewed across the flat water.

After paddling into some of the inlets of the pond, I saw that the same branch of the river I had paddled part way down reached all the way to the main pond, and I used it to return to the main channel. From there, I paddled upstream, back to where the little drainage ditch entered the river. I dragged the kayak across the wet leaves to the pathway and then lifted it to my shoulder for the short walk to the parking lot and my car. I had paddled no more than two miles, and it had taken me only an hour, even with stopping on the pond to take a few pictures. It would be easy, however, to spend many hours there, birdwatching, botanizing, fishing, or just drifting along.

Until there is an official public boat launch, however, I do not recommend putting into the river where I did. The New Common Pathway Committee of Peterborough has suggested the town establish such a launching area, and, with luck, better access to this lovely section of the Contoocook may appear.

November 2006

72
Norway Pond
Hancock NH

Norway Pond is close to the center of Hancock, easily visible from route 123, and the town's public beach is on the southern end. Until recently, I had never paddled around the pond, but an old friend, Joe Adamowicz, told me that the stream leaving the pond at its northern end could be paddled for quite a distance and was completely different from the main part of the pond. Joe's the author of *Hiking the Monadnock Region,* and I've always found his advice to be sound, so I decided to put my kayak onto Norway Pond.

I arrived at the boat launch area, adjacent to the beach, just before nine on a morning that held the promise of thunder showers by afternoon. Since I didn't expect to be on the water very long, that wasn't a problem. School was still in session for the year, so the beach was deserted, and there weren't any other boats on the water, either. There was one man sitting in a truck and enjoying the view over the water as he drank his morning coffee, a great idea.

I pushed off from the sandy shore and paddled up the main part of the pond toward the marshy northern end. There aren't very many houses on the pond, more on the western shore than the eastern, and the little lake is clean and lovely. As I neared the far end of the pond, I saw the stream exiting through an opening in the marsh grasses and flowing westward. The outlet was about five yards wide, and it quickly curved around to the right. In seconds, I was completely out of sight of the pond and paddling on a narrow stream winding through shrubs and high grass. There were no houses in sight. It certainly was a change from the open pond.

The water was shallow and pretty clear, and I watched a large snapping turtle swim past my boat about a foot beneath the surface. The big turtles always impress me, especially moving along through the water.

After paddling for less than a quarter of a mile, I came to a dam of logs and branches that made enough of an obstacle that I would have had to get out and drag the boat over it. I could see, however, that the stream looked open and deep for some distance beyond. It would be fun to find out how far it could be paddled, but I decided to save it for another day.

As I turned my boat around, I saw a movement a few yards into the marsh and a fairly large animal dove beneath the water, causing a large ripple. I watched for a minute, but it didn't appear. It must have been a beaver or muskrat. On the way back to the pond, another, much smaller, turtle swam close to my boat. A minute or so later, I saw an even smaller turtle resting on a small log above the water. I don't know what the stream is called, but Turtle Brook would be appropriate.

When I was back on the pond, I decided to paddle around the western edge on my way back to the boat launch. There was a sizable cove or inlet with a tree-lined and house- free shore line that provided another nice aspect to the lake. From there, it was only a few minutes back to the launch area, and I was loading my boat back on my car before ten o'clock.

My little kayak ride was a reminder that places which appear to have no hidden features or surprises often do. I had driven by Norway Pond many times and even stopped there for lunch on several bike rides, but I had the impression that although it was a pretty pond with a nice little beach, it wouldn't be interesting to paddle. I was wrong.

June 2007

73
Mountain Brook Reservoir
Jaffrey NH

From route 202, Jaffrey's Mountain Brook Reservoir appears to be a rather small pond with a gravel boat launch just below the highway. In fact, the waters of the reservoir extend to the west and south to form a considerable lake. It's a great place to paddle, with miles of shoreline and very few houses or other development.

I drove to the launch area, which is on the west side of route 202, just south of the center of town, on a Monday morning in early summer. The approach to the launch area, just before a bridge, was a little rough, but short. There wasn't much parking space, but there weren't any other cars. I put my kayak into the water and was paddling by 10:30. The reservoir ends at a dam just to the left of the launch area, and the water flows under the bridge on route 202 and down to the Contoocook River. I had looked at a map of the reservoir and knew that it extended a mile or more to the north and west where Mountain Brook itself entered, and I decided to begin by paddling as far as I could up the brook. Very quickly, I passed under a power line and by a couple of houses on the northern shore. Beyond that, the pond curved around to the right and a long arm stretched off to the north. I paddled by where Jacquith Road ended at the water's edge, its original course broken by the reservoir. There were very few signs of people, other than one boat with two people fishing and a couple boat landings. I saw what looked like a tent on the southern shore, with a truck parked next to it.

After paddling about twenty minutes, I was getting near the end - or beginning- of the reservoir where Mountain Brook flowed under

Gilmore Pond Road. There was one cottage on the water just before the road, with a nice little beach and a view down the reservoir. I paddled under the road through one of two steel culverts and a few yards beyond to where the brook splashed down from the wooded hillside. There were also quite a few splashes made by fish jumping in that end of the lake, and I saw a couple of herons looking for them.

On my way back, I explored the southern arm of the pond, which was very broad and had a great view of Monadnock. An island in the middle of the reservoir had hidden that section as I went by earlier. It was shallow and evidently sometimes has little water. It ended in a marsh that must serve to store more water when needed. There were no buildings visible on its edge, but I could see a couple of houses high on a hill to the east. Paddling on that section of the reservoir was like being on a separate lake.

I followed the shoreline around and back toward the narrower arm of the reservoir that I had first paddled. My course brought me by the tent I had seen earlier. There was a private property sign and two people sitting near a camp fire. They waved as I passed. Soon I was going under the power line again and paddling toward the dam. Two people were paddling a canoe along the northern edge of the lake, and as I approached the boat launch area I could see their car parked near mine.

I had been on the water for over two hours and covered at least three miles. The size of the reservoir had surprised me and so had the lack of boats on it. Only two other boats shared the water while I was there, but it was a splendid summer day and certainly a good place to paddle or fish. I have seen cars parked at the boat landing many times as I've driven by on 202, but I don't remember seeing it looking crowded. Of course, that's just another good feature of Mountain Brook Reservoir.

July 2007

74
The Contoocook River
Rindge to Jaffrey NH

The boat launch on County Road in Rindge provides access to Contoocook Lake, but it sits on what is really the uppermost stretch of the Contoocook River, which begins at the nearby outlet of Poole (or Pool) Pond. The lake itself is only a short distance straight ahead from the landing, and the channel there is well-marked with red and black posts. However, unless it's early on a weekday, there are many power boats on the lake, and that's not so great for canoes or kayaks. To the right and left, the water is nearly covered with water lilies and pickerel weed, but there are narrow channels of open water in both directions that make for good paddling.

I drove down route 202 to County Road, just south of the Rindge town line, on one of the fine, sunny mornings in late August. I launched my kayak at the public landing just beyond the intersection of County Road and the Jaffrey/Rindge Rail Trail at 8:30 that morning, and my car was the only one in the large lot.

Since it seemed quiet, I began by paddling down the main channel to the lake, and in a few minutes I was passing by the first of the many cottages that line the shore. Each cottage had at least one boat moored nearby, but I didn't see a single boat in the water at that end of the lake. The lack of activity was probably due, in part, to school having just started that week. Still, after a brief paddle around a small island, I decided to head back to the boat launch and paddle north toward the dam that sits just east of the highway in Jaffrey. I had paddled that stretch several years before and remembered going under a bridge on the old railway.

As I passed by the landing, I saw an older man had parked his truck there and was happily exercising his black lab, throwing balls out into the water for the dog to fetch. Just beyond the boat launch, I paddled by a tiny island a few yards from shore, most of which was taken up by a little cottage. No one seemed at home. Other than that, the river - or arm of the lake - had only a few houses on the eastern shore, and the general appearance and feel of being on the water there was far more natural. The rail trail went along the western bank, and I saw another older man walking across the little bridge I had remembered. Somewhere in that section, I had crossed from Rindge into Jaffrey. I noticed a number of large, time-blackened stumps rising from the water near the shore, and I figured they marked what had been the river's edge before the dams existed. The main channel turned left and passed under the bridge, but the water extended straight ahead before ending at a stand of trees. I made a loop around that marshy area and then paddled up to the bridge.

I had to keep low as I went under the heavy beams of the old bridge, which still showed the black charring from a fire years ago. On the far side, there was a house along the water's edge, and, to the right, I could see the top of the dam. I could hear the traffic on route 202. The river there was really covered with vegetation, so I decided not to paddle more than a short distance beyond the bridge.

After turning around, I paddled under the rail trail once more and then back up the channel to the boat launch. The man and his dog were gone when I got there, and once more mine was the only car on the lot. One of the real advantages of being even semi-retired is the freedom to visit places when they're not busy. On the other hand, I can't understand why I don't see at least *some* people more often.

September 2007

75
Pisgah Reservoir
Ashuelot NH

The Pisgah Reservoir is not the most accessible body of water in the Monadnock Region, but, as I learned on a lovely day in early September, the effort needed to get there with a kayak or canoe is well rewarded. First, I drove to the Reservoir Road entrance to Pisgah State Park on route 119, just west of Ashuelot Village. Next, I drove up the narrow, unpaved road for over a mile to a small parking area just before a gate across the road. The first section of the road is steep and narrow, and when I started up it, just before nine on a Tuesday morning, I was worried about meeting a car coming down. That didn't happen, and as I drove I noticed many wide spots where a car could pull off. As it turned out, I didn't see another car until I was back at the highway hours later.

The last step in getting to the water was the most difficult. After unloading my kayak, I had to get it up the remaining portion of the road to the reservoir. That stretch of road is very steep with frequent switchbacks, and it is over a half mile long. A strong, fit person could carry a light canoe with a portage yoke up the road, but a kayak of equal weight but with no portage yoke is harder to handle. I got my kayak to the water by using a two-wheeled kayak cart. It was still hard work pulling the boat, and I had to stop several times to rest and trade pulling arms. Oddly enough, a good portion of the road above the parking area was still covered with asphalt that must have been laid down many years ago. That made it easer on the wheels. I started up the road at about nine thirty, and it took me over twenty minutes to get to the water's edge.

I launched my kayak not far from the dam, which is at the

southern end of the mile and a half long lake. There are, of course, no buildings on the reservoir, although I did see the remains of what was probably a building associated with the reservoir's early days on the shore east of the dam. The lake's location within the huge state park and the difficulty reaching it almost guarantee solitude. There must be days in summer and on weekends when a paddler would not be alone on the reservoir, but I doubt the water is ever crowded.

My plan was to paddle by the dam and then follow the western edge of the reservoir to the northern end. On the way I passed several of the rocky islands that dot the lake and entered some of the many inlets. One of the islands was quite large, but most were just a few square yards of pine-covered rock. The water was deep and clean, but it grow shallower near the northern end. When I reached the far end, I was following narrow channels among the weeds and water lilies. I didn't see any, but it looked like a great place for moose. I did see a number of ducks.

From the top of the reservoir, I paddled slowly back down, following the eastern shore. It was a beautiful, peaceful ride. As I got close to the dam again, however, I heard what sounded like a large truck out in the woods. It proved to be just one ATV, ridden by a man and a woman. They crossed over the dam just as I was heading for shore below it. As I was landing, they stopped on the road a few yards above me, and the man asked how I had gotten onto the reservoir. I explained how I had pulled the kayak up the road with help of the cart, and he seemed impressed, They were off before I got out of the boat and probably went by my car before I had the kayak on its wheels.

The portage back to the car was easier, but not by much. I had to act as a brake for the boat on the steepest parts, and that was nearly as hard on my arms as pulling it u had been. It was quicker, though. I started down the road a little before twelve, and by a quarter after I was back at the car.

September 2007

76
Robb Reservoir
Stoddard NH

A few years ago, over a thousand acres of land around the Robb Reservoir in Stoddard were for sale, and there was talk of a housing development. Now the land is owned by the Trust for Public Land and will soon be officially part of the Harris Center's Super Sanctuary. The area is also a portion of what has been envisioned as a wilderness corridor extending from Mount Sunapee to the Quabbin Reservoir in Massachusetts. I paddled around the reservoir on the first day in October, and my little outing has made me very appreciative of the many groups and individuals who worked to protect it.

The reservoir is located near the junction of routes 123 and 9, not far from the Harris Center's Hancock headquarters. Small boats can be launched next to the dam, which is on the unpaved Keene-Concord Road. That road, which looks more like a private driveway, is off route 123, just east of the junction with route 9. A gate blocks the road at a small bridge near the dam, but there is room for one or two cars to pull off the road at that point. Just over the bridge, a very rocky access road leads up a short hill to the dam itself. There are plans for the state's Fish and Game Department to build a small parking lot, which would make access to the reservoir easier.

My visit began just past ten-thirty on a cloudy and mild first day of October. I put my kayak into the water next to the dam and paddled the length of the pond, keeping to the right hand shore. The water was mostly shallow, and many rocks either protruded above the surface or lurked just below. Since there were no visible signs of buildings or other development, save a few glimpses of old stone walls, I had the sense of being on a natural lake. I passed a number of small islands and pulled into a fairly deep inlet on my way up the pond. I didn't see a moose, but I'm sure they must be frequent visitors. I did see a flock of geese and another of ducks. The ducks flew away when they saw my kayak, but the bolder geese stayed on the water. I also saw what looked like a grebe, but probably not a pied-billed grebe, which is one of several endangered species found in the area.

Near the northeast end of the pond, I paddled by one of the larger islands, tree-covered and lovely. I came to the end of the pond, where a small stream entered on the left, flowing down over the rocks. I landed my boat near there and walked into the woods for a distance. One fork of the path led to the stream entering the pond, and the other headed in the general direction of route 123, but I didn't follow it long enough to discover if it reached the highway.

I returned to my kayak and paddled back toward the dam. I continued to keep the shore on my right, which took me close to the opposite side of the pond. Passing between an island and the shore, I scrapped the bottom of my boat on a rock, but there was no harm done. As I approached the end of my ride, I went by an artfully shaped boulder of the edge of the water, one of the largest I saw. I landed the kayak just before noon, ending the first of what I hope will be many visits to Robb Reservoir.

October 2007

Part Three
Cycling

77
Rail Trail
Jaffrey to Rindge NH

A good example of the success of the rails to trails movement is the trail from the center of Jaffrey through Rindge and into Massachusetts. Although the trail may be best known to snowmobilers, it makes a great mountain bike path. It's also a very convenient and safe trail with several road crossings for easy access, good parking opportunities for leaving a car or cars, and even several places for a lunch or dinner break.

On the last day of September, I parked at the strip mall across 202 from McDonald's in Jaffrey and set out for the Massachusetts border on the rail trail. To get to the trail, I took the rear exit from the parking lot, turned left at the first street, and just before the Jaffrey Legion took a right onto the old railroad bed. There are still many old ties on this stretch of the trail, so it's a bit bumpy. On the other hand, it doesn't last long, and you are soon at the new drug store in downtown Jaffrey where a broad, paved path leads you around the building and to the main intersection where 202 and 124 join. Traffic was light when I was there, and it was easy to cross. However, most of the time you should probably walk your bike across in the pedestrian crossing.

Just south of the intersection, the main part of the trail begins. There's a new street sign that reads Rails to Trails and then a gate marks the start of the trail. The trail from this point into Rindge is named the Jack Dupre Memorial Trail in honor of a Jaffrey man who was killed in a tragic snowmobile accident.

Soon after the gate, and about a half mile from the parking lot where I left my car, the Contoocook River appears on the right side of the trail. It's fairly broad and slow-moving at this point and covered with lily pads. Just past the one mile point, a low dam with a footbridge marks the actual starting point of the river as it exits the northern arm of Contoocook Lake. The trail now has water on both sides for a stretch, and there is an old railroad bridge that I walked my bike across.

The main part of the lake is east of the trail, and soon the water is on only the left side. It's a fairly narrow extension of the lake which opens up quite a bit eventually. There are a few houses near the trail at about two and a half miles, and there are two more gates where the trail crosses a road. There is also one tiny cabin on a tiny island just off the shore that looks like someone's real getaway.

After that crossing there's a nice stretch of trail leading into Rindge. There's a snowmobile bridge at about the three mile point, and then the Jack Dupre section ends just before Davis Crossing Road in Rindge. A sign identifies the surrounding land as the Contoocook Marsh Conservation Area. Route 202 is visible on the right and, just beyond, Poole Pond.

Next I came to the center of West Rindge, near Lilly's Restaurant, and the trail ended for a brief distance. I followed Goodall Road to West Main – just a few yards – and then turned left. A few more yards, and then I took a right onto the trail just before the West Rindge Basket Shop.

Then, very quickly, I found myself at route 119, which can be very busy. It's another spot where a rider usually should walk the bike across the highway. The trail south of 119 runs just behind the Market Basket supermarket and the attached strip mall, but little of it is visible from the trail. At about the five mile mark from the start of the ride, the trail crosses route 202.

From the 202 crossing to the state line is about three miles and includes some of the best riding of the trip. There are two paved roads and one dirt road to cross, but they are all lightly traveled, and I hardly had to slow down for them. The first is Hunt Hill Road, and after the trail crosses that road, it passes behind the FAMM Steel company, and their building is clearly visible. Next the trail goes behind both Wal-Mart and the Hannaford Super Store, but neither is noticeable. It's neat how you can be so close to so much hustle and bustle without seeing or hearing it.

About a mile from 202, I crossed under a power line, and then pedaled across Rand Road, which turns from paved to dirt just before it crosses the trail. There's another power line followed by a dirt road at the seven mile point. The dirt road is evidently an important snowmobile intersection since there are signs pointing the way to Keene, Jaffrey, Fitzwilliam and Massachusetts.

The last section of the trail that I traveled was bordered on both sides by an extensive marsh. A stone marker announced the state line, just a little before the eight mile mark on the trip. I went a short distance into Massachusetts to a point where evidently an old culvert has given way and the trail dips below the level of the water on the left side. Someone has built a rudimentary earthen dam there to keep the crossing dry, and it seems to be working. I'm sure it's underwater in spring. It was a good place to stop.The marsh on both sides offered a good view, and there were tons of lavender asters blooming along the trail.

On the return trip, I left the trail at Davis Crossing Road and took Woodbound Road back to Jaffrey. That took me along the eastern shore of Lake Contoocook, but I couldn't see the water until I passed the Woodbound Inn, just before the Jaffrey line. I took Squantum Road past the town beach with a great view of the lake, and before long I was back at my car.

The Jaffrey/Rindge Rail Trail is a good bike route. There are no real hazards on the trail, a few sandy spots and one short stretch of loose rock being the only problems. The highway crossings do require caution, however. Overall, it's a fine trail that even a novice rider can handle.

October 2002

78
Peterborough Bennington Loop NH

October was unusually cold this year with some days barely getting above freezing. We even had some measurable snow. At least partly because of the cold weather, I didn't get on a bike for the whole month. So when the forecasters said Indian Summer would arrive on the second weekend of November, I was ready to go for a ride. I was a little doubtful when I got on my bike, though, because the thermometer showed it was still in the low forties at eight o'clock.

I decided to take a twenty-five mile loop through Greenfield to Bennington and then back to Peterborough on route 202. That's a route which offers a variety of roads and scenery. There are only a few hills, and in the middle of a non-holiday weekend the traffic is light. The trip includes the centers of both Greenfield and Bennington, but mostly it goes by scattered houses, farms and woods. The town centers are small and easy to navigate. They also have nice general stores for coffee and snacks.

I began the loop on Concord Street in Peterborough and pedaled north along the Contoocook. It's a pretty stretch, especially beyond the businesses on the edge of the town. I've often seen deer crossing the highway going to or from the river, but the traffic can be heavy. Just before the North Peterborough bridge, there is a three-way intersection, and I took the middle road, which is the Greenfield Road or route 136.

That road is a narrow, two-lane highway with minimal shoulders, but cars travel pretty fast on it, so a cyclist has to be attentive. As noted above, however, on a November Saturday the traffic was not bad. The road is scenic as it rolls past first a dairy farm – with a flock of Canadian geese sharing a small pond with the cows – and then a

THE BENNINGTON COUNTRY STORE

string of houses on both sides of the road. There's also a large horse farm. The whole area has been growing in population over the last couple of decades, and more houses are being built on the side roads. There are a few minor hills, the last of which is just past the Greenfield town line, but the riding is basically easy.

On this ride, I stayed on 136 into Greenfield, but I've often turned left at the intersection with Forest Road and entered the state park. During the off-season, the park is a good place to ride. After the intersection, there is a rail crossing which is a bit rough and can be slippery in rain. The road then passes the new elementary school and comes to the center of town. I didn't stop this time, but Delay's General Store is a good place for a break. Just past Delay's, I turned left onto the Bennington Road, route 31.

I was quickly back in the countryside. I went past the entrance to Crotched Mountain Rehabilitation Center on the right and dirt roads leading into the state park on the left. The first part of the road to Bennington is mainly uphill, but it's not difficult. I passed the Half-Way Farm and the road leading to the boat launch on

Whittemore Lake, which isn't visible from the road. Soon I was on the long downhill that leads to the center of Bennington. I've pedaled up that hill several times, and I know it's easier to go from Greenfield to Bennington than the other way round. The hill flattens out just before the business section, and there is a beautiful stone wall around the grounds of a fine old house that I always admire.

When I reached the town center, I decided to stop at the Bennington Country Store for a cup of coffee and a home-style doughnut. It's a typical general store, packed with all sorts of goods and food. I sat on the stoop in front of the store, drank my coffee and noted that the temperature had climbed from the chilly forties into the fifties. Indian Summer had arrived.

From the center of Bennington, I rode past the Monadnock Paper Mill and got back on route 202. I headed south and was soon going by the Powder Mill Pond section of the Contoocook. The pond is a broad stretch of the river, formed by a dam, and it's a lovely area. For the next five miles the road is wide with a nice shoulder for biking. There are a couple of long hills to climb, but they aren't very steep. Just past the junction with Forest Road, the highway goes down a steep hill and passes a large marsh. When the highway reaches the Peterborough line, it narrows and there is almost no shoulder for the next two miles.

I covered the two miles of the "narrows" quickly and was soon passing Conval High School's athletic fields and the road was broad again. In a few minutes I was back in Peterborough.

November 2002

Note: The narrow section of route 123 going into Peterborough was greatly improved in 2006 and now has wide shoulders, great for cycling.

79

The First Pedals of Spring
Peterborough Hancock Greenfield NH

There are some hardy bicyclists who bike all year, but I'm not one of them. I remember seeing a man on a mountain bike riding on route 202 during one of our snowstorms earlier this year; he did not appear to be having a good time. Since the first of March, however, I have noticed quite a few cyclists out on the roads, and the arrival of really warm weather in mid-March convinced me it was time to take a ride.

Usually, the first flowers are unfolding their petals in sheltered, sunny spots on lawns before I start riding a bike. This year, all parts of most lawns in the region were still deep under snow when the weekend leading to St. Patrick's Day arrived. Along with the holiday, warm weather showed up, and by Sunday the thermometer read in the fifties! St. Patrick's Day began with temperatures in the thirties, but by mid morning it was in the forties and heading higher. It was time to put the pedals of my bike into action.

The bike I picked for my first ride was my hybrid with its wider tires. I knew there would be some puddles on the road from melting snow, and I expected to have to go onto some muddy road shoulders. The hybrid bike isn't nearly as quick as my road bike, but it's more rugged and stable. It's green, too.

I pedaled north from Peterborough on route 202. Just past EMS, the road gets very narrow, and there is almost no shoulder. It can be stressful when there is heavy traffic, but by late morning, there weren't so many cars. The road widens again right at the Hancock line, and a few yards beyond that, route 123 diverges from 202 and heads toward Hancock itself. There are some hills on that stretch, but the countryside it passes through is lovely. There are also many attractive homes scattered along both sides of the road. Just before the center of town, the houses quickly become more crowded, and then route 123 turns left and becomes the main street.

The center of Hancock is a picture-perfect New England village. The main street is lined with nineteenth century houses, all in splendid condition. Looking west, I could see the white spire of the church at the far end of the downtown section and, beyond that, the snowy shoulder of Mt. Skatutuakee. Perhaps the best known of the buildings is the Hancock Inn.

I rode the length of the street, turned around at the church and stopped at the little general store for a coffee. By that time the temperature was definitely in the fifties; it was a great day.

After a short break, I pedaled back the way I came until I reached the point south of town where Forest Road separates from route 123 and leads to Greenfield. Not far along that road there is a good view of north and south Pack Monadnock. The road crosses route 202 after a mile or so and then heads mainly downhill toward the Contoocook River. There is a fine covered bridge over the river, and the Greenfield/Hancock town line is posted inside, right over the center of the stream.

Just past the bridge, the access road to the boat launch area maintained by the state was blocked with snow, or I would have stopped there for a while. It's a popular spot for both fishermen and canoeists, and it's also a good spot to just sit and look at the river.

I continued the uphill climb on Forest Road and soon came to Oak Park, which is opposite the entrance to Greenfield State Park. The park has been developed nicely in recent years, and there are many events held there during the warm months. I always like to note the small park building with an attached front porch. I remember when it was the fire lookout's cabin on the top of Pack Monadnock. It was rapidly being destroyed by vandals after the fire tower closed, and local officials got permission to move it to Greenfield. When I was working at Miller State Park, I spent many rainy day hours in that cabin talking with Roy Finan, the long-time fire lookout.

From Greenfield, I followed route 136 back into Peterborough. By the time I was home, just a little after noon, it was over 60 degrees! The weatherman, however, was predicting a cold front.

March 2003

80
Country Ride
Keene - Surry - Gilsum NH

On Tuesday, April 15th, we were given a one day taste of really warm weather. We seem to get spring on the installment plan: a warm day here, a warm day there, with several cool, dreary days in between, and then it's black fly season. Despite it all, I still love spring.

Last Tuesday was a great day for being outdoors, and I went on a good bike ride from Keene to Gilsum and back. The weather forecasters had been promising a very warm day, and it was already in the fifties when I started my ride at nine o'clock. By early afternoon, it was in the mid seventies.

My ride began in Wheelock Park in Keene, and I took the Appel Way bike path over to Court Street. It's a fine trail for walking, running or biking, and it connects with the path along the Ashuelot River that leads to the park on West Street. I can remember many Aprils when the bike path was the final stretch of the old Spring Run-Off 10K race. Even though it was a great day, I saw only two other people on the path.

There was some traffic on Court Street as I went by the hospital, but then I turned onto East Surry Road where the traffic was light. The road goes by the Bretwood Golf Course and some well-scattered country homes. There were a few golfers practicing their driving when I went by, but I didn't see any out on the course at that time. I'm not a golfer, but I appreciate the outdoor beauty of the courses. They make good places to walk or ski during the off-season. Sometimes they are used for cross-country track courses as well.

I followed East Surry Road to Surry Dam Road where I turned

left and headed toward route 12A, the Surry Road. The short stretch of the dam road has several attractive structures on it, including the lovely old cider mill on its pond.

The Surry Road is narrow and there isn't much of a shoulder for bikes, but the traffic was really light. I'm sure it's very busy earlier in the morning when people are headed to Keene to work. The road passes the entrance to the Surry Mt. Recreation Area and then begins a gradual climb toward Alstead. I passed a small pond by the side of the road, and I heard the first spring peepers of the year. A little below the intersection with the Gilsum Road, the Ashuelot appears by the road side, and there is an old steel bridge that crosses the river to a woods road.

The Gilsum Road follows the river closely for over a mile. It was full of white water when I rode along its banks. I know people sometimes canoe it in the spring, but I didn't see anyone in the water. When the road moves away from the river, it starts to climb a little faster, and there are two steep, but short, hills before the intersection with route 10.

The intersection is at the part of the river known as the Ashuelot Gorge, and it's the site of the Gilsum Stone Arch Bridge. It was built in 1862, and it has the highest vault of any dry laid stone bridge in New Hampshire. The inside of its arch is thirty six and a half feet above the average level of the river. The bridge and the roaring river in the gorge are worth seeing.

I pedaled on route 10 into Gilsum's center to where the starting line for the DeMar Marathon crosses the main road. I knew it was going to be a lot easier getting back to Keene on my bike than it was the times I ran the race. I could have taken route 10 back and made a loop, but I wanted to enjoy the river again. I also wanted to stop at the Surry Mt. Recreation Area and sit by the lake for awhile.

There were only geese at the lake when I stopped, but when I passed the golf course, there were many people out on the links, all in short sleeves. I wasn't the only person enjoying the fine weather. Of course the forecast was for a cold rain beginning Wednesday afternoon.

April 2003

81
Tri-State Bike Tour
NH - Mass. - Vt.

Many days of this year's May were wet and cool, but we did have a few great days with blue skies and warm temperatures, and I tried to take full advantage of them. Unfortunately, May also means the arrival of black flies, which can make being outside on those few beautiful days a problem. The little bugs can make hiking in the woods or working in the garden a real problem. One way to cope with them and enjoy being outside is to go for a bike ride, and that's what I did on a perfect day in late May.

I biked a tour that I hadn't done in over ten years: a trip that starts on route 119 in Hinsdale, goes south on route 63 into Northfield, Massachusetts, and then follows Vermont 142 to just before the route 119 bridge in Brattleboro. I first learned of the route in the 1985 edition of *25 Bicycle Tours in New Hampshire* by Tom and Susan Heavey. My notes in that book showed that I hadn't followed the tour since 1990, but I remembered it as a great route.

I started from the parking lot of the Wal-Mart in Hinsdale and pedaled down route 119 to the junction with route 63 in the center of that town. The road was broad and straight for the first miles, with good, wide shoulders for biking. There were many views of the Connecticut River, which was often close to the highway. There was also the racetrack; its huge parking lot was empty when I passed it, but it was clearly the focal point of the area. Just before I got to the main part of town I could see the nuclear plant across the river in Vernon, Vermont. There was a nice roadside picnic area between the highway and the river, and then a short but steep hill led into the main part of town. I passed Hinsdale High School, and I soon found myself on route 63, crossing a bridge over the Ashuelot River.

Once I was south of the center of Hinsdale, the countryside changed. The road was narrower, but there was almost no traffic as I pedaled past many farms and scattered houses. It was mostly downhill or level, easy cycling, and the freshly green fields and trees provided a peaceful and lovely view. At the bottom of one of the few, small hills, I saw a large deer standing in the middle of the road watching my approach. I got within thirty yards of it before it turned and calmly bounded into some woods on the left side of the highway.

Soon after the deer, I passed through about a quarter mile long strip of Winchester and then entered Massachusetts. I pedaled by the Northfield Drive-In and came to the junction with route 10. Just beyond that I rode down the access road to the Pauchaug Brook boat landing area for a view of the river. Back on route 10, I rode up a short hill and entered the center of Northfield. Halfway up that hill I saw a roadside monument for one Nathaniel Dickinson, an early settler who was killed by Indians on that spot in 1747. Many fine buildings lined both sides of the road as I went through the center of town. From the beautiful Northfield/Mt. Hermon campus to the fine old homes on both sides of the road, Northfield had plenty to see.

I stayed on route 10, crossed the Connecticut, and turned right onto route 142. I was in the lightly-settled, western section of Northfield for a few miles, and then I entered Vernon, Vermont. I couldn't see the power plant from the road, but I did ride by a sign for the visitors' center. As I rode through the town, I thought about the monument to the 18th century settler just across the river from the nuclear plant, a monument to 20th century technology.

What I did see in Vernon as I headed north toward Brattleboro was beautiful countryside. The peacefulness and pastoral nature of that part of my tour was similar to the section through southern Hinsdale on the other side of the Connecticut.

As I got closer to Brattleboro, the river began to dominate the view, and after I entered the city limits, the surroundings became much less rural and more industrial. I went by a huge lumber yard and several trucking concerns before reaching the downtown area and the bridge back to New Hampshire. There was construction going on, traffic was backed up, and it was chaotic compared to what I had been riding through.

I had to walk my bike a bit to get onto the bridge, but it didn't take long. I was soon pedaling on the walkway part of the bridge, across the island and back to the Wal-Mart lot. I met a man walking back toward Vermont who said, "What a great day!" A few hundred yards later, I met another man – he said the same thing. They were right.

June 2003

THE SHARON ARTS CENTER ON ROUTE 123

82
Country Roads
Sharon NH

A few weeks ago, someone asked me if I knew any good bike routes in the Peterborough area. My first answer was that any of the roads in and around the town make good biking routes. I went on to describe a couple of specific trips, but my first answer was really true. It's not just true about Peterborough: all the towns in our region are surrounded by fine biking routes. Even our busiest highways aren't too crowded, and there are dirt roads and mountain bike paths as well. There are plenty of hills to climb, and there are long stretches of nearly level roads along our little valleys. The scenery, of course, is often spectacular. Finally, the many general stores and small restaurants in the area make for wonderful rest stops.

Near the end of the first week in September, I took a bike ride on one of those routes, starting from my house near the center of Peterborough. It was a ride that had many of the features I just named. There were lots of hills, lovely countryside, and a stretch of gravel road through undeveloped forest. Not only was the route really fine, but also the weather – it was one of those perfect days of September with blue skies, fluffy white clouds, mild temperatures and low humidity.

I began my trip by pedaling the half mile from my house to route 101 and followed it east to the Sharon Road, route 123. As soon as I turned onto 123, I had a hill to climb. That was only the first of a half-dozen steep but short hills I went up and down before turning off 123 and onto Nashua Road. The road parallels the long ridge of Temple Mountain, and it is really corrugated countryside. I was going downhill as much as uphill, but when you are on a bike or walking, going uphill takes so much longer than going downhill that it seems to be all up. It was fairly difficult, but I enjoyed the exercise. There were houses scattered along the road, but it was mostly woods. The most thickly settled portion was the cluster of houses surrounding the Sharon Art Center.

I followed Nashua Road to its junction with route 124, and then I pedaled west through the low land that borders the Gridley River. It was only the first week in September, but the swamp maples had already turned red.

Just beyond the bridge over the river, I turned right onto Swamp Road. It's a dirt road that has a gate, which was open. A sign near the gate indicated that trail bikes and ATV's are not allowed on the road. I was riding my hybrid bike, and I had chosen it for the ride because I knew the loose gravel on parts of Swamp Road would have been too much for my road bike.

I hadn't been on Swamp Road for several years, but I remembered it as a road through undeveloped woods and bordering the marsh through which the Gridley River winds. I also remembered it as being lovely, and it was. The first part of the road went through a stand of tall hemlocks and then downhill to where the marsh appeared on the right side of the road. It was a good place to see a moose, but I wasn't that lucky. I crossed the small metal bridge that spans the Gridley and then climbed a short hill to the pavement of Jarmany Hill Road. It was the best part of the whole ride.

I turned left and rode on Jarmany Hill Road to the junction with Spring Hill Road. Many new houses have been built in that part of Sharon over the last few years, but it is still mainly woods and fields. I coasted down the long hill that leads to Town Line Brook and Peterborough, and I was glad I wasn't pedaling up it. The only other cyclist I saw in Sharon that day was coming up the hill, but he seemed to be enjoying himself.

Back in Peterborough, I turned right onto route 202 and then took the Noone Falls bike path to Grove Street Extension. From there I pedaled past the Rivermead complex and turned left onto Powersbridge Road. I climbed the steep hill to route 101 and was back to where I began my ride.

September 2003

83
Honey Brook State Forest
Marlow NH

Since I read about it in Linda Chestney's excellent guidebook, *Mountain Biking New Hampshire's State Parks and Forests*, I've wanted to bike Honey Brook State Forest in Marlow. For one reason or another, I didn't do it until this May. The forest covers nearly a thousand acres in Marlow, Acworth and Lempster, but the trail described in Chestney's book is completely in Marlow.

It was a beautiful May morning as I drove north from Peterborough to Marlow, and I enjoyed the trip there almost as much as the cycling. I followed route 123 through Hancock and Stoddard to its junction with route 10. I continued north on route 10 to Marlow and parked at the large lot overlooking Stone Pond. There's great scenery on that trip, which passes several lakes and streams and goes over Pitcher Mountain.

I had decided to ride the six mile loop described in Chestney's book, and I began by pedaling across route 10 to Marlow Hill Road and riding up it for a mile. It proved to be the longest and steepest hill of the day. The first part of the road was paved, but the second half was gravel. At the top of the hill, there was a three-way intersection and a sign that read "Marlow Town Common Park," which stood on a small, grassy area. I turned right on Flagg Road, which was marked as a dead end, and followed it downhill past several houses. Just beyond the last house, the road became a dirt track and entered the forest.

The first stretch of trail was wet and muddy, but I was soon pedaling on a pretty good surface. I stopped to check the map in

CYCLING THROUGH A PINE FOREST

the guidebook, and I was quickly the center of a cloud of blackflies. I reminded myself to stay right at the first fork and then, after about a mile, to go left at the second. Then I got back on my bike and away from the flies. Blackflies don't keep up to a cyclist, even if he isn't going more than a few miles per hour. In another month or so, the deer flies will appear, and they are much harder to outrun.

I soon came to the first fork and remembered to keep right. The trail through the dense forest was wide enough for a four-wheeled vehicle, and there were some tracks, but no evidence of heavy use. There were no really steep or long hills, but the trail was almost never level, either. I crossed a few more muddy sections, and there were a few rocky, eroded spots, but mainly it was easy cycling for a woods trail. As I went along, I heard many birds, but I didn't see any wildlife other than the flies. If I had been willing to stop for a few minutes and put up with the blackflies, I might have seen many of the birds and some small animals.

When I reached the final intersection, I turned left and pedaled another half a mile through the forest to route 123A, just south of the Acworth-Marlow town line. I turned right on 123A and rode up a short hill to its intersection with route 10.

At that point, I had biked about five miles and my starting point was only a mile or so south. However, instead of going back to

Stone Pond, I decided to follow Chestney's advice and combine my ride in Honey Brook State Forest with a visit to Dodge Brook Forest, just up the road a few miles in Lempster.

I pedaled north on route 10 into Lempster, and after going a bit over two miles came to where Dodge Brook flowed along the west side of the road. I was looking for Gulf Road, which is the route into the forest indicated in the guidebook, but I didn't see any sign for it. I pedaled on into Lempster for another mile, and then I decided I had missed the road I was looking for and turned around. I wasn't surprised not to have seen a sign. There hadn't been any signs for Honey Brook State Forest either.

As I pedaled south on route 10, I came to a state highway lot and noticed a small, dirt road leading uphill into the woods next to it. I thought it might be the Gulf Road I was searching for since it was going in the right direction and was about two miles from the Honey Brook loop. I rode up the hill into the woods for about a half a mile. I saw boundary markers along the road which showed that it was indeed state property. At the top of the hill, there was some construction going on, and it appeared someone was building a house. Beyond that point, a snowmobile bridge crossed a small brook, and the trail narrowed and continued uphill into the forest.

I turned around and pedaled back to Stone Pond and my car. When I re-checked the map in my guidebook, it looked like I had found Gulf Road and Dodge Brook Forest. I thought the ride along route 10 to get there was as good as the little trip into the forest.

May 2004

84
River Road
Chesterfield and Westmoreland NH

We had a preview of summer in the second week of June, and I was fortunate enough to spend one morning cycling through Chesterfield and Westmoreland. My trip included terrific views of water, woods, farms and attractive homes. I passed by several reminders of the area's early history, and I got some beneficial exercise. All my tour was good, but the best part was the portion that followed River Road along the Connecticut River.

I began my trip at Chesterfield Gorge; the parking lot there is a convenient and safe place to leave a car. It was about nine and already in the mid sixties when I pedaled onto route 9 and headed west. I don't like riding on busy highways with fast traffic, but the shoulder was wide, and the pedaling was easy.

After riding about six and a half miles, I came to West Chesterfield Road and followed it down a winding hill toward the river. As I passed through the little town center, I was sorry to notice the general store was closed. I remembered stopping for lunch there a few years ago. Stopping at country stores is one of the things I like about bicycle touring. Just beyond the town center, I had a small brook on my left and woods on my right. Somewhere along there the road officially became River Road, and I soon saw the river itself.

There are houses along the road, but they are well spaced, and there is very little traffic. I passed an elderly couple who were walking along briskly and stopped at the boat launch area to look at the river for a while. The walkers had passed me by then, but I soon caught up to them, just as they made their turn and headed back toward the town. "Halfway there," the lady said as I waved.

They had turned at a small monument marking the first house built in Chesterfield by Moses Smith in 1761. That was just after the climax of the French and Indian War, and not very long after the French and their allies had attacked English settlements on the Connecticut as far south as Deerfield, Massachusetts. That was the first historical moment of my trip.

Not far past the Moses Smith monument, I crossed into Westmoreland. The river was farther from the road by then, but I could still hear the traffic on route 91 in Vermont, which provided a background to the birdsong that rose from the woods and fields along the road. Not far into Westmoreland, I came to the second historical reminder: the Canoe Meadow Cemetery, which was begun in 1764. I spent a few minutes looking at the old tombstones, many of which were so worn that their inscriptions could no longer be read. One that was still readable was for a Benjamin, who died in November, 1774, at the age of nine. Another stone, in a different family plot, was for a Susanna, who died just a month later, aged two. That winter, the last one before the beginning of the American Revolution, must have been a sad one for at least two families. People still suffer such losses, of course, but one thing we can be thankful for is that the death of young children is not as common now as it was then.

I was now moving away from the river, and plowed fields had replaced the river banks. I was also pedaling up some fairly steep hills. As I approached the Cheshire County jail, I noticed a sign for Cheshire County Nature Trails on the right of the road. I pedaled off the road into a small parking lot and read the signboard there. It showed a woods trail to the east of the road and a river trail along the Connecticut. I promised myself to walk both trails sometime in the near future.

I reached the spot where River Road joins route 63, and I pedaled north on 63 past Stuart and John's Sugar House to route 12. I followed that road a short distance to where North River Road begins and then turned around and pedaled back to 63.

When I reached the intersection with River Road again, I stayed on route 63 and pedaled up a steep hill to the Park Hill Meeting House, built in 1764 and moved in pieces in 1779. There are several other lovely old buildings in the old center of Westmoreland. A short distance from Park Hill, I came to a sign for the Nature Conservancy's Warwick Preserve - another spot with trails that I plan to visit. When I reached the center of Westmoreland, I stopped at the Village Store for a cold drink. It looked like a good place for lunch, but it was a bit early for that.

I continued my ride through the countryside, and after twenty seven miles I reached the shores of Spofford Lake. I rode along the lake side for a few yards where the road is close to the water. I saw that the lake's edge was yellow with pollen. I turned back a short distance to North Shore Road and followed it to route 12.

I was back at Chesterfield Gorge a little before one o'clock. It had taken me four hours to pedal thirty-two miles, but I had made several stops and taken my time. Next time I plan to take even longer.

June 2004

85
Rail Trail
Troy NH

My good friend, Steve Forte, and I spent a late summer morning pedaling our mountain bikes on the railroad bed from the center of Troy to Keene and back. It was a good ride through the woods with several interesting views. It was easy going, too, except for a sandy stretch at the beginning and a short but steep hill at the end.

I met Steve at the Gap Mountain Bakery, and since I got there first, I had time for a coffee and a super blueberry muffin, still warm from the oven. I always enjoy a visit to the little bakery on the common in Troy.

Steve arrived just as I finished my snack, and we started our ride from a point just north of the section of railroad bed that's being used for trucks involved in the clean-up at Troy Mills. The first part of trip passed under route 12, and it really was very sandy and hard to pedal. Within a few minutes, though, we were on a harder surface. It was easy pedaling from there all the way to Keene.

The best section of our ride was along the river just below the Swanzey line, where the highway cuts through the hills above the stream The railroad bed was high above the road for part of that section, and there were fine views.

One of the good parts of cycling on a railroad bed is the freedom from automobile traffic. It's nice to peddle side by side and not have to be concerned with cars coming up behind. There were a few crossings of small roads on our trip, but there were long stretches between the crossings with nothing but trees and the railroad bed.

THE OLD DEPOT IN TROY

Once we were in Swanzey, we passed behind some of the businesses on route 12, and we could see the fair grounds across the road. The track was a bit overgrown for a short distance, but it was never difficult. As we approached the Keene town line, we passed close to some houses and crossed another road. Then we reached the Swanzey Factory Road and the old railroad bridge across Otter Brook. Not too many years ago, there was a section of the bridge crossing the road, but it was removed, and now there is a short, steep downhill to the road and then a short, steep uphill to the remaining portion of the bridge.

We pushed our bikes up to the top of the bridge and paused to enjoy the view of the stream passing beneath. The bridge is a popular place for walkers, cyclists and, I imagine, snowmobilers. As we looked over the river, we wondered why there wasn't a path along its shore similar to that along the Ashuelot in Keene. We could see an old wall along the river bank, and we speculated that the highway once followed closer to the river.

The bridge was exactly eight miles from our starting point, and it had taken us a little under an hour to get there. We hadn't been in a hurry. After thinking about possible return routes other than the railroad bed, we decided going back the way we had come was the best choice.

About half way back to Troy, we stopped for a minute and watched a tiny snake crossing the track. He was probably born this summer, and he couldn't have been more than eight inches long. However, once he noticed me bending close to him, he coiled up just like a rattler and opened his mouth in an obvious threat. There he was, smaller than a nightcrawler and not as dangerous as a mosquito, but instinctively prepared to defend himself against a giant. We left him alone - he probably felt he had chased us away.

Soon we were pedaling above the river again and looking down toward the highway. Then, just as we were approaching the old, half-brick building that sits between the road and the railroad bed on the outskirts of Troy, we were startled by a very close gunshot. We were sure it was just someone target shooting, but the sudden noise really got our attention. We heard a second shot as we continued toward Troy, but no more. It was probably someone getting ready for hunting season. It won't be long before I'll be wearing something bright orange when I walk or bike in the woods.

As we were entering the town, we remembered the sandy section of the railroad bed and decided to avoid it. We pushed our bikes up the bank to the parking lot of the elementary school and pedaled the streets back to our cars.

September 2004

86
Annett State Forest
Jaffrey NH

Late in the afternoon of a cool, mid-October day, I pedaled my mountain bike around a seven mile loop that formed a rough triangle with Hubbard Pond at its center. My ride began and ended in Annett State Park, and over two miles of it was within the state forest, but most of the total distance was on paved roads or well-graded gravel ones.

The park is located between routes 124 and 119 in Rindge, just a mile north of The Cathedral of the Pines. The picnic area is relatively small, but there are trails leading down to Hubbard Pond and into the surrounding forest. I've never seen it crowded, and I was mildly surprised to see another car in the lot when I pulled in just after three o'clock. There were wooden picnic tables scattered among the trees, as well as a number of old fireplaces. However, only charcoal fires are allowed now, and the fireplaces look little used.

I unloaded my bike and set off on the paved road toward the Cathedral of the Pines. Almost immediately, I was coasting down a short but steep hill that ended in a sharp curve before starting back up. At the bottom of the hill, I passed the dirt road that led down to the dam on Hubbard Pond. A number of cars passed me, headed south, as I pedaled slowly up the hill, and I concluded a shift must have just ended at the nearby Millipore plant.

When I turned left onto Saw Mill Road, I left most of the traffic behind, and only a handful of cars passed me over the next three miles. As I pedaled down Saw Mill Road toward Old New Ipswich Road, I was surprised to see several houses that have been built on it, and I realized I had not been down that way for many years. I quickly came to the junction with Old New Ipswich road and turned left again. In the past I had followed that road only as far as the access road to the old boys' camp on Hubbard Pond, but I had the idea that there were few if any houses beyond that point. I soon discovered I was mistaken, for I passed many homes, including some quite old. It was a hilly stretch of road, too, and some of the houses had good exposure to the north. One newer house on a hilltop had a truly panoramic view of Temple Mountain and Pack Monadnock. The paved portion of the road ended not far beyond the junction with Saw Mill Road, but it remained smooth and well-graded. It passed close to the southern tip of Hubbard Pond, and I had a few glimpses of the water, but I was soon pedaling away from the pond and toward New Ipswich.

There were no houses for a short distance, and I noticed a small, green sign that indicated I had crossed the town line. In a few minutes I was passing more houses, and I noticed a street sign that read Pine Road. I was a little taken back since the trail map I had looked at before setting off showed that Old New Ipswich Road led directly to Hubbard Pond Road. I decided to believe the road merely had its named changed once it entered New Ipswich. When I reached a fork where another dirt road came in on my left, or from the west, I presumed it was Hubbard Pond Road, but I wasn't completely sure. However, I was sure enough to follow it for at least a few minutes.

There were a few houses near the intersection, but I quickly passed them, and the road narrowed. I noticed blue paint markers on some of the trees and a sign that proclaimed I was in a "Carry In, Carry Out" area, and I knew I was back in Annett State Forest and it was the right road.

The last mile and a half of my ride was through the forest and down to the dam at the north end of Hubbard Pond. Some parts were a bit steep, and the surface was rocky and loose, but it was fun. A small amount of water was flowing over the dam, and I had to step gingerly from one rock to another in order to cross the outflow just beneath the dam, walking my bike through the shallow water. After that, it was only a half mile up the gravel road to Cathedral Road and the park. I was back at my car less than an hour after beginning my ride.

October 2004

87
Russell-Abbott State Forest
Mason NH

The wooded hills near the Souhegan River, where Wilton, Greenville and Mason come together, include three attractive natural areas: The Nature Conservancy's Sheldrick Forest, the Society for the Protection of New Hampshire's Forests' Heald Tract, and the Russell-Abbott State Forest. The last, a nearly 900 acre woodland that features the lovely, undeveloped Pratt Pond, is excellent for mountain biking. The defunct Fitchburg Railroad bed, which passes through the forest on its way to Greenville, can be pedaled for nearly ten miles, and there are also several unpaved rural roads in and around the forest that offer more miles of good biking.

I drove east on route 101 to the intersection with route 31 in west Wilton. I turned south onto 31 and then immediately left onto the Isaac Frye Highway. That road very quickly crossed the Souhegan, and just past the bridge I turned right onto Capt. Clark Road. I was not surprised to see several new houses on that unpaved road, for the developers have been busy along route 101 in Wilton. I followed Capt. Clark Road for about two miles, passing the intersection with Abbott Mill Road. By then, I was in Mason, and the dirt road had become Pratt Pond Road.

Another half mile brought me to the pond itself, and I parked in the small lot on its eastern end. I got out of the car and was struck by the awful contrast between the pristine pond and the litter-covered parking lot. The trouble with carry in - carry out areas is that too many nocturnal visitors carry in only to carry *on* and leave a mess.

I unloaded my bike and pedaled to the nearby railroad bed, which comes up from Massachusetts and runs along the southwestern edge of the pond. From my earlier visit, I knew that I could ride northwest and then west to where the trail ends high above the Souhegan River and route 31. There was a railroad bridge there until about twenty years ago, and the massive supports are still to be seen. I remember that just before the bridge was torn down a local pilot flew his plane under it, to the delight of numerous spectators.

I pedaled along the shore of the little lake, on which I saw a pair of ducks and a beaver lodge. No one was fishing. The railroad bed beyond the pond was very wet in spots, and I had to walk my bike through a section that was flooded by the runoff of a marsh. The beavers had actually attempted to keep some of the water from escaping from the marsh by throwing up a small dam next to the trail. The trail passed under a power line, and there was a nice view to the north. I pedaled through a section that was cut from the hillside and had steep banks on either side. It was also mainly puddles. For one stretch, the land feel away steeply on the left, and since the leaves still weren't all out, I could see deep into the woods.

After about two miles, the trail turned more westerly and headed toward Greenville. By then I had left the actual forest and was within the town of Greenville. I passed one house and noticed signs prohibiting ATV's. I came to a road crossing and saw different signs on the gates, which showed the trail to be closed to all traffic until May twenty-third because of the mud. I had wanted to look over the old bridge site, but I turned around there and pedaled back to Pratt Pond.

Back at the pond, I rode a short way south on the railroad bed, passing under the same power line, and then returned to Pratt Road and pedaled west on it for a half mile or so. I passed under the same power line yet again. The road was hilly, and lots of mountain laurel grew among the trees that bordered it.

When I returned to my car, I had pedaled about ten miles. It would be easy to spend most of the day there; I know from my earlier visit that the railroad bed can be pedaled south for over five miles. There are other dirt roads, including the Old Starch Factory Road, that are good for biking. It would also be easy to spend the day right on the pond, picnicking, fishing, birding - or picking up trash. *May 2005*

88
Ashuelot Rail Trail
Keene - Swanzey NH

For the second time in two weeks, I had to leave my car at the dealership on Production Avenue in Keene for a few hours. This time I brought my mountain bike with me, and I rode an eighteen mile loop that included greatly varied surroundings and surfaces. Nearly half of the ride was on the Ashuelot Rail Trail, from the Keene State athletic fields to just south of the Winchester/ Swanzey line.

I pedaled away from the garage just after eight on a fine May morning and turned right onto route nine. For the first mile, I hugged the edge of the road as the early morning traffic buzzed by me. The traffic was still heavy when I turned south on Winchester Street, route ten, but all but a single car disappeared when I reached the side road leading to the KSC fields. The rail trail itself was a completely different world of green calm. Bird song replaced the sound of cars and trucks, and the only traffic I shared the trail with appeared in the first half mile: one man out for a walk.

After passing the man, I stopped to listen to a very pretty bird song. I searched for the bird with the small binoculars I had with me and located it near the top of a trail side tree. It was a rose breasted grosbeak. I listened to it for a few moments and then pedaled away. I looked back and noticed the walking man had also stopped at that point.

The Ashuelot River was never far from the trail on my ride, and I had a number of good views of it from my bike. For the first several miles, it was on my left, and from one road crossing I saw one of the covered bridges that cross the river in Swanzey. At times there were houses and small farms near by, and I noticed many horse tracks as I went along. I'm sure the trail is busy on weekends and in the evening. The surface was firm and dry for the most part, but there were many sandy stretches that made for harder pedaling, and I had to navigate a few large puddles. There was one section of a hundred yards or so in the middle of West Swanzey that I had to detour around on a town road. Those were minor problems, and I enjoyed seeing some of the old houses in the village.

The highlight of my ride was the old railroad bridge across the river about four miles south of the college area. It has been rebuilt for snowmobiles and pedestrian use, and I rested on it for several minutes, looking out over the river. At that point signs on some of the trees along the trail showed me that I was passing through the Yale Forest.

The river was on my right for the rest of my ride on the trail, but I couldn't see much of it from my bike. When I got to where the trail crossed route ten in Winchester, I had pedaled nearly nine miles from the car dealership, and I decided to head back to Keene on the highway. The traffic wasn't very heavy as I rode through Swanzey on route ten, and I was moving much faster. I could also see much farther on either side than when I was moving between the wall of trees on either side of most of the rail trail. I went by the homes and businesses along the road, and I passed another section of the Yale Forest.

I left route ten at the intersection with Base Hill Road and followed it back to route nine. There wasn't much of a shoulder for bikes on that winding road, and I was glad the traffic was light. I hope, for the sake of the people who live along Base Hill Road, that there won't be an increase of traffic on it once the Monadnock Marketplace is fully open.

It had taken me over an hour to get to where I left the rail trail in Winchester, but the ride back on the paved roads took only a little over half that. I was lucky when I hit route nine, for the traffic coming from the west was being held up, and I was able to pedal easily across the work area at the new bridge. My odometer had just hit eighteen miles when I rode into the dealership parking lot, and my car was sitting there, ready to go.

May 2005

89
The Sugar River Recreational Trail Newport and Claremont NH

The Sugar River Recreational Trail is a multi-use trail that follows the former Boston and Maine Railroad's route from Newport to Claremont. The trail begins on Belknap Ave., just north of the Newport town green and stays close to the Sugar River all the way into Claremont. The trail crosses the river several times, twice on wooden covered bridges. Although the trail also crosses two roads coming out of Newport and follows one gravel road for a short distance in Kellyville, most of it passes through woods along the river's banks. It's a beautiful ten mile ride, and the pedaling is easy except for a number of sandy stretches where motorized travel has churned the surface.

I drove up route 10 to Newport on a sunny July morning and parked near the large sign for the trail, just before the Newport Recreation Center's building on Belknap Avenue. I was on my mountain bike and pedaling at 8:15. I crossed the first of many bridges within a quarter mile and followed the trail and the river around a long bend, first to the north and then south. That part of the trail included the most difficult pedaling because it was very sandy. At times it was like pedaling through wet wallpaper paste. However, it was nearly level, and the views of the river were great.

For several miles, I didn't see another person on the trail, but I did notice a set of fresh footprints. Eventually, they led to an older man, who was carrying a walking stick in one hand and a leafy branch in the other, which he was using to wave away bugs.

Soon after, the trail crossed a road where several men had just parked and were heading down to the water with fly-fishing rigs. Just beyond that, I overtook another older man, who was walking with his dog, which looked like mostly poodle. He asked me where I had started, and I stopped to talk. He told me that he didn't like to walk from the center of Newport because the trail was so "chopped up" from the heavier traffic there so he always began his four mile walk in the middle of the trail where the surface was hard packed cinders. As I was about to pedal away, he said it looked like we were two senior citizens taking care of our health, and I agreed.

Just before the halfway point on the trail, I passed under route 103 and then came to the first covered bridge. The elaborate wooden construction was in good shape, and it looked as if it could still support a train. The bridge is in the Kellyville section of Newport, and Chandlers Mill Road runs close to it. The trail followed the road for a short distance, and I noticed a used book store, Hedgehog Publishers, occupying a large barn attached to a house. On my return trip I stopped in and found it to be well-stocked with thousands of books and operated by a very friendly and helpful lady.

The trail soon returned to the woods and the river bank, and I pedaled through the second covered bridge. By then, I was nearing Claremont, and the river was changing its personality. Most of the way, it was moving swiftly, often with white water, between steep, banks. Close to Claremont, it widened, slowed down, and curved amid small, grassy islands.

I also began to see people on the trail as I approached the city. Four joggers passed me, heading east, and then two older men riding ATVs went by in the same direction. Finally, I said hello to the only other cyclist I saw all day, who was riding a bike with a small trailer. The Sugar River Trail ended at a gate just south of route 103, but there was a continuation of the multi-use trail that ran into Claremont. I followed it for a mile or so, past several businesses and a strip mall and through a section of woods above a corn field to Monadnock Park, a nice area of playgrounds and ball fields. It was 9:45 when I reached the park. I took a short break and then turned around and pedaled back to Newport.

July 2005

90
Monadnock and Back
Dublin and Chesham NH

As I have written earlier, the entire Monadnock region is great for bicycling, and that makes it easy and enjoyable to plot out and follow a new route from time to time. On the first day of May, I pedaled, for the first time, a ride that took me from deep in the woods at the bottom of Mt. Monadnock to the traffic on route 101, along quiet country roads of Dublin and Harrisville, through the lovely old center of Chesham, and back to the mountain. All of that and more was in a thirteen mile trip that took only two hours.

The route began at the trailhead for the Dublin Trail on Monadnock. I left my car at the small parking area on Old Troy Road, about a mile and a half from the Dublin Lake golf course on Old Marlboro Road. I got there at ten on a partly cloudy morning and was just unloading my bike when another car pulled in. Two young men emerged and asked if I was going to ride up the mountain. By the time I laughed and said no, they were already headed up the trail, lightly dressed and carrying nothing but a water bottle each.

To begin my trip, I pedaled back on the rugged dirt and gravel surface of Old Troy Road toward Old Marlboro Road. Because half my route was on unpaved roads, I had chosen to ride my mountain bike. A good rider could use a road bike, but I was happy with my choice. I rode by the white fences of a large farm, passed a few houses and turned left on Old Marlboro Road. A minute later, I turned right onto Charcoal Road. That took me by the golf course and then over Charcoal Brook Beyond the brook, I pedaled up a short hill and by a couple of driveways leading to unseen homes.

Then I went downhill, passed a *visible* house and came to the waters of the Howe Reservoir on both sides of the road. A man was fishing there, his truck parked nearby.

A few yards beyond, I came to the intersection with route 101 and turned right, toward Dublin. Being on the busy highway was a huge difference, and I was glad to leave it in a half mile for a left turn onto MacVeagh Road. On that dirt road, I rode by green fields, thickly wooded hillsides, and rushing brooks. I did pass a farm set well back from the road, one house atop a hill, which was closer, and a couple of driveways leading back into the forest. Overall, it was a beautiful, pastoral mile and a half, and I didn't see a single car.

I turned left onto Brown Road, also unpaved. I passed the point where the Monadnock-Sunapee Greenway comes out of the woods above the Howe Reservoir and followed the white blazes up Brown Road to where they exited right. I pedaled up a short but steep hill and then down to the pavement of Chesham Road. That took me through the little town center and by its Community Church, built in 1785.

Then I was back on route 101 and heading east. Just before Charcoal Road, I stopped at the natural area overlooking the reservoir. I didn't have a lunch with me, but that would have been a good spot for enjoying one. After a short break to admire the view, I resumed pedaling and was quickly back on Charcoal Road. The fisherman was still there, and I stopped to ask him what fish were in the water. He told me there was a quite a variety: dace, perch, pickerel, horned pout and even trout. He explained the trout sometimes got into the pond from the brooks that fed it. "I catch one about every three years," he said.

I said goodbye to the friendly man and pedaled the three miles back to my car. Just as I ended my trip, one of the two young men I had last seen starting up the mountain came trotting out of the woods. "Hey, dude," he yelled, " ran down in thirty-four minutes! Great exercise, dude!" I asked where his friend was, and he told me he was "just walking" and would be along in a while. I found it easier to relate to the slower dude.

May 2006

91
The Road to Athens
Grafton - Townshend Vt.

My ever-youthful buddy, Steve Forte, and I have often pedaled a nice route from Bellows Falls through Saxtons River, Cambridgeport, Grafton and Chester, Vermont. This year, Steve suggested turning left instead of right in Grafton and riding along the South Branch River toward Townshend. He wasn't sure where that would take us, but a quick check of a road map showed us we could go south to the junction with Vermont Route 35 and take it back to the highway along Saxtons River. According to the map, we would ride through a town called Athens, just south of Cambridgeport.

We drove to Vermont on a Friday morning in mid July; it was foggy in Keene that morning, but by the time we reached Bellows Falls the sun had burned through, and it promised to be a warm day. We parked at the Health Center just west of where route 121 ends at route 5 in Bellows Falls and started our ride at 9:15.

Although the ride up route 121 to Grafton was familiar, its beauty was as pleasing as the first time I had enjoyed it, years ago. For most of the eleven miles, we were right on the banks of Saxtons River, riding through iconic Vermont countryside. The traffic was light, and we had only the briefest wait at the construction site on the bridge at Cambridgeport. As we rode through the town of Saxtons River, we noticed several newer businesses, but we were sorry to note the absence of the wonderfully named Pizza, Paul and Mary restaurant.

We had been pedaling uphill most of the way, but it was an easy grade. Nearing Grafton, the road did rise quite a bit above the river, but that only provided a different view of the stream. Grafton itself was as lovely as ever, but when we turned left at the inn and headed toward Townshend we found ourselves riding through territory new to us.

The South Branch River, a tributary of Saxtons River, flowed down a narrow valley with wooded hills on either side. For the first few miles we passed a mix of houses and farms, all prosperous looking. We noted we were going uphill slightly, and as the stream and its valley narrowed, we began going uphill more than slightly. We had wondered if the new part of the route would be hilly, and so it turned out. We reached the crest of the hill going out of the little valley and then enjoyed a long downhill. Before we reached the bottom, we came to the intersection with route 35 and started to climb once again.

The road to Athens took us uphill for a couple of miles. It wasn't too steep at first, but the last part was really tough. Steve pedaled all the way, but having reached the age of sixty-five, I got off and pushed my bike up the last few yards without feeling wimpy. We had passed very few houses and only one farm that seemed to be still in operation. It was a very sparsely populated stretch of road.

From the high point, we coasted down the road to where the pavement ended, next to a washed out bridge. A mile or so of dirt road ended at a small cluster of houses and farms, which was, evidently, Athens itself. There was no Acropolis, but we did ride by a very handsome old meeting house, which suggested a later site of the democracy that began in ancient Greece.

A few minutes later, we were back at the bridge work on route 121 in Cambridgeport. We stopped at the general store there for a cool drink, and we asked the proprietor why the short section of route 35 was unpaved. He opined that local residents preferred it that way, and that seemed sensible to us.

We continued back down route 121 and stopped for lunch at the general store in Saxtons River. From there, it was a short ride back to Bellows Falls. It was great to have enjoyed not only an old route we loved, but also to have discovered a fine new addition to it. Other cyclists who haven't already been over the route we traveled will certainly like it, and it would make a great Sunday drive as well.

July 2006

92
The Capital of Reading
Proctorsville - Felchville - Cavendish Vt.

Vermont is a wonderful place for cycling, and nearly every road in the state makes a great ride. For many years, I have been riding routes described in John Freidin's book, *Twenty-five Bicycle Tours in Vermont.* One of the tours I especially enjoy is the twenty-seven mile loop beginning and ending in Proctorsville and passing through Felchville and Cavendish. The ride includes farmland, a high forested hill, and the three picturesque towns. In the shape of a rough square, two sides of the tour are along the North Branch of the Black River and the last follows the Black River itself. Although the first seven miles are uphill and often difficult, the reward is an easy downhill or level ride for the remaining distance. It's a great trip.

Ten years ago, I rode around the loop alone, but this July I had the company of old buddy Steve Forte, who had never taken the tour. We drove up Vermont Route 103 to Proctorsville, parked at the general store, and began our tour at ten o'clock on a beautiful Wednesday morning. We pedaled east on Main Street, Route 131, for less than a quarter mile and turned left onto Twenty Mile Stream Road. A sign indicated that a bridge on the road was being repaired and directed cars back to Ludlow, but we trusted that bikes could get by and kept going.

Twenty Mile Stream Road was steep for the first half mile and then climbed more easily for several miles through a sparsely settled valley. We had no trouble crossing over the bridge, and soon after we did, the road's surface went from paved to dirt, and we began to climb more steeply. The last couple of miles were really rugged, and we stopped at a relatively level spot for a breather. When we did reach Tyson Road, a paved highway, we turned right and found ourselves pedaling up another steep climb. At last, we made it to the crest and stopped for a good rest.

From that point on, it was a super downhill run into Felchville. We passed a marshy area just below the top of the hill with woods on both sides of the road and not a house in sight. There was a moose crossing sign, and the landscape reminded me of the north country of New Hampshire, above Berlin. Evidently, the marshy area was the source of the North Branch of the Black River, and the stream grew larger as we descended. We began to pass houses and farms, including one with a great view of Mt. Ascutney. Soon we were nearing Felchville, but we were a bit confused by signs which told us we were in Reading.

At the very bottom of the long hill, Tyson Road (also called Kingdom Road) ended at route 106, the main street of what we by then weren't sure was Felchville or Reading. We stopped at the general store on the corner there and bought wonderful grinders for lunch. In the store there were large, framed photos of the town in earlier days. There were also caps for sale which read, Felchville, the Capital of Reading. The puzzle was solved; Felchville is a *section* of Reading, and -maybe- the greatest section.

We rode down route 106 for a mile or so, with the grinders, and stopped at a nicely mowed area on the roadside for our meal. The site was called Indian Stones and included a memorial to members of the Johnson family, who were captured by Indians in Charlestown in 1754. Mrs. Johnson was pregnant at the time and delivered a child at that spot.

After lunch, we continued down route 106 to the intersection with route 131. We passed more pretty country and had another, closer, view of Mt. Ascutney. At the intersection, we turned right and then pedaled along the banks of the Black River for several miles before reaching the center of Cavendish. Not many years ago, the Russian author, Alexander Solzhenitsyn, spent his self-imposed exile from Russia in the little town. A few minutes later, we were back in Proctorsville and our fine ride was over.

July 2006

93
Thirty Mile Loop
Winchester NH to Northfield Mass.

On a great day in early August, my cycling pal, Steve Forte, and I rode a super thirty mile loop from Winchester through Hinsdale, down to Northfield and Warwick in Massachusetts, and back to Winchester. The tour followed four roads and was in the shape of a rough quadrangle. It took us through several attractive small towns, miles of farmland, and thickly forested hills. It was a great bike ride, and it would certainly make a good fall foliage drive.

We began our ride at the junction of routes 119 and 10 in south Winchester. Steve parked in the most remote corner of the Rite Aid lot, and we started pedaling at a quarter to ten that morning. It was one of the many fine days of this August, with the temperature in the 60's, low humidity and bright sun.

The first leg of our trip was west on route 119, along the Ashuelot River. Most of the six or seven miles into Hinsdale took us right next to the water, but at times the road pulled away from the stream and, although the section was mostly downhill, there were a few hills to climb. The part of New Hampshire we rode through is certainly not unknown, but I think its beauty and charm are not as appreciated as they should be. For example, the old mill buildings and houses strung along the highway in Ashuelot are both interesting as reminders of earlier industry and lovely in their present state.

As we neared Hinsdale, we rode past three entrances to Pisgah Park, and in the center of town we noticed a nice park following the river's bank with many benches offering views over the water. We left route 119 for route 63, crossed the river and headed south toward Northfield. The next several miles, still in Hinsdale, took

CYCLISTS SOMETIMES HAVE THE ROAD TO THEMSELVES

us through a peaceful, pastoral countryside. It was very much like riding through rural Vermont.

Soon after we passed the state line into Massachusetts, we pedaled by the Northfield Drive-In, one of the few drive in movies still in operation. Before entering the town, we rode down the access road to the boat launch on the Connecticut and sat by the water for a few minutes. We talked with some people from Pennsylvania, who were waiting for members of their party to return from a boat trip. The boat launch is part of a new Massachusetts state park - the Connecticut River Greenway, which includes boat launches and natural areas along the river.

From the river's side, we returned to route 63 and pedaled into the center of Northfield. As always, I was impressed by the broad main street, lined with fine old homes and the buildings of the Northfield Academy. We turned left at the blinking light onto Warwick Road, which was marked by only a very small black and white sign, and began the third side of the quadrangle, which was the only portion completely new to me. I knew we would have to climb over the low mountains above Northfield, including Flower Hill and the shoulder of Mt. Grace, and sure enough, we had a seven to eight mile uphill ride before coasting into the center of Warwick.

It was the most difficult part of the trip, but none of the many steep climbs were overpowering, and there were several nearly level stretches. The road followed a small brook for much of the way, back to its source in a marshy area on the hill's top. There were very few houses along the road, but we did pass a number of unpaved driveways leading into the woods. For most of the ride, the forest was thick and close on either side.

At about a quarter to noon, we rode into the Warwick common. It was a quintessential New England scene: library, town hall, even an old horse watering trough turned into a fountain.
A large, white clapboarded building, which I thought was an inn, had a for sale sign and an old horse-drawn wagon in front of it.

From Warwick, we rode - or coasted - down route 78 through Mt. Grace State Forest. As we went along, I noticed the old picnic area appeared to have been removed; even the sign was gone. A couple of years ago, I hiked up Mt. Grace on the M&M Trail and looked at the remains of an old ski tow. I also saw a number of fireplaces and tables in the picnic area that didn't seem to be getting any use. I'm glad the hiking trails are still there.

Soon we passed the state line and were back in New Hampshire. We pedaled through a part of Winchester that people who know the tour only from driving through on route 10 would not recognize. It was a lovely, green valley with wooded hills on either side and old farm fields and pastures. Just before reaching the intersection with route 10, we passed a busy, outdoor food place named "Third Base, Last Stop Before Home." It looked tempting, but we decided to go for the home run and not a triple. At 12:15, we were back at Steve's truck.

August 2006

94
Bridge to Bridge
Connecticut River NH and Vt.

The roads near the Connecticut River, on both the Vermont and New Hampshire sides of the stream, make for great biking. Their popularity with cyclists is evidenced by the arrows and initials, in a rainbow of colors, that have been painted on the road surfaces over the years to mark the routes of many clubs and causes.

In mid August, my cycling buddy, Steve, and I rode a loop from the route nine bridge over the river in Chesterfield to Vermont, up route five to the route 123 bridge between Westminster and Walpole., and then down River Road back to route nine. It was a fine ride that took us from the busy traffic of the Brattleboro roundabout, through the small towns of Putney, Westminster and West Chesterfield, and - mostly - past miles and miles of field and forest. It was also a fairly demanding trip with many hills to climb.

Our tour began at the state store/ post office parking lot just before the bridge in Chesterfield. We started pedaling a little after nine that morning. A fog had just lifted from the river valley, and it was chilly as we crossed over the old bridge into Vermont. Being able to use the bike path and avoid the traffic on the new bridge was great, and it was nice to make use of the pedestrian crosswalk just before the roundabout. The next part of the trip, following route five north through the heavily developed stretch of north of Brattleboro, was the least relaxing part of the day, as we had to be very careful with the traffic and had only a narrow shoulder on which to ride.

Soon, however, we were beyond the busiest section of the trip and riding through East Dummerston and into Putney. We stopped in Putney for coffee at Mountain Paul's, across from the basket store. After that break, we found ourselves climbing the longest hill of the day, far from the banks of the river. The morning chill was long gone by then, and the sun was bright. The countryside we were passing through was lovely, with scattered houses and pretty farms. Among the interesting sights we pedaled by was Santa's Land USA.

Eventually, we came to the top of the long hill and coasted into Westminster. We pedaled through the center of town on the wide, tree-lined main street, stopping to admire the attractive homes and the town hall. Then it was a right turn under the railroad bridge and past a cornfield to the river. A train was running south on the bridge as we rode under it. Then we, too, had a bridge to cross, the route 123 bridge to Walpole.

We stopped for a moment on the middle of that bridge and took in the view down the river. By that time we had become quite familiar with the various route marks on the road, especially one featuring the letter M. For a while, we thought it might represent the Boston to Montreal bike route, but when the M's led us across the river into New Hampshire, we thought not.

In Walpole, we followed route 12 south for a short distance and then left that busy highway for the quiet of River Road. We rode through mile after mile of beautiful countryside, with only a very occasional car or truck sharing the road with us. The river was often in sight, and wild flowers bloomed along the road. A bicycle can be a time machine, taking the rider back to a quieter era, and it might have been the country of a half century or more ago that we were riding through. In fact, the hills we climbed probably outnumbered the cars we encountered. None of them were very long or high, but they tended to be steep.

Shortly past noon, we rode by the West Chesterfield boat landing and then had another short but steep climb up to the center of the village. Then we left River Road to follow Cross Road back to route nine. That also included a good climb, and just before we reached the highway, we noticed that one of the people marking the route in white paint had written "Whew!' at the crest of the last hill before the easy trip down route nine and back to the first bridge.

September 2006

95
Flowers, Leaves and Pedals
Hancock NH

Spring is at least as good a time to go out viewing foliage as fall. The process of spring is the reverse of autumn; instead of leaves turning and then falling onto the ground, green bursts from the earth and from the bare branches above. It's slow at first, more of a tease, often delayed or covered with late snow. Then the warming days speed up the operation, and the new growth unfolds and expands rapidly. If a person were to go away for a few days in May and then return to the Monadnock Region, he or she might think spring exploded in the interim.

I went on a bike ride in mid May that took me through miles of countryside and village streets, all glowing with flowers, blossoms, and bright new leaves. Except for a few miles, I could have ridden the route in a car, but the slower pace of the bike ride allowed me to appreciate the beauty more.

My trip began a little before ten o'clock on the Monday morning following Mother's Day. It was sunny and cool, almost chilly, at first, but by afternoon it warmed up to the mid seventies - a near perfect day. I pedaled my mountain bike north on Concord Street in Peterborough to Hunt Road and then took the Peterborough Pathway from Tarbell Road to Hancock. Those few miles were the only ones that I couldn't have driven in my car.

I left the rail trail at Cavender Road in Hancock and pedaled west. That road, with its scattered houses, open fields and mountain views, is always a delight. I crossed over the highway and followed route 123 into the center of Hancock. As was the case for the whole ride, I passed by and under spring flowers, still blooming forsythia bushes, azaleas, lingering daffodils, tulips, cherry and apple blossoms, and millions of new leaves on the trees that lined the roads and covered the hillsides.

Since it was too late for coffee and too early for lunch, I resisted the temptation to stop at the great general store in Hancock and rode through the village to Old Dublin Road. The next several miles, on that road and Jaquith Road, were the best of the trip. At first, the road dipped, but I was soon climbing steeply, and there were several really tough hills in the first few miles. I stopped for a break next to a pond that had a beaver lodge and, next to the road, a beaver dam. A number of old stone piers that once supported train tracks crossed the far end of the pond. Soon after I began riding again, the road's surface became dirt, and I was glad I was riding my bike with fat tires.

As I pedaled south, the hillside was on my immediate right, but the land fell off to my left, into a narrow valley, bordered by another ridge to the east. Much of the low land in between was wet, and a chain of ponds paralleled the road. Gradually the valley narrowed and disappeared. Not a single car passed me on Old Dublin Road, but I did pedal by a woman hiking along with a staff.

Just before noon, I reached the intersection with Jaquith Road. There was a beautiful farmhouse and barn there, with a great view to the south that included Mt. Monadnock. I intended to pedal east on Jaquith Road to route 137, but first I turned right and rode up the steep final stretch to its dead end. Then I turned around and rode back, crossed Old Dublin Road again and pedaled downhill. At the bottom of the hill, the wetlands on either side of the road were still full of water. People were working inside the huge old barn just beyond the ponds, and two trucks passed me as I climbed up the road from the barn. That was the most traffic I had to contend with since leaving Hancock.

From Jacquith Road I followed route 137 south to Sargent Camp Road. That took me through the Sargent Center and up to Windy Row in Peterborough. The view of the Wapack Range from Windy Row was spectacular, and the fields of the several big farms on that road were almost unbelievably green. To return home and avoid the center of Peterborough, I rode on MacDowell Road to High Street, followed that to the Middle Hancock Road, and then pedaled back on Hunt Road to route 202. I was home at a quarter after one, having ridden over twenty-four miles, feeling like I had just played a part in a travelogue.

May 2007

96
The Toonerville Trail
Connecticut River, NH and Vt.

On a beautiful day in early June with temperatures more like May, I rode my bike on a nearly thirty mile tour that started and ended in Charlestown. The trip included Springfield and Bellows Falls and lots of views over the Connecticut River, but the highlight of the day was the bike path along the Black River out of Springfield. The Toonerville Trail follows the old Springfield Electric Railway's route and is named for the old cars, which, in turn, were named after the comic strip trolley.

My ride began at the boat landing on the Connecticut River, just south of the center of Charlestown. There's a park there as well as a boat launch area, and it made a good place to leave my car. There were no other cars. I started pedaling just before 10 o'clock and went back up Lower Landing Road to route 12, Main Street, and rode north past the beautiful old homes that line the broad common. North of town, I turned left onto route 11, rode by the entrance to the Fort at Number Four, and crossed the Cheshire Bridge to Vermont.

The three mile long bike path began just beyond the bridge, and by a quarter past ten I was riding on it. It started on the north side of routes 5 and 11, but it quickly crossed the highway and passed under route 91. From there, I crossed route 5 and then rode under the route 11 bridge over the Black River. Next, the path joined an auto road, which had little traffic, for a short distance along the north shore of the river to the Paddock Bridge, which is closed to motorized traffic. On the far side of the bridge was a lovely bench and lookout with a view up the river to the falls just before the center of Springfield. There were even flowers, planted by a local club. From there, the path followed along the river for about a mile and a half, ending just before downtown. I met a number of people riding and walking along the path, but it wasn't crowded, not on a weekday. There were other benches, including one right above the impressive falls.

I stopped at the trailhead and then pedaled back to route 5, stopping for a short break at a convenience store at the junction. As I took my break, I thought about how people used to be able to take the trolley from the middle of Springfield into Charlestown. No doubt there were many people who went to work that way every day. Sometimes I long for the public transportation that used to be. From the store, I took route 5 south toward Bellows Falls.

The first couple of miles on the highway were very pleasant. There was little traffic; the road was level, and I had some good views of the Connecticut. When I reached a point just across from the boat landing where I had left my car in Charlestown, the first of three hill climbs made me work hard. The second hill was just before the junction with route 103, and the last was as I came into the town.

At the first bridge in Bellows Falls, I crossed the river again and pedaled through North Walpole on route 12. Between there and Charlestown, the road was close to the river, and I had it in sight for nearly the whole eight miles back to the boat landing. There was, however, a very narrow shoulder to ride, and the traffic was many times heavier than it had been on route 5 in Vermont.

I was back in Charlestown, pedaling down Lower Landing Road to the park, at one o'clock. A pickup was just leaving as I pulled in, and there was one other car parked in the lot. It must be a lot busier on weekends and evenings. Although the Toonerville Trail was the best part of my ride, all of it was good, even the three tough hills on the way to Bellows Falls.

June 2007

97
Cycling Around Mount Monadnock

By making use of two unpaved roads and several paved ones, I pedaled around the base of Mt. Monadnock, passing by all of the public trails that lead to the summit. Except for a few sections, it was a relatively easy twenty mile ride, but I used my hybrid bike rather than my road bike for its wider tires. If I do it again, I'll use my mountain bike.

I made my ride on a beautiful day in early July, and there were plenty of people hiking, but I didn't see another cyclist until I was more than halfway around the mountain. My plan was to park in the lot for the Gilson Pond area, just off Dublin Road, but it was closed for construction of the new camping area, so I decided to start my ride from the state park's headquarters. There was a line of cars at the toll booth when I arrived just after ten that morning. I had to wait for a few minutes, but since I am a certified New Hampshire codger, I didn't have to pay the fee.

By 10:15, I was on my bike, coasting back down the entrance road. I wanted to do the most difficult portions first, so I began a clockwise circumnavigation of the mountain by turning right onto Dublin Road. The first part of my ride took me by the Ark and the Shattuck Golf Club, and then I turned right again onto Mountain Road, route 124.

The few miles on that road included several steep but short hills and a bit of traffic, but it also took me by many impressive homes, several of which looked like they may have once been inns or hotels. I had a beautiful view as I pedaled around the curve by the Grand View Inn and Resort. Just beyond that, I reached the Old Toll Road Trail parking area. There were many cars parked in the lot, and it is probably the second most popular starting point.

MOUNT MONADNOCK FROM ROUTE 124

Next, I had a long, curving downhill ride to Perkins Pond. The road divides the pond, and I stopped for a few minutes to enjoy the view on both sides. There was a single boat on the left or southern half of the pond, and several houses stood on the shore. The mountain loomed over the other side of the pond, and in the very clear air the rocky summit appeared much closer than it was. Just past the pond, I had another steep but short climb to the junction with the first unpaved road, Shaker Farm Road South. It was ten minutes past eleven when I got there, seven miles into my ride.

There are only a few houses on that road, and the Marlborough Trail begins a quarter mile or so beyond the last one. The road is not plowed in winter beyond the last house. There were eight cars parked in the small lot near the trailhead, which made it nearly full.

I had driven, at one time or another, all of the route to that point. I was pretty certain that Shaker Farm Road would bring me to Old Troy Road, which I knew would take me by the Dublin Trail, but I had never tried it. The road quickly became narrow and went downhill. It was very eroded in spots, perhaps because of the April nor'easter, and I had to walk my bike for a bit. It was the stretch that made me wish for my mountain bike. There were no houses for a while, but after a mile or so the road improved, and I rode by what might have been the eponymous Shaker Farm. Right after, I reached the intersection of Shaker Farm Road North and Old Troy Road. There was a sign on a telephone pole indicating the Dublin Trail was two miles ahead.

There was a steady, but not difficult, grade up Old Troy Road, and it took me through a mature looking mixed forest. It was a very nice section of the trip, and there was no traffic. At noon, I reached the new parking lot for the Dublin Trail, which is in the process of having its trailhead moved west to avoid a lumber operation. The lot was large and had a porta-potty, but it was empty. However, the old, small, lot was full of cars when I passed it. I wondered why people out for a hike would prefer to avoid the nicer, more convenient new lot just to make their hike a third of a mile shorter.

I continued on Old Troy Road, passing a large horse farm, and reached the Dublin Golf Club and paved Old Marlborough Road at 12:15. I turned right yet again and rode east. It was on that section of road that I saw another cyclist, evidently heading back from the lake. Soon the Old Marlborough Road became Lake Road, and the waters of Dublin Lake were on my left. I passed the entrance to the Pumpelly Trail and reached route 101 at twelve-thirty. I had less than a third of the trip remaining.

After just a few yards on route 101, I turned onto Upper Jaffrey Road and began the easy, mostly downhill, last portion of the tour. It took me past Thorndike Pond, where I stopped to enjoy the view over the water and up to the ridge line that the Pumpelly Trail follows. Just after that, I pedaled by the Gilson Pond parking lot, and at one o'clock I was back on the entrance road to Monadnock State Park. There were still a few cars waiting at the toll booth.

July 2007

98
Five Town Tour
Peterborough, Hancock, Dublin, NH

A rough circle passing through the centers of five Monadnock towns - and along the edge of a sixth - makes a sometimes difficult and completely beautiful bicycle tour of over thirty miles. The five towns are Peterborough, Greenfield, Bennington, Hancock, and Dublin. I begin the ride on Concord Street, near my home in Peterborough, but the center of any of the five towns, including the park in Peterborough, would make a good place to start and end the tour.

I pedaled my road bike around the loop on a sunny day near the end of July, starting just before nine that morning and finishing around one, with a couple of morning breaks and a nice lunch included. Despite the easy pace, the many hills on the trip had me pretty tired by the end.

The beginning was easy enough, I pedaled north on Concord Street for just over a mile to the three-way intersection just before the bridge in north Peterborough. There, I took the Greenfield Road, route 136, and rode through the rolling countryside for about five more miles to the junction with Forest Road, close by the entrance to Greenfield State Park. I stayed on 136, crossed the railroad tracks, which can be slippery, and rode by the new elementary school into the center of town. I turned left onto route 31 and headed toward Bennington.

Almost immediately, I passed the sign for the Crotched Mountain Rehabilitation Center and then I was riding through more countryside with only scattered houses. There were a few minor climbs in the next few miles, but not long after I passed the

Bennington town line it was all downhill into the center of the third town on my trip. I stopped at the neat little country store for a cold drink and sat on the store's porch to drink it. To get to the next town, Hancock, it would have been more direct to stay on route 31 to its intersection with route 202, but instead I followed Antrim Road, which took me by several fine old houses along the river and then by Alberto's Restaurant and the big paper mill, a real scenic route.

I turned left onto route 202 and rode south to the junction with route 137, Pierce Hill Road. The next stretch included a fairly long climb up to the center of Hancock and lots more countryside. I passed the lovely fountain, rising from a flower-circled pool, and turned right onto Hancock's Main Street. I rode through what is perhaps the most picture-perfect New England town center and stopped for another short break on one of the tables overlooking the town beach on Norway Pond. From there, I took route 137, Bond's Corner Road, and began the toughest part of my ride.

It began with a steep, curving downhill, but soon I was pedaling the first of a series of climbs on the road to Dublin. Fortunately, there were easy stretches as well, but I had to pause for a rest at the top of one of the longer hills. Along the way to Bond's Corner and route 101, I rode through a portion of the eastern edge of Harrisville, hardly enough to count it as a sixth town.

When I reached route 101, I turned right and began the last tough climb of the day toward the center of Dublin. I didn't go all the way up to the flag pole, however, but stopped at the Dublin General Store for lunch. It was just past eleven thirty, and a line was beginning to form at the deli section. I ordered a grinder and sat at one of the tables on the back porch to eat it. It was well worth that last climb.

The rest of the ride back to Peterborough was mostly downhill or level. I left route 101 for the old Peterborough/Dublin Road, which took me to Union Street. Riding along the old road, it was hard to believe it used to be route 101, but I can remember when it was. I rode down Union Street, past the new "Little Stonehenge" at Teixeira Park in West Peterborough, to Main Street and then back home on Concord Street.

August 2007

Part Four
Observing

99
Nuts about Squirrels

I'm very fond of squirrels. Perhaps it's because gray squirrels were the first wild animals I became acquainted with as a child. Perhaps it's because they are so acrobatic, energetic, clever and cute. Perhaps it's because they are ubiquitous. Whatever the reasons, I like to watch squirrels. I'm far from alone in this attitude; most people feel the same. Even Sponge Bob is fond of a squirrel.

On the other hand, some people are at war with squirrels.The furry beasts do get into bird feeders, and nobody wants squirrels in the attic. I've had skirmishes with squirrels, trying to keep them away from my bird feeders. I had to get a baffle; then I had to move the post away from some bushes; finally, I had to cut some of the branches from the bushes so that the squirrels wouldn't jump from them to the feeders. I won that battle, but the squirrels still look longingly at the feeders, After heavy rains they even get to reach the feeders since the branches are bent over and some become good launching pads. I accept that as amusement.

It is fun to watch a gray squirrel attempting to climb a feeder post and defeat any obstacle in the way. Many people erect squirrel feeders that require the animals to perform acrobatics to get to an ear of corn or some other treat. I imagine the squirrels may feel a bit perturbed with us for making them earn their dinner that way, but I'm sure being entertainment is better than being a target.

The gray squirrel is an animal that has adapted very well to living with people. However, there are still plenty in the woods. In fact, squirrels remain one of the favorite game animals in the eastern United States. Our history is full of stories of the expertise of squirrel hunters. Some of them claimed they could "bark" squirrels out of trees without putting a hole in their fur by striking the branch a squirrel was on close enough to knock the squirrel onto the ground.

I'm sure the bushy rodents didn't move into our cities and towns to avoid being hunted, but that is one of the advantages they enjoy by being among us. They do have to contend with cats, dogs, and boys with BB guns. They also have to watch for cars. We've all seen many squirrels crossing roads and highways in front of us; their bodies and tails making a series of silver arcs that seem to chase one another. We've all also seen many examples of squirrels that didn't make it; their bodies for once and forever still. The dangers I just mentioned show that life close to people isn't carefree for the gray squirrel, but it's probably safer than the wild.

You can tell town squirrels feel pretty safe around people by their attitude. Yes, I believe squirrels have attitudes. I know when I make threatening gestures and even shout at the gray squirrel on my bird feeder it doesn't faze him a bit. He knows I'm not a threat as long as there is the patio door between us. Even when I open it, he shows no panic. To get him to run I have to charge out as if I really mean business. I'm sure a woods squirrel is a great deal more careful with a hunter.

The ability to gauge potential danger is one of the behaviors that show the gray squirrel is smart. It's ability to adapt to different environments is another. Their intelligence, athleticism and beauty make gray squirrels impressive animals. It's no wonder so many of us admire them.

I've been writing about gray squirrels, but they aren't the only kind of squirrel in our region. We also have red squirrels, flying squirrels, and chipmunks. I'm nuts about them, too, but they'll have to wait for another time.

November 2002

100
Frost on Leaves

It's hard to escape leaves in autumn. First they change colors and become a tourist attraction, and then they fall all over our lawns and driveways. For many of us, being outdoors in November means raking leaves. We spend whole days raking them up and disposing of them. There's a great deal of energy spent on that activity around here every year. And no matter how well we rake them up now, there are always more to be raked up in spring when the snow melts.

There's an urgency to raking because we all know snow and ice follow the leaves onto our properties. Cold rain followed by frost on fallen leaves causes conditions as slippery as ice, and once a real snow cover accumulates, it's too late for raking.

So, after the lovely colors and first rustling fall of crisp leaves, our attitude toward the deciduous debris may become if not hostile, then resolute.

This darker viewpoint was well expressed by Robert Frost in his poem, "A Leaf Treader."

All summer long they were overhead, more lifted up than I.
To come to their final place in earth they had to pass me by.
All summer long I thought I heard them threatening under their breath.
And when they came it seemed with a will to carry me with them to death.

Frost, of course, is reminding us of the temporary nature of all life, but he certainly put a spin on the usual autumn sentiment. In another poem, "Bereft," he uses leaves to create a startling and sinister image: "Out in the porch's sagging floor/ Leaves got up in a coil and hissed,/ Blindly struck at my knee and missed."

The autumn leaves weren't the only ones Frost wrote about. In "Nothing Gold Can Stay," the new leaves of spring are the subject.

Nature's first green is gold,
Her hardest hue to hold.
Her early leaf's a flower;
But only so an hour.
Then leaf subsides to leaf.
So Eden sank to grief,
So dawn goes down to day.
Nothing gold can stay.

Once again, there is the idea of the temporary nature of life. This time we might find ourselves thinking about how quickly youth is gone.

Well, as you can see, thinking about leaves in November can lead to some heavy thoughts. However, there are really many bright features of this month. For instance, without all the leaves you can see into the woods much easier. It's nice to see the stark loveliness of the trunks and limbs. Even the chill in the air is invigorating. The first snows often come in November, as they have this year, and bring a fresh beauty and the promise of winter outdoor activities. For the sports enthusiasts there is football, and for the hunters, deer season. Near the end of the month, when the days are really short, there is Thanksgiving, perhaps the warmest of our holidays.

I'll leave on that thought and get back to raking.

November 2002

101
Coping with Winter

Our current winter with its snow and cold has provided well for outdoor activities, but it has also made it harder to enjoy them As endless warnings on radio and TV have told us, even being outside for a few minutes in severe cold and high winds can be very dangerous. That means being outside for hours at a time really requires preparation.

By now all of us have learned to layer our clothing and cover as much of our flesh as possible when the wind chill factor is high. Most of us know that our extremities are especially important to keep warm, and we wear warm hats, gloves and footgear. We are also fortunate to have so many good choices of clothing. There are many fabrics that are both warm and lightweight; some also dry rapidly or even wick away moisture. Moisture is a real problem in keeping warm, and not just moisture from falling rain. Even in very cold weather heavy exercise such as snowshoeing or running causes perspiration, and when clothes become wet they give up their insulation value. That is especially true of down-filled clothing. Oddly enough, one of the very oldest fabrics, wool, is one of the best for being light and for retaining its warmth when wet. In fact, there are now new forms of wool clothing that retain the old values of wool and are both itch-proof and washable.

Even with all the advantages of modern gear, most of us spend more time indoors in the winter than during warm weather. We den up, just as many of our animal neighbors do. Some of them spend the whole winter in hibernation; others, gray squirrels for example, make appearances from time to time when the weather allows. There are also animals that share our houses for the winter.

FROZEN TREES ON MOUNT MONADNOCK

Mice invade and can be heard frolicking in our attics and walls. In the last few years we have noticed lady bugs clinging to our curtains, waiting for spring. Of course, some animals – and some people- avoid winter all together and head for Florida.

Those of us who remain here in the Monadnock Region and find ourselves spending more time than usual inside can use some of that time to plan activities for better weather, repair our gear, study trail guides, and read good books I have just read a great book that arrived at the Peterborough Library, appropriately, in early January. *Winter World*, by Bernd Heinrich, is all about how animals survive the winter. Heinrich is a professor at the University of Vermont, but he spends much of his time at a cabin in western Maine. Actually, he evidently spends a great deal of time outside his cabin in Maine. He is clearly fascinated with animal behavior, and he writes very well. His book includes descriptions of how animals from bears to wasps cope with the hardships of winter. Some of their practices are familiar to us in a general way, but the details Heinrich provides are sometimes startling He points out that even biologists remain puzzled by just how some animals survive. His observations on the behavior of the tiny kinglets, birds smaller than chickadees, tell us of the importance of insulation. He speculates as to how muskrats pass the winter in their lodges and suggests their dispositions must be very placid. He describes air-breathing turtles that spend the whole winter at the bottom of streams or ponds, and he writes of frogs that live with half their body liquids frozen.

Some of the most interesting parts of *Winter World* deal with the animals that remain active and outside all winter. The little kinglet, for example, has to find enough food to maintain a body temperature higher than ours. Heinrich wonders how it survives the long nights without eating. Flying squirrels do not put on extra fat – it would hinder their gliding, and they evidently don't always construct real nests as their gray cousins do although they sometimes construct very fine ones. They are also most active at night when it is coldest. Heinrich found that they sometimes congregate in hollow stumps or tree cavities, huddling together for warmth. He also writes about the predators that must learn to counter the measures taken by their prey. Weasles turn white for camouflage and crawl into the dens of hibernating chipmunks for dinner. Owls listen for the faint sounds of mice in their tunnels beneath the snow and pounce feet first, collapsing the snow around the rodents. The ways animals cope with winter are amazing, but the most important thing is that they have learned to endure, to be incredibly tough.

Reading a book like *Winter World* is one good way for us to cope with winter. It also makes us realize how easy we have it compared to our wild neighbors. It might even make us a bit more tolerant of mice in the woodwork.

January 2003

102
A Scent of Spring

February is really the middle of winter, and spring can seem very far away. Perhaps that is why the month begins with Groundhog Day, for we all want to know that spring is coming, and the sooner the better. The particular groundhog that gets the attention is Punxsutawney Phil, who appears right on schedule the second day of every February in the Pennsylvania town of the same name. Phil is famous, and his human handlers make sure he's right on time for the crowd and the cameras every year.

Another animal, not a rodent but a member of the weasel family, also appears this month, but he waits for a warmer night nearer the end of the month. That animal is the skunk, and when he awakes it is not due to the urging of keepers. He shows up due to urges of his own, for it is breeding time for skunks. That makes him a more reliable predictor than the groundhog, for the baby skunks are timed to be delivered when spring truly arrives in April.

This means you can expect to catch a whiff of the familiar skunk calling card sometime soon. You might even see one of the eager males wandering in search of a female, much like Pierre LePue in the old cartoons. Years ago I worked with a man who lived in an old house in Rindge. The lower floor of the house had originally been a workshop, and there was only a crawlspace under it. Every year, despite my friend's best efforts, a number of skunks managed to use the crawlspace for their winter den. Near the end of every February, he would come to work redolent of skunk and very fed up with their behavior. He said it was like living above the skunk Olympics.

A few years ago, I had a skunk in my barn, but it was in the summer. I didn't even know it was there until I noticed my cat seemed to be making a mess with his food dish. Then I noticed the cat wasn't even going into the barn. I investigated and discovered a very young skunk hiding behind some boxes. I used the water hose to drive him out of the barn and into the woods. He was so concerned with fleeing that he hardly sprayed at all.

Actually, as my experience showed, skunks are usually quite well-behaved. For example, many of them live in the state park where I worked as a night watchman last summer. I would see them late at night, wandering around occupied campsites in search of food, and I know campers would often encounter them, but they very seldom made a fuss.

Skunks don't have to spray often because their reputation is enough to discourage most enemies. Wild animals, pets, and people all learn to avoid them, and their vivid black and white coloring makes them easy to identify. They are proof that weapons don't have to be lethal to be effective. The federal government has even taken guidance from the skunk and developed a very potent chemical weapon to control riots with its odor. It's too bad we couldn't find a way to substitute stink bombs for nuclear warheads.

Even the skunk, however, is not without enemies. A very hungry fisher might settle for a skunk dinner, and the great horned owl regularly dines on them. That's one of the reasons so many skunks live so closely with us. They also like to forage for grubs on our lawns and dig in our trash for scraps. We see them in summer, often leisurely crossing the road or digging on our lawns. Usually they do not feel the need to employ their defenses. Unless there is a "skunk Olympics" under your house, you probably get along with your striped neighbors pretty well, too.

So, if you catch the scent of skunk on one of the warmer evenings this month, you can take it as a sign that spring is on its way. You can also be glad that it's not too warm to keep the windows closed.

February 2003

103
Yikes, Snake!

One recent afternoon my daughter, Ginny, who lives just up the street, called and asked me to get rid of a snake in her yard. When I got to her place, she and two of my grandchildren, Sam and Greta, were peering out a first floor window and pointing at the flowers along the foundation. I looked down and saw a two-foot, brown garden snake stretched out among the hostas. It was harmless, beneficial really, but my daughter, like so many people, is terrified of snakes, so I picked up the little fellow and transplanted him in the nearby woods.

It's a good thing snakes don't realize the power they hold over people. If a few of them got together, they could take over whole neighborhoods just by showing up at dinner. Most humans would be happy to provide them with an unlimited supply of bugs and vermin just as long as they promised to stay out of sight. Of course, that's just about what does happen, because there are many more unseen snakes than the ones we notice.

Some snakes are dangerous, and there are probably a few rattlesnakes in our region. I remember reading about a lady in Hooksett who was bitten by a rattler while mowing her lawn a few years ago, but there are so few of them in our state that scientists fear for their survival. What's remarkable about rattlers is that even where there are many of them, people seldom see them. If you should meet up with one, leave it alone. A common way people sometimes do get bitten by snakes is foolishly handling them. Even a non-venomous snake can give a nasty bite as can any animal with teeth, including chipmunks and people. The main thing to remember is that here in the Monadnock region, nearly all snakes are harmless.

The fear most people have of snakes is no doubt a defensive adaptation of long standing, and even those of us who aren't terrified of snakes have to admit they do get our attention when they appear. They have a talent for startling us, even when we see them in places where we expect them. In her poem, "The Snake," Emily Dickinson wrote "His notice sudden is." In the last stanza of her poem, Dickinson confesses to feeling as many people do upon encountering a snake:

But never met this fellow,
Attended or alone,
Without a tighter breathing,
And zero at the bone.

I felt a bit of that chill last week when I was fishing in the Contoocook from one of the railroad bridge abutments along the pathway. A large water snake swam up next to me and started to climb up on the concrete with me. I'm sure he would have made a considerate guest, but my reaction was to splash the water with my rod. That was when he noticed me, and having much more reason to fear my company than I his, he swam away.

When I consider what a snake's life must be like, I have to feel more pity than fear. Imagine being just one long tube with no limbs at all. If you have ever been in a pie-eating contest, you know how hard it is to eat without using your hands. For a snake, life is a perpetual pie-eating contest, but the "pies" have legs or wings and don't sit still. They often bite back as well. There are plenty of creatures that like to make meals of snakes including hawks and cats. Finally, there are all the people whose first reaction upon seeing a snake is to pick up a rock and bash it.

Come to think of it, maybe a snake would be a good participant in a pie-eating contest. This summer, you might want to enter an anaconda in the pie-eating contest at the local fair. He would probably win just by showing up because all the other contestants would make a hasty exit I don't think he would get any hugs for winning, either.

June 2003

104
Late Summer Color

Mid-way through September, people in New England begin to speculate about how good the "color" will be this year. They mean, of course, the color of the fall foliage. The autumn leaves are an important part of the season. Everyone enjoys the bright display of red and gold, and it helps to dispel the gloom that comes with the waning sunlight and increasingly cold temperatures.The foliage is also an important source of revenue, especially for Vermont and New Hampshire. It's not hard to understand why such a source of both beauty and income receives so much attention.

Hardly any notice is given another wave of color that arrives a little earlier in the year. From late August until the first frosts, the last flowers of summer brighten the sun dried fields and roadsides. Goldenrod and asters are everywhere. There are billows of white and lavender asters along our roads, and whole fields of goldenrod echo the dandelions of spring. They are very democratic blooms: they are more impressive in the aggregate than individually. A single aster in a vase would be out of place.

There are other, less conspicuous flowers in late summer. On a recent walk near my house, I decided to look more closely at some of the small flowers growing along the road and on the edges of some lawns. There were some dandelion-sized yellow flowers on tall stems on the lawns, and I found one small bush with odd-shaped little yellow flowers. I also found a small bush near a pond that had tiny orange flowers with a trumpet shape. When I was back home, I used a field guide to identify them. I had seen hawkweed, birdsfoot trefoil, and spotted touch-me-not. The touch-me-nots were the orange flowers. They were particularly complex and delicate.

I enjoyed examining and identifying the flowers I found on my walk. As I get older, I pay more attention to the little things in nature, including the flowers. I can understand, now, why so many nineteenth century writers were so happy to spend time doing what they called "botanizing." The flowers are worth the attention.

If you stop to admire these late summer flowers, you might notice – as I did – that other creatures are attracted to them. Bees and other insects swarm around the asters and goldenrod. (They don't visit the dull colored ragweed whose airborne pollen plagues so many.) That is another feature of the late summer flowers that I admire: they are still in business. Their colors are a part of life, a welcome, even a seduction. The colors of the autumn leaves are a sign of the death of the year. They are a farewell, and each bright leaf will soon lose its grip and fall to the earth. The trees themselves are not dying, but they are cutting back, getting ready for a sort of hibernation. In a way, the trees' method of coping with winter is one of resignation; the flowers', one of hope. We can, of course, see the foliage as a celebration of the summer that has just ended and a promise of the spring to come, but no figurative thinking is required to understand the living colors of the flowers.

September 2003

105
Franklin Pierce Geese

Just about anyone in the Monadnock region could tell you that the Franklin Pierce College athletic teams are known as the Ravens, but if you were to visit the campus, you might conclude they would be more appropriately called the Geese. Canadian geese are very much in evidence on the lovely campus overlooking Pearly Pond, but ravens, if any are around, must be sought in the wooded hills nearby.

I have a part time job at the college, and I have grown very used to seeing geese on the lawns and walkways of the college. When I walk from my car to my post just before eight every morning, the only living things I see more of than geese are the freshmen walking slowly to class with their heads down. The geese, being wide awake, neatly dressed, and already hard at work, are easily distinguished from the freshmen at that early hour.

There is, of course, a good reason for the freshmen to keep their heads down as they walk to their classes; they are watching their steps. One area in which the geese are deficient is sanitation. They spread their waste liberally on both the lawns and the walkways. That is really no laughing matter, as any groundskeeper at the college and at many golf courses will agree.

Over the last decade or so, we have all become aware that many geese have become nearly year-round inhabitants of our region. At first they were a novelty, but now they have become nearly as common as pigeons. Despite their ubiquity, I had never looked at them as closely as I have at the college. They are very large birds up close, and I often think that if our country were in a depression like the Great Depression of the thirties, the geese would quickly disappear.

I am fascinated not only by their size but also by their attire. They really do have a neat appearance, and their gray, black and white coats would be suitable for cadets at a military academy. Their webbed feet are so black and rubbery that they look artificial, like boots purchased in large lots from a military supply house.

Sometimes I have to step around a goose or two on the walkway. I know that even barnyard geese can be aggressive and that those bills can give a painful nip, so I give them a wide berth. (I was cycling past a farm in southern Vermont once, and a goose chased me for a not inconsiderable distance, flapping its wings and offering to do me great damage.) One morning, when I stopped to look at one of those walkway geese, it returned my stare and opened its mouth wide. I expected a great hiss, but the goose only stuck its purple tongue out in silent reproach.

As you can gather, geese are the prominent bird at FPC. Nonetheless, I hope to see or at least hear a raven at the college, perhaps when I'm walking on one of the trails. They are, after all, birds of more discretion. However, even if there are no ravens croaking from the trees on campus, I don't expect to hear anyone cheering "Go, Geese!" at Crystal Field.

November 2003

106
The Man on the Mountain

Last year many people were saddened by the news that the Old Man of the Mountain was no more. The great stone profile, which has been the symbol of New Hampshire for so long, had fallen. The story was covered world wide, and millions of people who had viewed the Old Man in Franconia Notch felt a loss.

Some years earlier, the Monadnock Region lost another old man of the mountain: Roy Finan, who was for over forty years the fire lookout at the summit of Pack Monadnock Mountain in Peterborough. The old fire tower sat in the middle of Miller State Park, and thousands of visitors to the park thought of Roy as being as important to their visit as the view. For most visitors, a climb to the top of the tower and a visit with Roy was essential.

When he wasn't looking for fires or answering the questions of visitors, Roy spent some of his time carving handsome eagles from blocks of wood. His craftsmanship was fine, and no one would ever have suspected that the carvings were done one-handed.

Roy lost his left arm in an industrial accident as a young man, but he didn't allow his loss to keep him from doing things he loved. In addition to the woodcarving, he was an expert mechanic, carpenter and outdoorsman. For years he was the man who set off the fireworks on the Fourth of July in his hometown, Hancock. Although it was certainly admirable that Roy was able to do so much on his own, the thing I remember as most admirable about him is that despite having only one hand, he was always willing to lend it to someone in need

I learned that the first time I met him. It was my first day as the manager of Miller State Park, a cold April morning, and I was trying unsuccessfully to pry off the boards that had been nailed over the door to the little park building at the summit. I hadn't any tools with me, and I was about to give up and go home for some when a rugged featured, ginger-haired older man dressed in a khaki and green uniform appeared and said, "Let me give you a hand."

The offered hand was large and strong and had in its grip a pry bar. In a moment the heavy boards were removed and the door was free. It was only then that I noticed the man had only the one hand. We introduced ourselves, and for over a dozen summers we worked together on the mountain. During that time he gave me a hand many times, and I saw him do the same for many others.

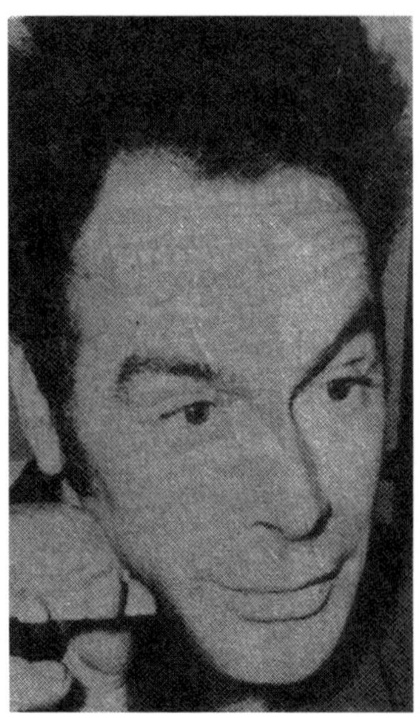

ROY FINAN

One of the ways he often helped visitors to the park was with their cars. Hardly a week would go by without someone having car trouble. Overheating was a common problem; fan belts would break, and people would lock themselves out of their cars. Roy would often be the person who came to the rescue. Once I saw him crawl under a bus – which should not have made the trip to the top at all – and fix something that allowed the driver to get the unloaded vehicle back to the highway.

Roy also extended that helping hand to the smaller creatures that frequented the mountain. He began every day by putting out food for the chipmunks, and they would be waiting nearby for him. From a wildlife manager's point of view, it was probably not a good thing to do, and the chippies did fight amongst themselves over the food. However, I know Roy's only motive was to help them. I often saw him feeding the little animals by hand, and chipmunks frequently sat contentedly in his huge paw and stored sunflower seed in their cheeks. I know that he also fed a family of raccoons at his home in Hancock, and I remember him telling me how to pet a porcupine on its nose.

Roy retired in the early 1980's and died soon after. The tower was manned for another year or so, but it wasn't the same. Finally, the tower was abandoned, and the cab at the top was removed. Part of the structure is still standing in the center of the parking lot at the top of the mountain, dwarfed by other towers added in recent years. The little cabin that stood just beneath the summit and was used by Roy in cold and wet weather is gone as well – moved to Greenfield. There is no longer a fire lookout on the mountain.

However, whenever I visit the summit, I can still envision the familiar cab at the top of the tower, and I like to think Roy's spirit still looks out over the hills of the Monadnock Region.

March 2004

Note: A new fire tower on Pack Monadnock has replaced the one from Roy's day.

107
Heron Morning

The last Saturday in June began with clouds and the threat of showers. The paper arrives early on Saturday, and I looked at it before setting out on a run. The front page was dominated by a color photo of four nesting herons in Stoddard. It was quite a picture, and it reminded me of the six herons I had seen in early spring on one of the first lakes to thaw. Usually I see them one at a time, and although it's not at all unusual to see them, they always make an impression.

I started running a few minutes after reading the paper. It wasn't raining as I left town and ran north along the river, but it was getting darker, and I knew I would get at least a little wet. Sure enough, as I approached the bridge at the junction of routes 202 and 136, a few raindrops began to fall. It wasn't cold, though, and a light rain in warm weather is fine for running.

Whenever I cross that bridge over the Contoocook, I always look down at the water. I often see people fishing, and once I saw an Osprey perched on one of the rocks in the shallow water below the dam that is just south of the bridge. Sometimes I see a heron fishing there, and one was just below me as I stopped on the bridge for a look. Usually when I stop to look at one of the huge birds from that vantage point, it quickly notices me and takes off in a lumbering flight upriver. I'm sure the one I saw that day noticed me as soon as I appeared, but he decided to ignore me for a while That was because he was in the midst of subduing a very large fish. I think it was a trout, and it was a good twelve inches long. It was the biggest fish I had ever seen caught there by man or beast.

The bird was standing on the largest rock in the pool below the dam, and he had the fish pinned against it with his beak. He was trying to get just the right grip on the fish, I guessed. In a few seconds he was satisfied, and he stretched out his long neck and beak. Herons look large in their normal postures, but when this one had his beak and neck in one perpendicular line above his body, he appeared nearly six feet tall from my point of view. At the very apex of this sight was the fish, held headfirst in the beak. Then the bird opened his mouth a bit, and the fish slid downward and out of sight into the bird.

As soon as his meal was safely stored in his insides, the bird took to the air. He wasn't bothered enough by being watched by one old man in shorts to abandon his catch, but he didn't appreciate the audience enough to stay around. I wondered what it felt like to take off with the big fish, probably still alive, on board.

I began running again and crossed the bridge. By that time it was raining pretty hard, but I was comfortable and bemused by what I had witnessed. A heron catching a fish is really no more out of the ordinary than a robin catching a worm, but I felt lucky to have seen it. Nature provides us little gifts, if only we are there to see.

Later that day, I took my fishing rod, parked by that same dam, and tried to imitate the heron. I didn't catch a thing.

July 2004

108
Year of the Locust

The media have given much attention this spring to the seventeen year cicadas, which are making their periodical appearance in much of the eastern United States. Cicadas don't live in central New England, however, so we won't be seeing them or listening to their astoundingly loud summer songs.

Although I have been living in New England since Uncle Sam sent me to Fort Devens in 1960, I grew up in south central Pennsylvania, and I can remember listening to the cicadas - not just the seventeen year variety, but also the ones that made more frequent appearances. Their drawn-out, buzzing sound was a background noise for summer afternoons. The creatures themselves were seldom seen, but their music was as familiar a part of the season as mosquitoes, baseball and thunderstorms. The seventeen year cicadas were really special, though, and the articles I have been reading about them have made me think back to when I was a witness to one of their years.

It wasn't 1987. President Reagan was in office and the cold war was nearing an end. The most popular song that year was Whitney Houston's "I Wanna Dance with Somebody." The Twins beat the Cardinals in the World Series that year, and gas was about $1.10 a gallon. It wasn't 1970, when the president was Nixon, the war in Vietnam was raging, and hippy communes were popping up in the Monadnock region. The biggest hit that year was "Bridge Over Troubled Waters" by Simon and Garfunkle. The Orioles defeated the Reds in the series, and gas was only thirty-five cents a gallon. It was 1953. Eisenhower was in the White House; the Korean War had just ended, and the Hit Parade's top ten songs of the week didn't

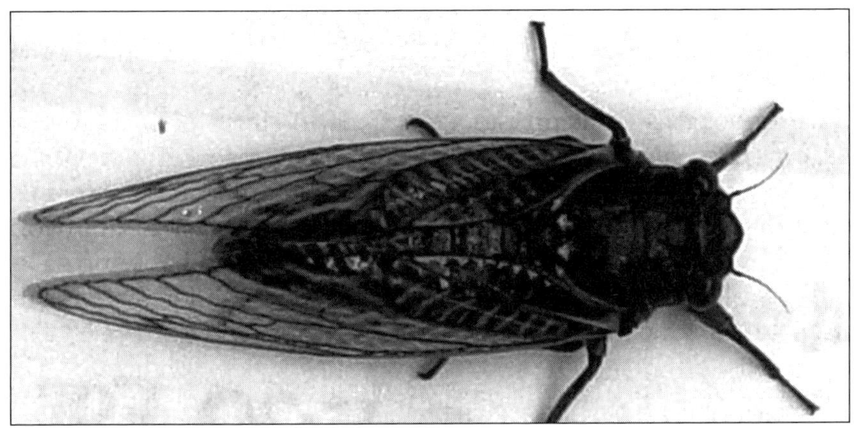

CICADA

include rock and roll. The top hit that year was "Don't Let the Stars Get in Your Eyes" by Perry Como. Five dollars would fill your gas tank, and the Yankees were winners over their cross town rivals, the Brooklyn Dodgers, in the series. I had my twelfth birthday that summer.

That was the only cicada year that I remember. However, we didn't call them cicadas in central Pennsylvania. They were the seventeen year locust. The name always made me think of one of the plagues on Egypt, but they were hardly that. What I remember, however vaguely, is that their chrysalises, or "shells" as we called them, littered the ground. I don't remember seeing a live locust, but I know I saw thousands of the yellow-brown, transparent chrysalises. It seemed like, upon arriving on the bright surface of the world after living so many years underground, the insects felt the need to strip for the beach. We might not have seen many of the living cicada, but we certainly heard them. I'm sure people who live in that part of the East are getting tired of listening to them this summer.

The noise of the cicadas might be a real pain, but seventeen years between visits is a long time - plenty of time to recover from the racket. Having to listen to the bugs once in a generation isn't much to complain about. Our summer insects don't make so much noise, but they show up every year. Wouldn't it be great if we had seventeen year black flies or seventeen year mosquitoes? We might find ourselves looking forward to their arrival.

July 2004

109
Crickets

At some point in mid-summer every year, I begin to notice small black bugs leaping across the grass in front of my lawn mower, and I know that the crickets have arrived. It's not that they have been away, exactly, but that they have arrived at that stage of their development where they are recognizably crickets.

By the end of summer there are hundreds, probably thousands, of them living in my back half acre, and the male members of the horde are singing up a storm in their efforts to attract the opposite sex. I try not to run over them with the mower when I'm cutting the grass, but I suppose a man with a mower just serves as another predator along with birds and snakes, helping control the cricket population.

By the end of summer, crickets also begin appearing in the house. Until I did a little research in the Stokes Natural Guide to insects, I thought the crickets in my house had inadvertently found their way inside. Now I've learned that there are house crickets as well as field crickets, and I'm no longer sure the ones I find inside are as domestic as the house mice or field crickets that have lost their way and become trapped under my roof.

Despite my new knowledge, I continue my practice of catching the little fellows in my hands and releasing them outdoors. I try not to damage them in the process, but I know sometimes I have broken a leg or two, and I can't be sure every cricket I return to (or introduce to) the wild will survive.

Sometimes during a early fall evening, my wife will call from the living room: "There's another cricket in here!" and I will abandon

CRICKET

my study and rush into to capture it. It frequently takes several attempts since I am handicapped by kindness from being too aggressive. However, I soon make the capture and one-handedly open the door and deposit the creature outdoors. Often I make two or three catches a night.

I do this partly because there is something about a cricket that makes it impossible to fear or even dislike. It's not just that they don't sting, bite, or secrete smelly substances. Their close cousins, the grasshoppers, aren't really threatening either, but I don't have the same feelings for those hoppers, and they don't come into the house anyway. I'm not alone in this. I've read that in China people keep crickets as pets, and I remember the scene in the movie *The Last Emperor* when the young future emperor is given a cricket in a cage by a kindly older man. Perhaps a character in another movie, on I saw as a very young boy, also helped me think of crickets as amusing. That movie was *Pinocchio*, and the character was, of course, Jiminy Cricket. Who could help but love Jiminy?

Disney's cricket was a real talker, and the crickets in our back yards are noisy too, but not exactly vocal. The males make their familiar sound by scraping one of their front wings over the underside of the other.

We humans associate the resulting music with summer and fall evenings. As the evenings get colder, their songs slow down. The timing of the song of one type of cricket, the snowy tree cricket, can be used to know the temperature. One just has to count the number of chirps in 13 seconds and add 40. Since one would have to be certain it was a snowy tree cricket chirping, it might be better to look at a thermometer.

Crickets that get into a house, whether house or field crickets, can keep singing right into the winter. I remember being told as a child that a cricket singing in the fireplace was good luck. In his poem, "The Grasshopper and the Cricket," Keats depicted the grasshopper as providing some of nature's poetry in the summer and the cricket taking its place in winter:

On a lone winter evening, when the frost
Has wrought a silence, from the stove there shrills
The Cricket's song, in warmth increasing ever,
And seems to one in drowsiness half lost,
The Grasshopper's among some grassy hills.

Maybe that's one reason why we like crickets: faced with the coming of winter's ice and cold, they help us to hold onto the memory of summer.

September 2004

110
Welcome to the Flock

It was just after sunrise on the next to last Sunday in October, and I was out for my daily run. It was cloudy and chilly, and since it was Sunday, there was no traffic on Summer Street as I ran toward the beginning of the Peterborough Pathway. I was approaching the last few houses before the point where the pathway leaves the road and enters the woods next to the river when I noticed a flock of turkeys on a lawn next to the road. I had seen turkeys along Summer Street several times before, but never so many, so close.

I thought they would move away as I drew near them, but the big birds stayed put, even when I ran by within a few feet of the lawn where they were scratching for food. I counted well over a dozen as I passed, but didn't have time to count them all as I ran by. Some of them did turn their heads to look at me, but none of them showed any fear. As I ran by the flock, I imagined they might be speculating about me as well: "Hey, what's that going by? It has crow's feet. Look at those chicken legs and neck! Nice little dewlaps. I don't see any beard. Could be an old buzzard. Nah, it's just a big turkey."

A minute later I was running through the woods along the Contoocook, enjoying the lovely pathway, which was covered with yellow maple leaves. However, I continued to think about the turkeys and how commonplace it has become to see them. I thought about how smart they must be to know how to avoid hunters during not one, but two hunting seasons every year.

As I ran north on the pathway, I passed two walkers headed back toward the center of town. I wondered if the turkeys would move away from twice as many people, moving even slower than

I did. When I reached Hunt Road, I turned around and began the return trip. By then, I had decided there was little chance of seeing the turkeys again that morning.

A mile later, I was quite surprised to see the flock still assembled in nearly the same place. They had just crossed to the opposite side of Summer Street; two were still in the middle of the road as I ran toward them again. This time, I slowed enough to count the entire flock. There were twenty-three birds. When I passed very close to the last turkey to cross the road, he turned to look at me and seemed to be saying, "Well, are you coming?" It was a nice invitation, but I declined, having a flock of my own.

MALE WILD TURKEY

Later, I went to the New Hampshire Fish and Game web site and learned some more about turkeys. I already knew that there were no wild turkeys remaining in our state not long ago, and that there had been a program to bring them back. On the web site, I read that they were successfully reintroduced to New Hampshire in 1975, and there are now over 25,000 of the big birds in our state. The fall hunting season is for archery only, but in the spring shotguns may also be used. The spring season is limited to bearded turkeys, which are mainly males. I noticed the web site also includes information on how to prepare a wild turkey for a meal.

I hope to see those turkeys, or others, again this fall. And, as the end of November nears, I half expect to see members of the flock carrying picket signs reading: Thanksgiving is Unfair to Turkeys!

November 2004

111
Spring Peepers and Friends

When it's fall in the Monadnock Region, we have leaf peepers. They arrive in cars from Boston and New York, and they come to peep at the foliage. The sound many people associate with them is the jingle of cash registers. In spring, we have quite different peepers, and the peeping they do is one of the distinctive sounds of spring in New England. They are tree frogs, which hibernate through the winter and come out peeping in the April warmth.

I heard my first peeper chorus this year during the second week of April. I was running on the Peterborough Pathway, along the Contoocook River, and they were in the trees that border one of the permanent little ponds between the pathway and Summer Street. I don't think I've ever heard just one peeper; they are always in choirs. Even though many sing together, each one is quite loud. For creatures less than two inches long, their volume is spectacular. I heard them from a considerable distance, and as I ran I thought about how the sound of the tiny toads is so familiar a part of the season that after the first time we hear them each year, their song quickly becomes a barely noticed background music. However, it was my first peeper chorus of the year, and I not only noticed but also welcomed it. The sound hushed as I ran past, for they are alert as well as noisy, but it picked up a moment later. The force that drives them to song can't be silenced long by the passing of one old man in sneakers.

I heard the peepers, but I never saw one. Seeing one would have taken patience, stealth, and wading through the pond to one of their trees. I did see a large number of their friends and close relatives, wood frogs. In the same long, shallow pond above which the tree frogs were singing, a great many wood frogs were basking in the warmth of the sun. I noticed a small splash in the water as I trotted along the path, and when I looked at the spot, I saw a medium sized, pinkish -tan frog suspended just below the surface of the water. Its legs were in a wide bow, for stability, I supposed. I noticed one frog and then another and another. Like their little cousins, the wood frogs must have just ended their hibernation, but unlike the tree toads, they were still recharging their batteries. The surface of the pond was dotted with a flotilla of frogs, all equidistant from each other, all in the exact same posture. It looked like a frog Coney Island on a hot August day.

Seeing and hearing those amphibians put a spring in my step for the rest of my run. On the rest of my route I thought about what a miracle every spring is. I also thought about how we long for it when winter gets old and seems to be lasting forever. Then, spring is a wish that can't come soon enough. When it gets here, though, it arrives with such an acceleration of life that we can't keep up. Peepers, birds, leaves, grass, black flies, and flowers all come upon us too fast to be completely appreciated. All we can do is pay attention to one part of the miracle at a time.

April 2005

112
Observations on Pack Monadnock

I have a special fondness for Miller State Park on Pack Monadnock Mountain for several reasons. First, it's beautiful and near my home, so I can visit it often. Second, it's located right on the Wapack Trail, which makes it a great place for hiking. Finally, I worked at the park for over twenty years and can't help identifying with it.

Although the mountain itself remains unchanged, there have been changes to the park in recent years. Two of the most interesting were put into effect over the last year: a fire lookout has returned to the summit and the New Hampshire Audubon Society has developed a Raptor Migration Observatory a short walk from the fire tower.

I had been surprised to see the new cab on top of the old tower on a visit to the mountain top in late summer. Somehow I had missed the news that the state had decided to once again have a manned lookout on Pack Monadnock. The previous cab had been closed back in the eighties and fell into disrepair. Finally, it was taken down and replaced with a massive, ugly radio tower. For the first dozen years that I worked in the park, I often visited with Roy Finan, the longtime lookout, and he taught me the names of all the mountains and hills visible all the way up to Mt. Washington.

When I looked up and saw a new cab, complete with lookout, I immediately climbed up and found myself once more looking out over 360 degrees of rolling countryside, river valleys and mountains. The new lookout, Ernie Kirouac, was just as friendly and helpful as Roy Finan had been. We chatted about how many of the towers had been out of use for a time, and we agreed that it was

HAWK WATCHERS ON PACK MONADNOCK

good they were back in operation. He gave me a pamphlet with information on the sixteen fire towers now in operation. Obviously the state is interested in support for the towers, and the pamphlet described a program called Fire Lookout Tower Quest, which invites visitors to any of the fifteen towers that are open to the public. (One tower, on Croydon Mountain, is on private property.) Once a person has visited five of the towers, he or she can submit a form to the state and receive a colorful patch, certificate and letter of recognition.

That same day, I looked over the new path that leads from the summit parking lot to the new hawk observatory. It was prior to the migration, however, so no one was manning the site. That gave me a good reason to return to the park when the hawk migration was on. Therefore, on a beautiful weekday in late September, I decided to hike up the Marion Davis Trail from the parking lot off route 101 to the summit.

I hadn't been on that trail for a couple of years, but it was so familiar that I recognized almost every step of the way. As I climbed, I was thinking about the number of times I had driven, biked, walked, and even run to the top of the mountain, and I arrived at a total of at least 1600. Of course, most of those climbs were by car, but I have been up and down both the Marion Davis Trail and the section of the Wapack Trail in the park hundreds of times.

When I arrived at the summit, just before 11a.m., I was disappointed to see the tower was not manned that day. However, several cars parked near the newly improved path to the observatory indicated that it was staffed. I walked out to the rocky point and found a group of men and women with binoculars pressed to their eyes, watching for hawks gliding from north to south over the Contoocook Valley. One of them was Brendan Clifford, a representative of the Audubon Society. He told me that it had been a pretty good year for sightings, but since it was the first year that the observatory has been staffed every day, he had no way to compare the numbers with previous years. He had a chart posted which showed the types and numbers of raptors sighted that day as well as the total since the first of September, which was 4,480.

I spent a few minutes speaking with Clifford and one of the other observers, and then I began my walk back to the base of the mountain. On my way down I thought about how nice and useful it was to add the two observatories - the fire lookout and the hawk watch - to the mountain, but I reminded myself that the greater number of observations are made by the thousands of visitors who climb the mountain every year to see whatever they can.

September 2005

113
Recycled Bridges

An interesting side effect of the never ceasing development and expansion of our highways and roads is the conversion of abandoned structures to pedestrian uses. Most successful has been the transforming of railways to trails. Hundreds of miles of old railroads are now multi-use trails, many of them under the auspices of the Rails to Trails Conservancy. However, there are also highway segments no longer used by cars that have been put to use by walkers and bicyclists. In the Monadnock Region, the Otter Brook Falls trail in Keene is a fine example.

Old bridges, large and small, have also been put to new uses. The old route 9 bridge in Chesterfield over the Connecticut River was retrofitted as a pedestrian bridge by the company that built the new one. Another large bridge, over part of the Piscataqua River in Newington, and once part of routes 4 and 16, is now used by fishermen, walkers and cyclists.

There are smaller bridges that have been closed to cars but remain open to pedestrians as well. On an early February morning, I walked from one such bridge in Peterborough to another. I began at the Old Sharon Road bridge over the Contoocook River near the Noone Falls mill buildings. That bridge was closed to cars and trucks several years ago, but it gets quite a bit of use from walkers, cyclists, and anglers. Instead of crossing it, however, I walked south along route 202 toward the newer Sharon Road and another abandoned bridge over the river.

The first half mile of my walk was both scenic and a bit scary. It was scenic because of the broad expanse of the river with its little islands and marsh grasses, but it was a bit scary because of the cars and trucks rushing past just a few feet away. The shoulder was pretty wide, though, and it wouldn't take much to create a walkway connecting Noone Falls with the Sharon Road.

Once I reached that road, I passed the new SDE building, and crossed over the river on another, still in use, bridge. For the next half a mile or so, I had the very full, rushing river on my right. There are only a few buildings along that stretch, and, although there is some traffic, it's a good place to walk. It's a popular fishing spot in spring, too, and there are a few places where cars can be safely parked off the road. Tall pines, oaks and hemlocks border the road for most of the way.

My destination was the old, stone bridge over the river just before the Harris Company's sand pit. It leads from the present Sharon Road to route 202, but many years ago the connecting road was closed. Steel railings block the road from the highway now, and the bridge is closed to all but pedestrian traffic by a mound of earth. The old structure is quite handsome, formed by two arches, but people driving by see mostly the top of the bridge, which looks like just a section of old road.

I walked across the bridge and up the old stretch of road to route 202. The pavement was visible in places, beneath the remaining patches of snow, and it appeared to be crumbling away. A number of footprints showed me that some walkers do use the old bridge and road, perhaps as a short cut to the highway, or even as part of a walking loop from the exercise center or the ball-bearing plant. I know many people use the area for fishing, for the old road runs close to the river.

As I walked back to Noone Falls, I thought what a nice little picnic area could be made of the bridge and the nearby road. Who knows, some day it may happen. Meanwhile, the well-built old bridge isn't going anywhere, and it's worth a visit just as it is.

February 2006

114
Famous Shoes

Famous Shoes is not a discount shoe store but the name of a character in several books by Larry McMurtry, all sequels to his most known work, *Lonesome Dove*. Famous Shoes is a Kickapoo Indian and the best tracker on the Texas frontier. He has an almost supernatural ability to find and interpret the tracks of man and beast, and he is often employed by the Texas Rangers. He is also an eccentric, given to disappearing on trips to far off places in search of relics of the old days.

In a time and place when nearly everyone goes on horseback, Famous Shoes travels by foot. He believes he can see and understand much more with his feet on the ground. It's not only that he is moving at a slower speed, either. In fact, the mounted rangers are always surprised by how he keeps ahead of them and far out of sight most of the time. Even trotting along at a good pace, Famous Shoes is closer to the ground than he would be on the back of a horse, and he is also able to concentrate on what he is seeing more than he would be if part of his attention was on a horse.

The ability to pay more attention to one's surroundings while on foot is just as true today, especially when our usual mode of transportation involves horsepower rather than horses. To a driver, miles fly by in a blur, but to a walker, a single mile is full of details. However, even walkers must be willing to pay attention. I went on a few short walks over two days recently and made an extra effort to notice and pay attention to the details around me. That meant, like Famous Shoes, I had to stop frequently to look and ponder.

One of my little walks was in Shieling Forest, just up the road from my home. It was late afternoon on a cool, clear day, and the

MACDOWELL LAKE

angle of the sun shining through the trees illuminated the forest with a crystal clarity. Among the details I noticed were a milk weed pod's cottony display, ripples on a pool, lavender turtlehead flowers, and the silent flight of an owl through the trees.

Later that day, just after the sun had set, I was walking by the old cemetery on Concord Street and watched a flock of more than a dozen turkeys pecking at the grass among the tombstones.

Early the next morning, I went walking at the MacDowell Dam recreation area. My route took me down the dirt road from Spring Road to the lake, and I noticed the hoof prints of horses. I also saw the tracks of a deer crossing the road. Once at the lake, I watched the mist rising from the water and noticed many wild flowers still blooming along the shore. I was happy to see several people walking their dogs, too.

None of the things I saw were particularly unusual - except the turkeys - but they were all worth my attention, and they were all beautiful. They were reminders of how walking is more than good exercise. Although I thought I did pretty well in paying attention, I can only speculate about how much old Famous Shoes would have noticed.

September 2007

Recommended Reading List

Adamowitz, Joe, *The New Hiking the Monadnock Region,* 44 Nature Walks and Day Hikes in the heart of New England, University Press of New England, (2007) ISBN 978-1584656449

Brandon, Craig, *Monadnock: More than a Mountain,* Surry Cottage Books, (2007) ISBN 978-0979506710

Cantele, Andi Marie, *Backroad Bicycling in New Hampshire,* The Best Routes for Road and Mountain Bikes, Countryman Press, (2004) ISBN 978-0881506105

Chestney, Linda, *Bicycling Southern New Hampshire,* University Press of New England (2000) ISBN 978-1584653622

Daniell, Gene and Burroughs, John, *Southern New Hampshire Trail Guide,* Appalachian Mountain Club Books (1999) ISBN 978-1878239730

DeLorme, David, *New Hampshire Atlas and Gazetteer.* DeLorme Publishing (2005) ISBN- 978-0899332420 The essential guide with topo maps of the entire state in a convenient book. There are also versions for Massachusetts and Vermont.

Freiden, John S., *Backroad Bicycling in Vermont,* Countryman Press (2006) ISBN 978-0881506921

Hayes, John and Wilson, Alex, *Quiet Water New Hampshire and Vermont, Canoe and Kayak Guide,* Appalachian Mountain Club (2001) ISBN 978-1878239945

Monkman, Jerry and Marcy, *Discover Southern New Hampshire,* AMC Guide to the best Hiking, Biking and Paddling, Appalachian Mountain Club (2002) ISBN 978-1929173150

Older, Julia and Sherman, Steve, *Nature Walks in Southern New Hampshire,* Appalachian Mountain Club, (1994) ISBN 978-1878239358

Smith, Steven and Daniell Gene, *Southern New Hampshire Trail Guide,* Appalachian Mountain Club (2005) ISBN 978-1929173600

Acknowledgments

For their efforts in maintaining trails and protecting public lands, I want to thank the following: The Friends of the Wapack, The Monadnock-Sunapee Greenway Trail Club, The Nature Conservancy, The Audubon Society, The Society for the Protection of New Hampshire Forests, The Windmill Hill Pinnacle Association, the state parks and fish and game departments of New Hampshire, Vermont, and Massachusetts, the National Park Service, and the conservation committees of the towns in the Monadnock Region.

I also want to thank my two long-time teaching partners, Steve Forte and Bob Ganley, for their companionship on many of my outings.

Finally, my appreciation to two people who made this book possible, my editor at *The Monadnock Shopper*, Michelle Green, and the editor, publisher and instigator of this book, Craig Brandon.

For my father

Place Names Index

Other Publications About the Monadnock Region from Surry Cottage Books

Monadnock: More than a Mountain by Craig Brandon. An encyclopedia full of information about the most climbed mountain in North America. *The Boston Globe* called it " a fascinating anthology of history, literature and recreation."

The Heart of Monadnock by Elizabeth Weston Timlow. The story of a mystical experience on the side of Mount Monadnock, described by a children's author and private school principal who moved to Fitzwilliam to be next to the mountain.